BREAKING BOUNDARIES

AN ANTHOLOGY OF ORIGINAL PLAYS

FROM THE FOCUS THEATRE

BREAKING BOUNDARIES

AN ANTHOLOGY OF ORIGINAL PLAYS

FROM THE FOCUS THEATRE

edited by

Steven Dedalus Burch

Carysfort Press

A Carysfort Press Book
Breaking Boundaries: An Anthology of Original Plays from the Focus Theatre
Edited by Steven Dedalus Burch
First published in Ireland in 2013 as a paperback original by
Carysfort Press
58 Woodfield
Scholarstown Road
Dublin 16, Ireland
ISBN 978-1-909325-42-5
©2013 Copyright remains with the authors
Typeset by Carysfort Press
Cover design by eprint
Printed and bound by eprint limited
Unit 35
Coolmine Industrial Estate
Dublin 15
Ireland

Table of Contents

Acknowledgments

I wish to thank my colleagues Brian McAvera and Joe Devlin whose commitment drove the project, and our editor Dan Farrelly, who with Lilian Chambers kept us, me especially, on our toes. But the bulk of my gratitude goes to these wonderful playwrights whose work you can read here. Or, rather, some of their work. Each of their plays deserves publication and production.

Steve Burch

Introduction

In this book are seven plays, original works, which had their premieres at the Focus Theatre, and which grew out of the history, the artistic aims, and the personalities of the Focus Theatre. There have been many others, too many to cram into an anthology intended as an introduction to the styles and artistic voices that have been and continue to be found in this theatre company, voices such as Mary Elizabeth Burke-Kennedy, Declan Burke-Kennedy, Michael Harding, Elizabeth Moynihan, Brian McAvera, Mike Poblete, and Aiden Harney. Let me explain.

In 1963 the 23-year-old Deirdre O'Connell, child of Irish immigrants to New York City in the United States, became an immigrant herself when she moved to Dublin, determined to bring the 'new' theatre of Konstantin Stanislavski to the Irish theatre. She had been a *Wunderkind* at the Actors' Studio which had been co-founded and run by the late Lee Strasberg, who was perhaps the most famous acolyte of Stanislavski in America. Admitted when she was eighteen, Deirdre made her mark very early with her superb acting and singing talents, and within a couple of years was teaching at the studio. From all accounts Deirdre had a bright future ahead of her as an actress, as talented as any of the other young actors making their way to the Studio (as it came to be called) in the late 1950s and 1960s, including Julie Harris, James Dean, Geraldine Page, Rod Steiger, Ben Gazzara, Rip Torn, Lois Wilson, Paul Newman, Dennis Hopper, Jo Van Fleet, Martin Sheen, Anne Bancroft, Shelley Winters, Estelle Parsons, Ellen Burstyn, and Al Pacino. But Deirdre had a vision of a theatre company.

In 1963, Deirdre opened the Stanislavski Studio in Dublin with the aim of providing training in an acting technique which allowed actors to reach for emotional truths without having to rely on 'inspiration', maddeningly imperfect and intermittent at best. Stanislavski, co-founder of the Moscow Art Theatre (MAT) in 1894, spent years studying and analysing how actors prepared for their roles on stage, and over the years, in acting classes at MAT, built up a series of exercises which would allow each actor to work for an emotional level of truth in their performance. Stanislavski once defined acting as 'living truthfully in imaginary circumstances' and set about creating exercises which would allow the actor/student to find a psychophysical truthful reaction to a series of stimuli which would bring their character to life on stage and, most importantly, be repeatable from performance to performance. By the 1920s, following the Soviet Revolution and Civil War, many of Stanislavski's troupe of actors had fled their homeland and, armed with their teacher's training, set out to bring the technique to the various theatre capitals of the Western world. In the United States, several American actors, teachers, and directors, including Harold Clurman, Stella Adler, and Elia Kazan, created the Group Theatre from these principles, offering an extraordinary level of theatrical playing not seen in generations. And what emerged from these performances was not only well acted and well received productions of stage classics, but the beginning of a new playwriting which took advantage of these new *techniques, in plays by such young and up-and-coming writers as Clifford* Odets and, later, Tennessee Williams and Arthur Miller. By the late 1940s, the American theatre had grabbed a powerful place for itself in world theatre.

In Ireland in the early 1960s, the general level of acting was largely mediocre and lamented by many of the drama critics of the day. Still, when a brash twenty-three-year-old American actress landed in Dublin and announced that her aim was to teach Irish actors how to act, her announcement was greeted with derision and distaste. Undeterred, Deirdre proceeded, opened her acting training studio, and five years after that opened her theatre, the Focus Theatre in Dublin, where it remained and continues to this day, fifty years after her arrival, training actors and staging plays both old and new.

At first, the Focus produced largely known works, classics such as Ibsen's A *Doll's House,* Sophocles' *Antigone,* Chekhov's *Uncle Vanya,* Turgenev's *A Month in the Country,* Albee's *A Delicate Balance,* Strindberg's *Miss Julie* and *The Father,* as well as 'new' plays from London and New York, such as Livings' *Kelly's Eye,* Melfi's *Birdbath,* Williams's *Talk to Me Like the Rain,* along with modernist works by Beckett *Happy Days,* Pinter *Old Times,* and Andreyv *He Who gets Slapped.*

The Dublin critics were mainly ecstatic. They were now seeing superb ensemble productions of classic theatre which hadn't been produced in Dublin in generations. And as happened in the American theatre, new plays and new playwriting became sought after which would embrace the training, utilize the insights now being reached in a system which could free each actor and allow them, regardless of the style of writing and playing demanded, to seek and reveal.

The seven plays in this anthology do just that. Their styles range from Lewis Carroll's fantastical world, to a couple on the brink of a philandering weekend disaster, to a one-man show about Jonathan Swift with several characters all played by the same actor; an examination of two shoplifting thieves and the would-be writer who gets in their way, a battle royal between two sides of a world-famous painter, the reactions of multiple New

Yorkers to that moment on September 11, 2001 when their world was changed forever, to the final days of an iconic movie star.

Listing them chronologically: the earliest of these plays, *Alice in Wonderland* (1979) by Mary Elizabeth Burke-Kennedy, is a witty, theatrical, and highly accessible adaptation of what remains perhaps the most beloved avant-garde work of all time. For those at the time who were used to seeing largely 'realistic' works on the Focus stage, this came as a revelation, especially seeing what Stanislavski-trained actors could bring to the wonderfully illogical logic of Carroll and what the director (its author) could achieve on the small, cramped spaces at 6 Pembroke Place (Focus's home base). The result was pure theatre and a re-invigorated Focus.

The Day of the Mayfly (1980) by Declan Burke-Kennedy feels at first to be a standard, Focus-style realistic comedy/drama of two married lovers calling for performances that are deeply felt, through the techniques and training of the studio. But Burke-Kennedy also calls for a sense of colouring, lighting and sound design that opens the play to a sharing of emotions and desires with its audiences.

Talking Through His Hat (2003) by Michael Harding, presents Jonathan Swift and his guests at a dinner party, all performed by a single actor in a tour-de-force, recreating a time of Dublin's Georgian society and celebrating the art and craft of the performer.

Pinching for My Soul (2011) by Elizabeth Moynihan is a three-character play that is made up of single and singular monologues. Moynihan's characters are all defined through their obsessions and lives which revolve around the act of shoplifting (pinching): a young drug addict, a middle-aged politician's wife, and a young Irish-African security guard who dreams of being a writer.

Francis & Frances (2011) by Brian McAvera is a highly theatrical, disturbing, and brilliant meditation on art, sexuality, and morality as it examines the contentious and shocking life and disruptive art of the great painter, Francis Bacon.

New York Monologues (2011) by Mike Poblete presents us with a large cast of characters who reveal, argue, and share their experiences of that momentous morning on September 11, 2001 in New York City as the twin towers of the World Trade Center were brought down in a shocking act of international terrorism. The connections between New York and Ireland are all too apparent in this deeply-felt play.

Hollywood Valhalla (2012) by Aiden Harney examines the end of film star Rock Hudson's life in a series of scenes between the dying star and his fitness instructor.

Each of these scripts is followed by a short note, a memory of the production and in some cases its aims by its author. As will become quite clear, there is no single Focus play, no play which perfectly captures the spirit, the aesthetic aims, the physical abilities of this continually surprising fifty-year-old company.

6 Pembroke Place, where each of these was performed, is no more the home for the Focus Theatre. It closed its doors in April 2012. Since then Focus has survived by performing in other theatres and as of this writing is searching for a new home base. A fuller story of the Focus Theatre is to be found in a companion to this anthology, *Stanislavski in Ireland: Fifty Years of the Focus Theatre*, also published by Carysfort Press (2013). The situation looks quite promising and Focus continues to generate emotional support for its mission. Its effect on the acting industry of Ireland is quite palpable, with many of its former members and students popping up in films and on television, acting, directing, designing, and writing. Enjoy these plays. Read them aloud. Find a place to perform them. Share them with friends, teachers, local theatre groups. Support each other and support the Focus Theatre.

Steven Dedalus Burch, Theatre History, University of Alabama

Alice In Wonderland

Adapted For The Stage

by

Mary Elizabeth Burke-Kennedy

Carrigahorig
Nenagh
Co. Tipperary
Ireland
Tel: 0909747322

Character List With Doubling:

1. Alice
2. Dr Trilby / Mad Hatter / Caterpillar / Gryphon
3. Dr Hare / March Hare / King / Frog
4. Mrs Cruikshank / Queen of Hearts / Pigeon
5. Mrs Smithson / Duchess / Mock Turtle
6. Mr Dodgson / White Rabbit / Dodo
7. Miss Lilley / Mouse / Two of Hearts / Cook
8. Edith / Dormouse / Parrot
9. Jack / Cheshire Cat / Knave / Duck

SCENE ONE

A picnic has just been eaten and the party has broken up into groups. Mrs Cruikshank and Mrs Smithson are gossiping over tea, Miss Lilley is listening to Dr Hare and Dr Trilby arguing. Edith is reading. Jack is climbing a tree. Alice is on a swing being pushed by Rev. Dodgson. Jack utters a piercing shriek and jumps down out of the tree beside the two gossiping ladies. Mrs Cruikshank and Mrs Smithson leap up in consternation.

Mrs Smithson. What on earth? Oh!

Mrs Cruikshank. What is the meaning of this outrageous behaviour?

Jack. I saw something in the tree, aunt.

Mrs Cruikshank. Saw what, Jack?

Jack. A serpent.

Mrs Smithson. A serpent? In a tree?

Mrs Cruikshank. Never!

Mrs Smithson. They're only ever in the grass.

Mrs Cruikshank. Exactly. English snakes know their place.

Jack. I tell you it's up there, aunt. Look! You can just see its tail.

Mrs Cruikshank and Mrs Smithson gaze up at the tree. While they are distracted, Jack grabs a plate of cakes and runs off with it. The ladies look down and discover they have been tricked.

Mrs Smithson. He's been fooling us. He stole our tarts!

Mrs Cruikshank. My sister, Maud, is forever bragging about how clever her beloved Jack is. She'll change her tune when I tell her that her pet is a liar and a thief.

Mrs Smithson. Greedy little pig.

Mrs Cruikshank. My sister Maud indulges her children.

Mrs Smithson. A good dose of castor oil. That's what I'd give that fellow.

Mrs Cruikshank. Spare the rod and spoil the child.

Mrs Smithson. That's the moral of the story.

Mrs Cruikshank. I developed my discipline when I was in the colonies with Colonel Cruikshank. My husband always insisted that we should treat the natives as children. They're better off when they have no say.

Mrs Smithson. I always tell my children to emulate yours. 'why can't you be like the Cruikshanks?' I'm forever saying to them. That's the proof of the pudding.

Mrs Cruikshank. How gratifying to know that I have set a standard. Like our own dear queen. And now, Mrs Smithson, be so good as to fetch some tarts to replace the ones that Jack has purloined. Tea without a cake is like bread without butter.

Mrs Smithson. Like soup without pepper, you'd be surprised how many cooks neglect to put pepper in soup. That is the first question I ask when I have to engage a new cook. How much pepper does a broth require...

Mrs Cruikshank. Mrs Smithson, the cakes!

Dodgson stops pushing the swing and Alice slows down.

Dodgson. There you go, Alice. You're on your own.

Alice. Just ten more pushes.

Dodgson. Sun's too much for me, I'm afraid. Push yourself with your feet.

Alice. Just five more, then.

Dodgson begins to push her again.

Dodgson. It's all very well for you, madam, you're sitting down.

Alice. The swing makes a nice breeze. Can't you feel the breeze too?

Dodgson. You're like the ancient mariner in the poem.

> Swiftly, swiftly flew the ship
> Yet she sailed softly too.
> Sweetly, sweetly blew the breeze.
> On me alone it blew.

Miss Lilley joins them.

Alice. (*Stopping herself swinging.*) I don't know that poem. Will you recite it for me?

Dodgson.

> It is an ancient mariner,
> He stoppeth one of three,
> 'by thy long grey beard
> And glittering eye,
> Now wherefore stopp'st thou me?'

Miss Lilley. You are not going to recite the whole poem, are you, Mr Dodgson?

Alice. Why not?

Dodgson. It is very, very long.

Miss Lilley. It is, more to the point, quite unsuitable for a fanciful young girl.

Dodgson. Oh! I see.

Alice. I don't see. What are you talking about?

Dodgson. Miss Lilley is referring to the fact that the ancient mariner is full of dead men and ghosts and all kinds of terrifying apparitions. On the ocean.

Alice. Really! Would I be scared?

Dodgson. Shaking in your shoes. I promise you.

Miss Lilley. Alice has just learned a more appropriate poem with me. Recite, 'How doth the little busy bee', Alice.

Alice. Must I?

Dodgdson. Yes, Alice.

Alice. (*Whispering*) A trade, then, for the ancient mariner?

Miss Lilley. Begin.

Alice.

> How doth the little busy bee
> Improve each shining hour,
> And gather honey all the day
> From ev'ry op'ning flower!
> How skilfully she builds her cell!
> How neat she spreads the wax;
> And labours hard to store it well
> With the sweet food she makes.

That doesn't really rhyme properly, does it Mr Dodgson, 'wax' and 'makes'? You could do better than that, couldn't you?

Miss Lilley. The rhyme doesn't matter, Alice. It's the next stanza that matters.

> In works of labour or of skill,
> I would be busy too;
> For satan finds some mischief still
> For idle hands to do.

Listen to what you are being told there, Alice, about idleness. That is what is important. Not the rhyme.

Alice. I like a poem to have a story. And good rhymes. Not a lesson.

Dodgson. Tell you what, Alice. I'll go and have forty winks over there on the riverbank and you make up a poem for me. When you've finished, wake me up. Be sure you call me before six o'clock, for I need to be wide awake if I'm to play cards with your mother's guests.

Alice. Very well.

Miss Lilley. Come, my dear. Let us go and sit with Dr Trilby and Dr Hare. They are much cleverer than Mr Dodgson, you know. They talk about important things. May we join you, gentlemen? You were having such an exciting discussion earlier, all about turtles. (*To Alice.*) They were talking about an explorer called Mr Darwin and the discoveries he's made.

Dr Trilby. It was hardly a discussion. My learned friend here has no grasp of what I have been saying, any more than you, dear lady, if I may be so bold.

Dr Hare. You're trying to tell us, Trilby, that we human beings were once all apes, swinging from tree to tree! What about Adam and Eve?

Dr Trilby. What about them? Fine mess they made of things. Hardly the most advanced form of life, if you ask me.

Dr Hare. Steady on, Trilby. Is this one of your charges, Miss Lilley? One of the Liddell girls? I doubt if the Dean would approve of Darwin's ideas being pushed down his daughter's throat.

Dr Trilby. You're supposed to be an academic scholar, Hare. Now you're hiding behind the pinafore of a child.

Dr Hare. Take that back. I'm dashed if I'll be insulted by someone who embraces one fad after another! That's not scholarship. Like a woman changing her hats.

Dr Trilby. So I'm a woman am I?

Dr Hare. I suppose you'd rather be an ape!

Miss Lilley. Come on, Alice. The gentlemen seem to be somewhat over-excited.

Dr Trilby. Simmer down, Hare. Any time any one comes out with a new idea, you go hopping mad.

Dr Hare. You've got to admit it, Trilby, you are utterly gullible.

Miss Lilley. Let's find that young Jack Harte and the two of you can help me with the card tables for later.

Dr Trilby. Darwin is a scientist.

Dr Hare. His theory of evolution is just a fairy story, and that's flat.

Dr Trilby. Like the earth, I suppose?

Dr Hare. It's a waste of time arguing with you.

Hare moves off

Dr Trilby. You're running away, Hare.

Miss Lilley. We shall have to check all the packs of cards and take out the jokers and we must be sure everybody has a pencil and a pad to write on.

Alice. But I have to make up a poem.

Miss Lilley. Follow me.

Alice and Miss Lilley find Jack, leaning against a tree, stuffing the last of the cakes he has stolen into his mouth. The empty plate lies beside him.

Miss Lilley. Still eating, Jack?

Jack. (*With his mouth full*) I don't know you.

Miss Lilley. This is Alice Liddell and I am her governess, Miss Lilley.

Jack. Are there any more of those tarts with the jam in them?

Miss Lilley. I should think you have had enough already. And stand up when you are in the presence of ladies!

Jack. (*Still chewing*) I can't move. I'm too full. (*He belches.*)

Miss Lilley. Well I never!

Jack. You never what?

Miss Lilley. I never encountered such rudeness.

Jack. Anyway you're not ladies. You're just a governess and she's just a girl.

Alice. Miss Lilley happens to be the best governess. I bet I know tons more than you do.

Jack. More what?

Alice. More poems, more history, more geography, more everything.

Jack. That stuff is easy. Bet you can't play the piano with crossed hands.

Miss Lilley. Let's ignore him, Alice. We'll do the card tables by ourselves.

Jack. (*In a prissy voice, mocking Miss Lilley*) 'Let's ignore him Alice'.

Miss Lilley. I shall tell Mrs Liddell about you. You won't be invited here again. (*Exits*)

Jack. Oh how terrible! Best pack some more tarts in then.

Moves away. Mrs Cruikshank and Mrs Smithson promenade towards Alice.

Mrs Cruikshank. Athletics, of course must be encouraged in children. Too much reading is bad for boys. You can never tell what is going on in a boy's head.

Mrs Smithson. Girls are easier to bring up.

Mrs Cruikshank. You are wrong, Mrs Smithson. Girls can become even more fanciful and dangerous than boys. I'll prove it to you. You, girl, come over here.

Alice. Yes, Ma'am.

Mrs Smithson. Who have we here?

Mrs Cruikshank. One of the Liddells, I should think.

Alice. I'm Alice, Ma'am.

Mrs Cruikshank. 'I'm Alice, *if you please* Ma'am.'

Alice. I'm Alice, if you please, Ma'am. Are you the lady who has just come back from Ireland? Is it true that there are fairies there?

Mrs Cruikshank. See what I mean? Head full of rubbish.

Mrs Smithson. Quite. But rather (*spelling*) p r e t t y, don't you think?

Mrs Cruikshank. Not in the slightest bit. In comparison to the Cruikshank girls she is quite P L A I N. And much TOO I N Q U I S I T I V E.

Mrs Smithson. What was that?

Alice. Inquisitive.

Mrs Cruikshank. What are you doing, girl, moping around the garden on your own?

Alice. I'm making up a poem for Mr Dodgson. He wants one with rhymes and nonsense in it.

Mrs Cruikshank. What did I tell you, Mrs Smithson? Rhymes and nonsense.

Mrs Smithson. You are uncanny, Mrs Cruikshank. You are the proof of the pudding.

Mrs Cruikshank. Your hair needs cutting, girl. (*To Mrs Smithson*). I shall advise the mother to have it cut.

The ladies sweep off. Alice goes to Edith and tries to read over her shoulder.

Alice. What's your book about?

Edith. Shhhh!

Alice. Are there any pictures?

Edith. There aren't any pictures in a novel. Don't be so stupid.

Alice. Can we read the conversations? I'll be one person and you can be the other.

Edith. There are no conversations. And shush, please.

Alice. No wonder you're in a bad temper, trying to read that sort of stuff.

Edith. Be quiet, Alice. You really are the worst nuisance of a sister anybody ever had. Why can't you amuse yourself? Make a daisy chain.

Alice. It's too much trouble. I'm too tired. It's too hot.

Edith. Go to sleep then and let me read in peace.

Edith moves away with her book towards the swing. Alice sits silently, alone except for the sleeping Dodgson.

SCENE TWO

Alice. Going to sleep is so boring. It's all grown ups ever want you to do. I'll just put my head down for five minutes and think about my poem and then I'll waken Mr Dodgson. He'll talk to me.

Alice stretches out, her head on her arm.

White Rabbit. Oh dear! Oh dear! I shall be too late!

The White Rabbit consults his watch and charges off.

Alice. (*Rubbing her eyes*) I've never seen the like of that! That rabbit had a waistcoat! And a watch! And he spoke! Wait for me, Mr Rabbit! Wait for me!

White Rabbit. Can't stop now.

During the following Alice pursues the White Rabbit around the stage.

Alice. Wait for me Mr Rabbit, wait for me.

White Rabbit. Oh my ears and my whiskers, I shall be so late, so late.

Alice. Mr Rabbit...Mr Rabbit...

White Rabbit. Oh my dear paws, the duchess, the duchess...

Alice. Oh please wait for me Mr Rabbit.

Alice and the White Rabbit finally meet, but he immediately disappears.

Alice. Oh, he's vanished. He must have gone somewhere. What have we here, a rabbit hole. He must have come this way. Oh, it's very dark and narrow in here. Let me just look in. I'll squeeze myself through, oh, oh, I'm slipping, I'm falling, I'm falling.

Alice tumbles for a while, but finally gets her balance.

It's turned into a well! It must be very deep or I must be falling very slowly. What a strange well it is, with cupboards full of books and maps and marmalade. Perhaps if I could see a map I'd know where I am. I wonder how many miles I've fallen by this time? I must be getting somewhere near the centre of the earth. I wonder if I shall fall right through the earth. How funny it'll seem to come out among the people who go about with their heads downwards. The antipathies, I think. I shall have to ask them what the name of the country is. 'please, Ma'am, is this Australia or New Zealand?' what an ignorant little girl she'll think me for asking. Perhaps I shall see it written up somewhere. Dinah'll miss me very much tonight. I hope they remember her saucer of milk at teatime. Dinah, my dear, I wish you were down here with me. There are no mice in the air, but you might catch a bat and that's very like a mouse. Do cats eat bats, I wonder? Do cats eat bats? Do bats eat cats? All this falling is making me sleepy. (*Yawns*) Now, Dinah, tell me the truth. Did you ever eat a bat?

Alice thumps down on the ground and sprawls. The White Rabbit appears beside her with his watch.

White Rabbit. Oh! My ears and my whiskers how late it's getting!

Alice. There he goes again!

White Rabbit. The time, the time, she'll have my head as sure as...

The Rabbit disappears. Alice explores the space. She discovers the little door. A key appears on a hook in the air beside her. She takes it and opens the little door. She kneels down and peers through.

Alice. Oh my! I never knew there were such colours. That must be the most beautiful garden in the world. I must get in there but how can I? Even if my head would go in it would be very little use without the rest of me. Oh, how I wish! (*She stands up*) If only I could shut up like a telescope. I think I could if only I knew how to begin.

A bottle with a label saying, drink me, appears beside Alice. She replaces the key on its hook and takes the bottle.

Alice. (*Reading*) 'Drink me'. Indeed I shall not. You might be poison. Still, you don't look like poison and there aren't any warnings. (*She takes out the cork and sniffs.*) Cherry tart! (*She sips.*) No? Custard!

(*She sips again.*) No? Pineapple! (*Sips*) No, roast turkey! No. Ice cream! No, no! Hot buttered toast!

Alice begins to shrink down.

What a curious feeling. I'm shrinking. Oh! Oh! I hope it doesn't go on. I don't want to go out like a candle when it burns down. I nearly forgot! The little door. Now I'm the right size to get through. Where did I put the key?

The key is now far above her and she cannot reach it.

Alice. Why didn't I put the key in the lock? Now I've become really tiny and I still can't get into the garden. Edith is right. I really am a stupid, stupid girl.

A cake box with the words eat me appears in front of her.

'eat me'. Why not? If this makes me grow taller I can reach the key. If it makes me smaller, I can squeeze under the door. Either way, I can get into the garden.

Alice eats the cake. She puts her hand on top of her head to try to gauge which way she is going.

Curiouser and curiouser. Now I'm opening out like the largest telescope that ever was. Goodbye feet! I wonder who will put your shoes and stockings on for you now? I shan't be able to.

Alice grabs the key from on high. When she goes to the door she opens it and lies down.

This is worse than ever. I'm too big to even see in much less get in. I'll never get to explore that beautiful place now. I'm locked out forever.

White Rabbit. Oh! The duchess! The duchess! Won't she be savage if I've kept her waiting.

Alice. If you please, sir...

White Rabbit. Good heavens! What sort of thunderous noise was that?

The White Rabbit drops the fan and the gloves and rushes off.

Alice. How could he not hear what I said? How could he not have seen me? How weird everything is today. And yesterday things went on as usual. I wonder if I changed in the night. Let me think. Was I the same when I got up this morning? But if I'm not the same, the next question is, who in the world am I? Let me give myself a test. 4 times 5 is 12. 4 times 6 is 13. 4 times 7 is...I don't know. London is the capital of Paris and Paris is the capital of Rome. Those aren't the right answers. Let me see if I can remember my poem about the little busy bee.

How doth the little crocodile
Improve his shining tail,
And pour the waters of the Nile
On every golden scale!
How cheerfully he seems to grin,
And neatly spreads his claws,
And welcomes little fishes in,
With gently smiling jaws!

I'm sure those are not the right words

Alice begins to cry and the sound of the pool of tears builds up. Alice picks up the Rabbit's fan and gloves, slipping one on to her hand.

Oh, I wish that someone would put their head down and tell me who I am. It's awful being all alone here. (*Alice adopts a bossy tone with herself.*) You ought to be ashamed of yourself, a big girl like you blubbering in this way. Stop this moment, I tell you. But I can't help crying. Everything's going wrong.

Alice looks at her hand in the glove.

Alice. How did I manage to put this little glove on? I'm ten times bigger than that rabbit. I must be growing small again. (*Looking at the fan.*) This must be what's doing it. I don't want to shrink away altogether. (*She drops the fan.*) Now I'll fit into the garden. And I'll be able to explore it and find out...everything.

Alice runs to the garden door. The key is no longer in it. Instead it is hanging high above her as before. She jumps to try and reach it.

How did that get up there again? I'll reach you. I will!

Alice slips with a splash and falls into the pool of tears.

SCENE THREE

Alice. I wish I hadn't cried so much. I shall be punished for it now I suppose, by being drowned in my own tears.

Another splash heralds the arrival in the pool of the mouse. They swim around each other.

How do you do, Mouse? Mr Mouse? Mrs Mouse? Reverend Mouse? Professor Mouse, Miss Mouse? Oh, she doesn't seem to understand English? Do you speak French? Où est ma chatte?

Mouse. (*Swimming frantically away from Alice*) Aaaaaaaagh!

Alice. Oh good!

Mouse. What do you mean, 'oh good'?

Alice. I mean you can see me and hear me.

Mouse. I hear you only too well! Talking about cats. In a sneaky way. In French.

Alice. I beg your pardon. I forgot you don't like cats.

Mouse. Would you like cats if you were me?

Alice. Well perhaps not. Don't be angry about it. Yet I wish I could show you our cat, Dinah. I'm sure you would take a fancy to cats if only you could see her. She is so sweet and quiet. She sits purring by the fire, licking her paws and washing her face and she is lovely to cuddle. But she can be really fast when she's after mice.

Mouse. Aaaaaaaaaagh! You really are outrageous.

Alice. Oh dear! We won't talk about her any more if you'd rather not.

Mouse. We indeed! As if I would talk on such a subject. Nasty, low, vulgar things. Never let me hear the name again.

The parrot, the duck and the dodo enter the pool noisily.

Alice. I'll not mention it. Are you fond of dogs? There is a nice pup near our house. A little terrier with bright eyes and tangly curls. He fetches things when you throw them. He's really clever at finding them. And he puts out his paw to shake hands. The farmer who owns him says he's the best dog he ever had for getting rid of the rats in the barn.

Duck. Eats them alive does he?

Mouse. (*Furious*) Did you hear that?

Parrot. We heard. We heard.

Dodo. No respect.

Mouse. My nerves!

Duck. You're too fussy, you are.

Parrot. Her nerves! Her nerves!

The mouse swims away from Alice.

Alice. I've offended you again. I'm so thoughtless! Dear Miss Mouse, please come back and we won't mention cats. Or dogs either if you don't like them.

Mouse. Let us go to the shore, then, and I'll tell you my history. You'll soon know why it is I hate those creatures.

Alice. Shall we all swim ashore? Follow me.

The creatures arrive at the shore, wet and cranky.

Dodo. I thought I'd seen everything, until now. This is the last straw! 'What is wisdom?' You may well ask, when any day at any time disaster may be waiting...

Duck. Give over! A swim never hurt anyone. How'd you like my life – stuck in the bloomin' water all the time, never a break? I ask you – what right you got to complain about the odd duckin'? Ha ha! You got a duckin'.

Dodo. I'm older than you and I know better what it is...

Parrot. Older and better. Older and better.

Duck. Watch it, Polly.

Dodo. Please! When you are as old as I...

Alice. How shall we get dry?

Dodo. You must not interrupt your elders, girl. When you are as old as I...

Duck. You know very well how to get dry. Did you hear that? I made a rhyme.

Alice. Tell us how, please, Mr Dodo.

Dodo. I don't know how to get dry. What I was saying was, when you are as old as I...

Alice. How old are you anyway?

Dodo. What an impertinent question.

Duck. Perfectly pertinent, if you ask me.

Parrot. Nobody asked you. Nobody asked you.

Mouse. Sit down all of you and listen to me. I'll soon make you dry enough.

Alice and the birds all sit around the mouse.

Ahem! Are you ready? This is the driest thing I know. Silence all round if you please. William the Conqueror, whose cause was favoured by the Pope, was soon submitted to by the English, who wanted leaders and had of late been much accustomed to usurpation and conquest. Edwin and Morcar, the Earls of Mercia and Northumbria...

Duck. Uughh!

Mouse. I beg your pardon. Did you speak?

Duck. Not I.

Mouse. I thought you did. I proceed. Edwin and Morcar, the Earls of Mercia and Northumbria declared for him. And even Stigia, the patriotic Archbishop of Canterbury, found it advisable...

Duck. Found what?

Mouse. Found, 'it', of course. You know what, 'it', means.

Parrot. It. It. It. It.

Duck. I know what 'it' means well enough when I find a thing. 'It's' generally a frog or a worm. The question is, what did the archbishop find?

Mouse. Found it advisable to meet William and offer him the crown. William's conduct was at first modest. But the insolence of his followers...how are you getting on my dear?

Alice. As wet as ever, I'm afraid. It doesn't seem to dry me at all.

Dodo. In that case, I move that the meeting adjourn for the immediate adoption of more energetic remedies.

Duck. Speak English. I don't understand the meaning of half those long words and what's more I don't believe you do either.

Parrot. Don't believe you! Don't believe you.

Dodo. What I was going to say was, the best thing to get us dry would be a caucus race.

Alice. What is a caucus race?

Dodo. The best way to explain is to do it. This is the race course. The exact shape doesn't matter. You go here. You go there. You here. You here. Set off any time you like. And run, two, three, four. Run, two, three, four. Off we go.

Everyone runs in different directions and at different speeds.

Dodo. The race is over.

They all run panting to where the dodo is.

All. Who won, who won?

Dodo. Everybody has won and all must have prizes.

Parrot. Prizes! Prizes!

Alice. Who is going to give the prizes?

Duck. Not I.

Dodo. Why she, of course.

They all cluster around Alice.

All. Prizes. Prizes.

Alice digs into her pocket and produces a bag of sweets, which she distributes.

Alice. I have just enough fruit drops for each of you to have one.

Mouse. But she must have a prize for herself.

Dodo. Of course. What else have you got in your pocket?

Alice. Only a thimble.

Dodo. Hand it over here. We beg your acceptance of this elegant thimble.

The dodo presents the thimble with great solemnity. Alice bows and everyone cheers.

Duck. Waste of money, these sweets. No taste. Absolutely none.

Dodo. Now when I was young, you knew what you were eating. This could be anything. This could be a pebble.

Parrot. (*Choking*) Help! Help! Help! Help!

Duck. Will you stop repeating yourself.

Parrot. Slap my back! Slap my back! (*All slap her back*) Enough!

Dodo. Well I really must be getting home. The night air doesn't suit my throat.

Parrot. Very bad for the throat, very, very, very, very, very.

Dodo. Farewell young lady.

Alice. So nice to meet you. Please, Miss Mouse, you promised to tell us your story of why it is you hate, ahem, c.a.ts & d.o.gs

Mouse. (*Gathering her tail up in her arms*) Mine is a long and sad tale.

Alice. It certainly is a long tail, but why do you call it sad?

Mouse. Listen and you shall hear. Fury said to the mouse that he met in the house, 'let us both go to law: I will prosecute you...come I'll take no denial: we must have a trial; for really this morning, I've nothing to do.' Said the mouse to the cur, 'such a trial, dear sir, with no jury or judge would be wasting our breath.' 'I'll be judge, I'll be jury', said cunning old fury. 'I'll try the whole case and condemn you to **death**.' You are not attending. What are you thinking of?

Alice. I beg your pardon. You had got to the fifth bend, I think.

Mouse. I had not!

Alice. A knot? Let me help undo it.

Mouse. I shall do nothing of the sort. You insult me by talking such nonsense.

Mouse scuttles off.

Alice. I didn't mean it. But you're very easily offended. Please come back and finish your story.

The mouse turns and growls before leaving.

Duck. Well, I declare!

Alice. What a pity it wouldn't stay. If Dinah was here, she'd soon fetch it back. Dinah's my cat. She's super at catching mice. And as for birds! I wish you could see her after birds. They never stand a chance against Dinah.

Duck. Time I was off.

Parrot. Me too. Me too.

Alice. Must you all go?

Duck. 'fraid so. Don't like all this talk about, 'not standing a chance'. (*To the parrot as they scuttle off*) She's all right I suppose. But she seems to have some nasty friends.

Parrot. Nasty. Nasty.

Duck. Can't you ever say anything original?

Parrot. Not a chance! Not a chance!

Duck. You'll drive me mad, you will.

Parrot. I will. I will.

Alice. I wish I hadn't mentioned Dinah. Nobody seems to like her down here. And I'm sure she's the best cat in the world. Oh my dear Dinah, I wonder if I shall ever see you again. And if I do, will you remember me? Will you have changed too, I wonder? Will your whiskers be grey?

SCENE FOUR

Dreamy exotic music. Enter an enormous caterpillar with a long tail. He is slightly stoned, smoking a hookah. Alice goes to him.

Caterpillar. And who are you?

Alice. I hardly know, sir, just at present – at least I know who I was when I got up this morning but I think I must have changed several times since then.

Caterpillar. What do you mean by that? Explain yourself.

Alice. I can't explain myself I'm afraid, sir, because I'm not myself you see.

Caterpillar. I don't see.

Alice. I'm afraid I can't put it more clearly, for I can't understand it myself to begin with and being so many different sizes in a day is so confusing.

Caterpillar. It isn't.

Alice. Well perhaps you haven't found it so yet but when you have to turn into a chrysalis and then after that into a butterfly, I should think you'll feel a bit odd, won't you?

Caterpillar. Not a bit.

Alice. Well perhaps your feelings are different. All I know is it would feel extremely odd to me.

Caterpillar. You, indeed. The question is, who are you?

Alice. I think you ought to tell me who you are first.

Caterpillar. Why?

Alice is dejected by the abruptness of the caterpillar and turns to move away.

Caterpillar. Come back. I've something important to say.

Alice turns back to him.

Caterpillar. Keep your temper.

Alice. (*Annoyed*) Is that all?

Caterpillar. No. (*It resumes smoking its hookah ignoring her for some seconds*). So you think you've changed, do you?

Alice. I'm afraid so. I can't remember things like I used to and I don't keep the same size for ten minutes at a time.

Caterpillar. Can't remember what things?

Alice. Well, I tried to say, 'How doth the little busy bee', and it all came out different.

Caterpillar. Repeat. 'You are old Father William'.

Alice.

'you are old Father William,' the young man said,
'and your hair has become very white;
And yet you incessantly stand on your head —
Do you think at your age it is right?
'in my youth,' Father William replied to his son,
'i feared it might injure the brain;
But now that I'm perfectly sure I have none,
Why I do it again and again.'
'you are old,' said the youth, 'and your jaws are too weak
For anything tougher than suet.
Yet you finished the goose, with the bones and the beak —
Pray how did you manage to do it?'
'In my youth', said his father, 'I took to the law,
And argued each case with my wife;
And the muscular strength which it gave to my jaw
Has lasted the rest of my life.'
'You are old', said the youth, 'one would hardly suppose
That your eye was as steady as ever;
Yet you balanced an eel on the end of your nose —
What made you so awfully clever?'
'i have answered two questions, and that is enough,'
Said his father. 'don't give yourself airs!
Do you think I can listen all day to such stuff?
Be off, or I'll kick you down-stairs!'
Caterpillar. That is all wrong.
Alice. I'm afraid some of the words got altered.

Caterpillar. It was wrong from beginning to end. What size do you want to be?

Alice. I'm not that fussy about size but I'm so small at the moment, I feel quite ridiculous.

Caterpillar. There's nothing ridiculous in being small.

Alice. But I'm not used to it.

The caterpillar begins to slither away.

Caterpillar. One side will make you grow smaller — the other side will make you grow larger.

Alice. Of what...(*urgently*) sides of what?

Caterpillar. (*Off stage*) Of the mushroom.

Alice. (*Alice finds a mushroom where the caterpillar has been sitting.*) Which side is which, I wonder? Eeeny, meeny, miney, mo.

She nibbles a bit off the left hand side. She shrinks rapidly. Then she stuffs some of the right hand piece into her mouth and suddenly extends.

SCENE FIVE

Alice is suddenly chest deep in greenery – the tops of trees.

Alice. What can all that green stuff be? And where has the rest of me got to? Where are my hands?

Alice wiggles her hands and the undergrowth shakes.

I can't get my hands up to my face. Maybe I can get my face down to them.

Alice bends her head down and as she does so, the pigeon pokes up her head from out of the branches.

Pigeon. (*Screaming*) Serpent!

Alice. I am certainly not a serpent! Let me alone.

Pigeon. Serpent, I say again! Serpent. I've tried every way, but nothing seems to suit them.

Alice. I haven't the least idea what you're talking about.

Pigeon. I've tried the roots of trees, I've tried banks, I've tried hedges! But those serpents! There's no stopping them.

Alice. I don't understand.

Pigeon. As if it wasn't enough trouble hatching the eggs but I must be on the lookout for serpents night and day. I haven't had a wink of sleep these three weeks!

Alice. I'm very sorry you've been annoyed.

Pigeon. And just as I'd taken the highest tree in the wood and just as I was thinking I'd be free of them at last, one must come wriggling down from the sky. Ugh!

Alice. But I'm not a serpent. I'm a... I'm a...

Pigeon. Well, what are you? I can see you're trying to invent something.

Alice. I'm a little girl. Sometimes.

Pigeon. A likely story indeed! I've seen plenty of little girls but never one with a neck like yours. No! You're a serpent and there's no use denying it. I suppose you'll be telling me next that you've never tasted an egg?

Alice. Of course I have. But little girls eat eggs just as much as serpents.

Pigeon. What does it matter to me whether you are a 'little girl' or a serpent?

Alice. It matters a great deal to me.

Pigeon. You're looking for eggs, I know that much.

Alice. I'm not looking for eggs and if I was, I wouldn't want them raw.

Pigeon. Well take yourself off then, and rob someone else!

Alice ducks her head down and the forest withdraws. She nibbles the mushroom.

Alice. I think I'd better remain small for a while longer while I'm here. At least until I get into the garden and then perhaps I can be myself again.

SCENE SIX

The Frog staggers in carrying an enormous card and written on it – 'for the Duchess. An invitation from the Queen to play croquet'. He reels around, falls under the card, struggles up, props it up and reads it.

Frog.

'For the Duchess, an invitation from the Queen to play croquet.'

'For the Duchess, an invitation from the Queen to play croquet.'

Alice. Excuse me but do you by any chance know where the beautiful garden is around here?

Frog. 'From the queen, an invitation for the duchess to play croquet.'

Alice. Excuse me but do you by any chance know where the beautiful garden is?

Frog. I shall lie here till tomorrow.

Alice. There's a little door that leads into it. How am I to find my way back to the little door? Could you direct me, please?

Frog. I shall lie here till tomorrow – or the next day maybe.

Alice. There's no use talking to him.

Frog. Ought you go there at all? That's the first question, you know.

Alice. Everyone in this place argues — no matter what you say, they *will argue*.

Frog. I shall sit here, on and off, for days and days.

Alice. But what am I to do?

Frog. Anything you like.

Alice. What's the point in talking to you?

Frog. What's the point? What's the point?

The Duchess emerges into the playing area. She is carrying a baby in a bundle and regards it with obvious distaste. Over her head appears the head of the Cheshire Cat – in one of the upper apertures of the setting. The Cat grins and meows. The Duchess lavishes it with affection, tucking the baby unceremoniously under her arm while she does so. The Cook accompanies her with a large saucepan, which she is stirring and beating. She has a pepper pot in her apron which she keeps sprinkling everywhere. Everyone sneezes throughout.

Frog.

> 'For the Duchess, an invitation from the Queen to play croquet.'
> 'For the Duchess, an invitation from the Queen to play croquet.'

Oh, what's the point, what's the point! (*Exits*)

Alice. Please would you tell me why your cat grins like that?

Duchess. (*Gurgling to the cat*) Because it's a Cheshire cat.

Cat. (*In a man's voice*) Miaowww.

The baby begins to howl.

Duchess. (*Screaming at baby*) Pig.

Alice. I didn't know that Cheshire cats always grinned. In fact I didn't know that cats could grin.

Duchess. They all can and most of 'em do.

Alice. I don't know any that do.

Duchess. You don't know much and that's a fact.

She turns from the cat and begins jiggling the baby around.

Alice. Oh careful. Mind his little head.

Duchess. I mind my own business. That's what I mind. If everybody did likewise the world would go around a great deal faster than it does.

Alice. Which would not be an advantage. Just think what would happen to day and night. You see the earth takes twenty-four hours to turn on its axis...

Duchess. You'd better not let the Queen hear you talking about axes. She'll chop off your head.

Alice. Twenty-four hours, I think, or is it twelve?

Duchess. Oh! Don't bother me. I never could abide figures.

The baby howls even louder. The Duchess sings to it and shakes it.

> Speak roughly to your little boy
> And beat him when he sneezes.
> He only does it to annoy,
> Because he knows it teases.
> I speak severely to my boy.
> I beat him when he sneezes.
> For he can thoroughly enjoy
> The pepper when he pleases.

Duchess. You mind him for a bit if you like. (*She dumps the baby in Alice's lap*) I must go and get ready to play croquet with the Queen.

Duchess exits. The Cook sprinkles pepper on the baby and Alice and exits.

Alice. (*Sneezing*) It's no wonder you're crying, you poor little mite. Here let me wipe your nose. (*Alice cleans the baby's nose with her hankie.*) You have a very turned-up nose haven't you? And your eyes are very small for a baby. Your eyebrows are all bristly and yellow. In fact you're rather like a pig.

The baby grunts.

Alice. What was that?

The baby grunts again.

You are a pig. Well you'd better get along for I can't mind you. Find yourself a nice, smelly pigsty with a big fat sow in it.

Alice puts the pig down and it trots off.

Alice. It's just as well it turned into a pig, for it would have made a dreadfully ugly person, whereas it's quite a nice pig.

Cat. And what about me? Am I not a handsome cat?

Alice. Yes, indeed you are, Mr Cheshire. And now, would you tell me please which way I ought to go from here?

Cat. That depends a good deal on where you want to get to.

Alice. I don't much care where-

Cat. Then it doesn't matter which way you walk.

Alice. – so long as I get *somewhere*.

Cat. Oh you're sure to do that if you only walk long enough.

Alice. What sort of people live about here?

Cat. In *that* direction lives a hatter. And in *that* direction lives a march hare. Visit either you like. They might invite you to tea. They never stop eating. They're both mad.

Alice. But I don't want to go among mad people.

Cat. Oh you can't help that. We're all mad here. I'm mad. You're mad.

Alice. How do you know I'm mad?

Cat. You must be or you wouldn't have come here.

Alice. And how do you know that you're mad?

Cat. To begin with, a dog's not mad. You grant that?

Alice. I suppose so.

Cat. Well then you see a dog growls when it's angry and wags its tail when it's pleased. Now I growl when I'm pleased and wag my tail when I'm angry. Therefore, I'm mad!

Alice. I call what cats do, purring, not growling.

Cat. Call it what you like. I growl. Do you play croquet with the Queen today?

Alice. I should like that very much but I haven't been invited yet.

Cat. You'll see me there.

The Cheshire Cat disappears. Alice stares at the place from where it has gone. Suddenly it reappears.

Cat. What became of the baby?

Alice. It turned it into a pig.

Cat. I thought it would.

The Cheshire Cat vanishes. Alice is left deciding where to go. She looks to right and left. Suddenly the Cheshire Cat appears again.

Cat. Did you say pig or fig?

Alice. I said pig. And I wish you wouldn't keep appearing and vanishing so suddenly. You're making me dizzy.

Cat. (*Slowly vanishes all but its grin*) That's all right.

Alice. We'll I've often seen a cat without a grin – but a grin without a cat. It's the most astonishing thing I've seen in my life. This is the way to where the March Hare lives. Yes, I can see the chimneys of a house – and they're shaped like ears! And the roof is thatched with fur. It seems like quite a large house. I wonder if he is raving mad? He can't be any madder than some of the people I've met already. He just might be able to tell me the way to the garden. Anyway, I really could do with a nice hot cup of tea.

Interval

SCENE SEVEN

Hatter, Hare and Dormouse are seated at a table set with tea things. They are all scrunched up at one corner of it. Alice enters determinedly.

Hatter/March Hare/Dormouse. No room. No room.

Alice. There's plenty of room.

March Hare. Have some wine.

Alice. I don't see any.

March Hare. There isn't any.

Alice. Then it wasn't very civil of you to offer it.

March Hare. It wasn't very civil of you to sit down without being invited.

Alice. I didn't know it was your table. It's laid for a great many more than three.

March Hare. That doesn't mean you were invited.

Hatter. Your hair wants cutting.

Alice. You should learn not to make personal remarks. It's very rude.

Hatter. Why is a raven like a writing desk?

Alice. Oh great. Riddles. I love riddles. Now let me try to guess that. Why is a raven like a writing desk? Yes I think I can guess that.

March Hare. Do you mean you think you can find out the answer to it?

Alice. Exactly so.

March Hare. Then you should say what you mean.

Alice. I do. At least I mean what I say. That's the same thing.

Hatter. Not the same thing a bit. You might just as well say that 'I see what I eat' is the same thing as 'I eat what I see'.

March Hare. You might just as well say that 'I like what I get' is the same thing as 'I get what I like'.

Dormouse. You might just as well say that 'I breathe when I sleep' is the same thing as 'I sleep when I breathe…'

Hatter. It is the same thing with you.

March Hare. All change!

They propel Alice around the table, only to return to the same places.

Hatter. (*Examining his watch*). What day of the month is it?

Alice. The fourth.

Hatter. Two days wrong. I told you butter wouldn't suit the works.

March Hare. It was the best butter.

Hatter. Yes, but some crumbs must have got in as well. You shouldn't have put it in with the bread knife.

March Hare. (*Takes the watch and dips it in his teacup*) It was the best butter you know.

Alice. What a funny watch. It tells the days of the month but doesn't tell what o'clock it is.

Hatter. Why should it? Does your watch tell you what year it is?

Alice. Of course not. But that's because it stays the same year for such a long time.

Hatter. Which is just the case with mine.

Alice. I don't quite understand you.

Hatter. (*Pours tea on the Dormouse's nose.*) The Dormouse is asleep again.

Dormouse. Of course. Just what I was going to remark myself.

Hatter. Have you guessed the riddle, yet?

Alice. No. I give up. What's the answer?

Hatter. I haven't the slightest idea.

March Hare. Nor I.

Alice. I really think you might do something better with the time than wasting it in asking pointless riddles.

Hatter. If you knew time as well as I do, you wouldn't talk about wasting 'it'. It's him.

Alice. I don't know what you mean.

Hatter. Of course you don't. I dare say you never even spoke to time.

Alice. Perhaps not. But I know I have to beat time when I learn music.

Hatter. Ah! That accounts for it. He won't stand beating. Now if only you kept on good terms with him, he'd do almost anything you liked with the clock. For instance, supposing it were nine o'clock in the morning – just the time to begin lessons: you'd only have to whisper a hint to time and round goes the clock in a twinkling! Half past one, time for dinner.

March Hare. I only wish it was.

Alice. That would be grand, certainly, but I shouldn't be hungry for it.

Hatter. Not at first – but you could keep it to half past one as long as you liked.

Alice. Is that the way you manage?

Hatter. Not I. We quarrelled last March – just before he went mad – you know (*pointing with his tea-spoon at the Hare*). It was at the great concert given by the Queen of Hearts. I had to sing –

> 'Twinkle, twinkle little bat!
> How I wonder what you're at!'
> You know the song perhaps.

Alice. I've heard something like it.

Hatter. It goes on, you know, in this way

> 'Up above the world you fly
> Like a teatray in the sky
> Twinkle twinkle'

Dormouse. Twinkle, twinkle, twinkle, twinkle, etc.

Hatter. (*Hare pinching the Dormouse till it stops singing*) Well I'd hardly finished the first verse, when the Queen bawled out 'he's murdering the time. Off with his head!'

Alice. How dreadfully savage!

Hatter. And ever since that he won't do a thing I ask. It's always six o'clock now. It's always teatime and we've no time to wash the things between whiles.

Alice. That's why you keep moving 'round I suppose.

Hatter. Exactly so. As things get used up.

Alice. But what will you do when you get to the beginning again?

March Hare. I'm getting tired of this. I vote the young lady tell us a story.

Alice. I'm afraid I don't know one.

Hatter/March Hare. Then the Dormouse shall.

March Hare. Wake up Dormouse.

Dormouse. I wasn't asleep. I heard every word you were saying.

March Hare. Tell us a story.

Alice. Yes, please do.

Hatter. And be quick about it or you'll be asleep again before it's done.

Dormouse. Once upon a time, there were three little sisters and their names were Elsie,Lacie, and Tillie and they lived at the bottom of a well.

Alice. What did they live on?

Dormouse. They lived on treacle.

Alice. They couldn't have. They'd have been ill.

Dormouse. So they were. Very ill.

Alice. Why did they live at the bottom of a well?

March Hare. Take some more tea.

Alice. I've had nothing yet. So I can't take more.

Hatter. You mean you can't take less. It's very easy to take more than nothing.

Alice. Nobody asked your opinion.

Hatter. Who's making personal remarks now?

Alice has some bread and butter.

Alice. Why did they live at the bottom of a well?

Dormouse. It was a treacle well.

Alice. There's no such thing.

Hatter/March Hare. Shh! Shh!

Dormouse. If you can't be civil you'd better finish the story for yourself.

Alice. No, please go on. I dare say there may be one. I won't interrupt again.

Dormouse. One indeed! And so these three little sisters – they were learning to draw – you know.

Alice. What did they draw?

Dormouse. Treacle.

Hatter. I want a clean cup. Let's move on one place.

They move around the table – Alice finding herself in a messy place and expressing discomfort.

Alice. But I don't understand. Where did they draw treacle from?

Hatter. You can draw water out of a water well – so I think you could draw treacle out of a treacle well. Stupid!

Alice. But they were in the well?

Dormouse. Of course they were. Well in. They were learning to draw and they drew all manner of things – everything that begins with an m.

Alice. Why an m?

March Hare. Why not?

Dormouse. (*Falling asleep. It is pinched by the Hatter*) Such as mousetraps and the moon and memory and muchness. You know you say things are 'much of a muchness'. Did you ever see a drawing of a muchness?

Alice. I don't think so.

Hatter. Then you shouldn't talk.

Alice. Well in that case, I'll go away.

Hatter. Excuse yourself.

Alice. Excuse me and good-bye. You can be sure I won't ever come to your house again.

March Hare. You weren't invited in the first place.

Hatter. The Dormouse is asleep.

March Hare. Pour more tea on him.

Hatter. Doesn't work.

March Hare. Into the teapot with him then.

Hatter. Into the teapot.

SCENE EIGHT

Alice comes and sits downstage.

Alice. I'm so tired of arguing and answering questions about who I am. I wish I could go home and be the same size for a while. I wish I could find a set of steps that would lead me back up above the ground to where Edith was reading. Oh, if only I'd found my way into that beautiful garden.

The garden appears behind her. Alice moves into the garden.

Alice. At last I've found it.

Alice explores. Without noticing Alice, Two enters with a can of red paint and proceeds to start painting the white rose bushes red.

Alice. Excuse me? What are you doing?

Two continues painting frantically.

Alice. Oh dear! How disappointing! It seems as though the people here are just as rude as in the other place. Excuse me. What are you doing?

Two sees Alice and falls on his hands and knees, bowing.

Alice. Oh please! You don't need to do that. Please get up.

Two. Oh don't tell her. Don't tell her.

Alice. Don't tell who? What?

Two. Oh you've seen, so you'll be bound to tell.

Alice. But I've seen nothing.

Two. You've seen it all. I'll be reduced to a pulp.

Alice. You will if you keep crying like that. But I'm not going to do anything to you.

Two. You won't tell her?

Alice. You'll have to tell me what it is I'm not to tell her. And you'll have to tell me who 'she' is.

Two. I did it by mistake. Planted white roses. And she wanted red roses. So if I can't disguise them...ooh!

Alice. What will happen?

Two. She'll cut off my head.

Alice. Who will?

Two. (*In agonies, throwing himself on the ground – flat out*) The Queen of Hearts.

Fanfare of trumpets.

Here she comes. It's the Royal procession. Lie down. Lie down.

Alice. But then I won't see anything. What's the use of a procession if you can't see it?

Enter King, Queen, White Rabbit.

Queen. Who is this?

White Rabbit. Just a girl.

Queen. Idiot! Simpleton! What's your name child?

Alice. My name is...

Queen. And who is this?

The Queen points at Two, who is trying to hide his paintbrush.

Alice. How should I know? It's no business of mine.

Queen. Off with her head.

All gasp.

King. Consider my dear. She is only a child.

Queen. (*To Two*) Turn over!

Two manages to flop over.

Queen. What have you been up to with that paintbrush?

Two. A mistake. It was all a mistake.

Queen. (*Examining the rose bush*). I see. You have been painting white roses red! Off with his head! Off with his head!

She shuts her eyes and screams and stamps her feet. While she has her tantrum, Alice and the White Rabbit grab Two and push him off stage. The Queen's fit subsides.

Queen. Is his head off?

Alice. His head has gone Your Majesty.

Queen. Good. Can you play croquet?

Alice. Yes.

Queen. Come on then.

White Rabbit. It's a very fine day. (*Whispering*) I think she's forgotten to behead you.

Alice. Isn't the Duchess meant to be here? She was invited to play croquet with the Queen.

White Rabbit. She's under sentence of death too. She boxed the Queen's ears. Don't laugh. The Queen will hear you and remember. Laughter means a plot's afoot. That's what she always says.

Queen. Where are the things! Where are the croquet thring-throug-triangily-trang things!

Enter Two, with flamingos and hedgehogs. He distributes them and he himself becomes the croquet hoop hopping from place to place while the others hit the hedgehogs through his legs. The Queen keeps bashing everyone else's flamingo with hers and hitting the hedgehogs all over the stage. Alice draws aside with her flamingo which keeps staring at her. The Cheshire Cat appears and sits beside her.

Cat. How are you getting on?

Alice. I don't think they play at all fairly and there don't seem to be any rules.

Cat. There is one rule. The Queen always wins.

Alice. But that's not a rule at all.

Cat. It is here.

King. Who are you talking to?

Alice. It's a friend of mine, a Cheshire cat.

King. I don't like the look of it at all. But it may kiss my hand if it likes.

Cat. I'd rather not.

King. Don't be impertinent and don't look at me like that.

Alice. A cat may look at a king. I've read that somewhere.

King. Too much reading is bad for children. Your Majesty, my dear, I wish you would have this cat removed.

Queen. Off with its head!

King. I'll fetch the executioner myself. (*Looking at Alice dangerously*). Too many people around here are getting off scot-free.

The King exits. The Duchess enters and sits beside Alice.

Duchess. (*To the Cat*) Off you go my pet. By the time he gets back he'll have forgotten all about you. That's the way they all are here. As I always say.

Cat. Right! I'll vanish.(*To Alice*) But I'll still be around, you know.

The Cat slinks off.

Duchess. You can't think how glad I am to see you again, you dear old thing. You're thinking about something that makes you forget to talk. I can't tell you just now what the moral of that is. But I shall remember it in a bit.

Alice. Perhaps it hasn't one.

Duchess. Tut tut child. Everything's got a moral if only you can find it. (*She kisses Alice.*) Oh, 'tis love, 'tis love that makes the world go 'round.

Alice. Somebody said that it's done by everybody minding their own business.

Duchess. Ah well! It means much the same thing. And the moral of that is 'take care of the sense and the sounds will take care of themselves'. I dare say you're wondering why I don't put my arm around your waist – the reason is that I'm doubtful about the temper of your flamingo.

Alice. Yes. He might bite.

Duchess. Very true. Flamingos and mustard both bite. And the moral of that is 'birds of a feather flock together'.

Alice. Only mustard isn't a bird.

Duchess. Right as usual. What a clever way you have of putting things.

Alice. It's a mineral I think.

Duchess. Of course it is. There's a large mustard mine near here. And the moral of that is 'the more there is of mine, the less there is of yours'.

Alice. Oh I know. It's a vegetable. It doesn't look like one but it is.

Duchess. I quite agree with you. And the moral of that is 'be what you would seem to be' – or if you would like to put it more simply 'never imagine yourself not to be otherwise than what it might appear to others that you were, or might have been was not otherwise than what you had been would have appeared to them to be otherwise.

Alice. I think I would understand that better if I had it written down; but I can't quite follow it as you say it.

Duchess. That's nothing to what I could say if I choose.

Alice is silent.

Duchess. Thinking again?

The Duchess squeezes Alice.

Alice. (*Pulling away*) I've a right to think.

Duchess. Just about as much right as pigs have to fly and the moral –

The Queen arrives beside Alice and the Duchess.

Queen. Morals. Mottoes. Fat lot you know.

Duchess. A fine day Your Majesty.

Queen. Now I'll give you fair warning. Either you or your head must be off. And that in about half no time.

The Duchess scuttles off.

Queen. The game is over and I have won. Have you seen the Mock Turtle yet?

Alice. No, Your Majesty. I don't even know what a mock turtle is.

Queen. It's the thing mock turtle soup is made of.

Alice. He's made into soup?

Queen. You will find them over there.

Alice. Them. Is the Mock Turtle two creatures?

Queen. Don't contradict.

Alice. But Your Majesty, I didn't contradict. I simply asked...

Queen. You ask too much. 'they' are the Mock Turtle and the Gryphon. And if you keep on contradicting and asking stupid questions, I shall have all your heads off. I shall have a trial. Yes, I shall have a trial!

SCENE NINE

The Queen charges off. The Gryphon and the Mock Turtle appear upstage singing. Alice watches them.

Mock Turtle.

> 'Beautiful soup so rich and green,
> Waiting in a hot tureen!
> Who for such dainties would not stoop?
> Soup of the evening, beautiful soup!
> Soup of the evening, beautiful soup!

The Gryphon joins in the chorus.

> Beau – ootiful soo oop!
> Beau – ootiful soo oop!
> Soo oop - of - the – evening
> Beautiful, beautiful, soup.'

Gryphon. Never mind.

Mock Turtle. (*Sobs*) Never mind.

Alice. You must be the Gryphon. Is that the Mock Turtle.

Mock Turtle. (*Sobs*).

Gryphon. What an intelligent young lady.

Alice. That's the nicest thing anyone has said to me since I came here.

Gryphon. Beware of compliments!

Mock Turtle. (*Sobs*).

Alice. What makes him so sad?

Gryphon. There's nothing the matter with him at all. It's all just his fancy. This here young lady, she wants for to know your history she do.

Mock Turtle. Once. Once I was a real turtle.

(*Prolonged sobbing*).

Alice. Oh please! Don't tell me any more if it upsets you so much!

Gryphon. Don't mind his tears. Let him go on.

Mock Turtle. When we were little we went to school in the sea. The master was an old turtle. We used to call him tortoise.

Alice. Why did you call him tortoise if he wasn't one?

Mock Turtle. Really you are very dull! We called him tortoise because he taught us.

Gryphon. He taught us! No wonder the Queen is upset with you! Drive on old fellow. Don't be all day about it.

Mock Turtle. Yes, we went to school in the sea, though you may not believe it.

Alice. I never said that.

Mock Turtle. You did.

Gryphon. Hold your tongue.

Mock Turtle. We had the best of educations – with extras.

Alice. Yes. Me too. French and music are my extras.

Mock Turtle. And washing?

Alice. Certainly not.

Mock Turtle. We had extras; French and music and washing.

Gryphon. French and music and washing.

Alice. But why did you need washing? Living at the bottom of the sea!

Mock Turtle. I couldn't afford the extras anyway. I took the regular course.

Alice. And what was that?

Mock Turtle. Reeling and writhing of course, to begin with. And then the different branches of arithmetic. Ambition, distraction, uglification and derision.

Alice. What else did you have to learn?

Mock Turtle. Well there was mystery. Ancient mystery. Modern mystery. The mystery of the present times. And seography. And drawling. The drawling master was an old conger eel that used to come once a week. He taught us drawling and stretching and fainting in coils.

Alice. What was that like?

Mock Turtle. Well, I can't show you. I'm too stiff.

Gryphon. I never learnt that. I went to the classics master. He was an old crab, he was. He taught laughing and grief.

The Gryphon and Mock Turtle both weep and laugh.

Alice. And how many hours a day did you do lessons?

Mock Turtle. Ten hours the first day, nine the next and so on.

Alice. What a curious plan.

Gryphon. That's the reason they're called lessons. Because they lessen from day to day.

Alice. Then the eleventh day must have been a holiday.

Gryphon. Of course it was.

Alice. And the twelfth day?

Mock Turtle. A teacher's meeting.

Gryphon. To decide how to go on.

Alice. And the thirteenth day?

Gryphon. The teachers went on and on.

Mock Turtle. And on and on.

Gryphon. Until tea-time and then there was games.

Mock Turtle. And we danced the lobster quadrille.

Alice. That must be a very nice dance.

Mock Turtle. Would you like to see a little of it?

Alice. Very much indeed.

Gryphon. We can do it without lobsters. Which of us shall sing?

Mock Turtle. Oh you sing. I've forgotten the words.

Gryphon. I've forgotten the words too.

Mock Turtle. Very well. I'll sing.

Mock Turtle, and Gryphon dance and sing while Alice watches.

> 'Will you walk a little faster,' said a whiting to a snail,
> 'there's a lobster close behind us and he's treading on my tail.
> See how eagerly the lobsters and the turtles all advance!
> They are waiting on the shingle – will you come and join the dance?
> Will you, won't you, will you, won't you, will you join the dance?
> Will you, won't you, will you, won't you join the dance?
> You can really have no notion how delightful it will be
> When they take us up and throw us with the lobsters out to sea!'
> But the snail replied, 'too far, too far', and gave a look askance.
> Said he thanked the whiting kindly but he would not join the dance.

Alice. That was a very interesting dance.

Gryphon. Why is a whiting called a whiting? Do you know?

Alice. Because it's white, I suppose.

Gryphon. That's another dull answer. It's called a whiting because it does the boots and Shoes, of course.

> Would not, could not, would not, could not, would not join the dance.
> Would not, could not, would not, could not, would not join the dance.
> 'what matters it how far we go?' his scaly friend replied.
> 'there is another shore, you know, upon the other side.
> The farther off from England, the nearer 'tis to France –
> Then turn not pale, beloved snail, but come and join the dance.
> Will you, won't you, will you, won't you, will you join the dance?
> Will you, won't you, will you, won't you, won't you join the dance?'

Mock Turtle. What does your boots and shoes? What makes them so shiny?

Alice. They're done with blacking, I believe.

Gryphon. Boots and shoes under the sea are done with whiting.

Alice. And what are they made of?

Gryphon. Soles and eels of course. Any shrimp could have told you that.

Queen. (*Offstage yelling*) The trial is beginning. Anyone who does not attend will be beheaded.

Alice. Oh there she is. We had better go.

Gryphon. Not us.

Mock Turtle. Not us.

Gryphon. We're going back down.

Mock Turtle. Back down under. Farewell. (*Sobs*). Farewell.

The Gryphon and the Mock Turtle exit.

SCENE TEN

The White Rabbit recruits eleven of the audience as jurors. He gives them pads and pencils.

Enter the court with the King and the Queen. On a table is a large plate of tarts. There is uproar.

King. Silence in court!...silence in court!...silence in court. This trial is now in session.

The White Rabbit blows his trumpet. The King and Queen and jurors all start writing.

Alice. What are they doing. They can't have anything to write down, the trial has not yet begun.

White Rabbit. They're putting down their names for fear they might forget them by the end of the trial.

Alice. Stupid things!

King. Silence in court! Call in the prisoner.

White Rabbit. (*Trumpets*) I call the Knave of Hearts.

Enter the Knave in ball and chains.

White Rabbit. (*Pointing to the Knave*). The accused. Write down his name. Write down all the evidence.

King. Silence in court. Read the accusation.

White Rabbit.

'The Queen of Hearts, she made some tarts

All on a summer's day.
The Knave of Hearts, he stole those tarts
And took them quite away.' (*uproar*)

King. Silence in court! Consider your verdict.

White Rabbit. Not yet. Not yet. There's a great deal to come before that!

King. Call the first witness. And remember. No jokers.

White Rabbit. Call the Hatter.

The White Rabbit blows trumpet. Enter Hatter with a piece of bread and a cup, followed by the Dormouse.

Hatter. I beg your pardon Your Majesty for bringing these in, but I hadn't quite finished my tea when I was sent for.

King. You ought to have finished. When did you begin?

Hatter. (*Looking at his watch*) The 14th of March, I think.

Dormouse. Or the 15th.

Hatter. Or 16th.

King. (*To jury*) Write that down. Now add them all up. And give your answer in shillings and pence. (*To the Hatter*) Take off your hat.

Hatter. It isn't mine, Your Majesty.

King. Ah. Stolen. (*To jury*) Write that down.

Hatter. I keep them to sell. I've none of my own. I'm a hatter.

The Queen begins to stare at the Hatter fixedly. She continues staring at him all through the next sequence.

King. (*To the Hatter*) Give your evidence. And don't be nervous or I'll have you executed on the spot.

Queen. I know this face. I remember this face. The concert...twinkle twinkle...bring me a list of singers at the last concert.

King. (*The White Rabbit exits. Hatter trembles and bites his cup*) Give your evidence or I'll have you executed, whether you're nervous or not.

Hatter. I'm a poor man Your Majesty, and I hadn't yet finished my tea – not above a week or so – and what with the bread and butter getting so thin, and the twinkling of the tea...

King. The twinkling of what?

Hatter. It began with the t.

King. Of course twinkling begins with a t. Do you take me for a dunce? Go on.

Hatter. I'm a poor man and most things twinkled after that – only the March Hare said...

Dormouse. He didn't.

Hatter. He did.

Dormouse. I deny it. (*Nods off to sleep*).

King. (*To jury*) Are you writing that down? Leave out that bit.

Hatter. Well at any rate, the Dormouse said...

They all look at the Dormouse who is by now asleep.

Dormouse. Zzzzzzzzzzzzzzz!

Hatter. After that I cut some more bread and butter.

King. What did the Dormouse say?

The White Rabbit returns and gives a piece of paper to the Queen.

Hatter. That...I can't remember.

King. You must remember or I'll have you executed.

Hatter. I am a poor man, Your Majesty.

King. You are a very poor speaker. If that's all you know about it you may stand down.

Hatter. I can't go no lower. I'm on the floor as it is.

King. Then you may sit down.

Hatter. I'd rather finish my tea.

King. You may go.

Queen. (*Finishing reading the list of singers*) I thought so. He murdered the time. Remove him and his head.

The Hatter charges out. Uproar.

King. Silence! Call the next witness.

WhiteRabbit. The Cook! I call the Cook.

Trumpet. Enter the Duchess's Cook. Everybody begins to sneeze.

King. Give your evidence.

Cook. I will not.

White Rabbit. Your Majesty must cross-examine this witness.

King. Well if I must, I must. What are tarts made of?

Cook. Pepper mostly.

Dormouse. Treacle.

Queen. Collar that Dormouse. Suppress him. Behead the Dormouse. Pinch him. Off with his whiskers. Turn that Dormouse out of court.

Everyone gets into an uproar. The Dormouse is stuffed into a bag and carried out. The Cook shakes the pepper. Everybody sneezes. Exit Cook.

King. Settle down. Settle down. Never mind. Call the next witness. Really my dear, you must cross-examine the next witness. It quite makes my forehead ache.

White Rabbit. (*Blowing the trumpet and reading out*) Alice. I call Alice.

Alice comes forward.

King. What do you know about this business?

Alice. Nothing.

King. Nothing whatever?

Alice. Nothing whatever.

King. That's very important.

White Rabbit. Unimportant Your Majesty means.

King. Unimportant of course I meant. Important. Unimportant. Important. Unimportant.

(*To jury*) Write that down. Silence. Rule 42. All persons more than a mile high to leave the court.

Everybody looks at Alice.

Alice. I'm not a mile high.

King. You are.

Queen. Nearly two miles.

Alice. Well I shan't go at any rate. Besides that's not a regular rule. You invented it just now.

King. It's the oldest rule in the book.

Alice. Then it ought to be number one.

King. Consider your verdict.

White Rabbit. There's more evidence to come yet, please, Your Majesty. This paper has just been picked up.

King. What's in it?

White Rabbit. I haven't opened it yet but it seems to be a letter written by the prisoner to somebody.

King. It must have been that, unless it was written to nobody, which isn't usual, you know.

White Rabbit. It isn't directed at all. In fact there's nothing written on the outside. It isn't a letter after all: it's a set of verses.

Queen. Are they in the prisoner's handwriting?

White Rabbit. No, they're not and that's the queerest thing about it.

King. He must have imitated somebody else's hand.

Knave: Please, Your Majesty. I didn't write it and they can't prove I did. There's no name signed at the end.

King. If you didn't sign it, that only makes matters worse. You must have meant some mischief or else you'd have signed it like any honest man.

Queen. (*Applauding and indicating to the jury to do the same*) That proves his guilt.

Alice. It proves nothing of the sort. Why you don't even know what the verses are about.

King. Read them.

White Rabbit. Where should I begin please Your Majesty?

King. Begin at the beginning and go on 'till you come to the end and then stop.

White Rabbit.

'They told me you had been to her,
And mentioned me to him:
She gave me a good character
But said I could not swim.
He sent them word I had not gone
(we know it to be true):
If she would push the matter on,
What would become of you?
I gave her one, they gave him two,
You gave us three or more;
They all returned from him to you,
Though they were mine before.
My notion was that you had been
(before she had this fit)
An obstacle that came between
Him, and ourselves, and it.
Don't let him know she liked him best.

42

For this must ever be
A secret kept from all the rest,
Between yourself and me.'

King. That's the most important piece of evidence yet. So now. Let the jury decide.

Alice. If any one of them can explain it, I'll give him six-pence. I don't believe there's an atom of meaning in it.

King. If there's no meaning in it, that saves us a world of trouble, you know, as we needn't try to find any. And yet I don't know, 'said I could not swim...' (*to the knave*) You can't swim can you?

Knave. Do I look like I can?

King. 'We know it to be true' – that's the jury of course. 'I gave him one, they gave her two'. Why that must be what he did with the tarts...

Alice. But it goes on, 'They all returned from him to you'.

King. And there they are . Nothing can be clearer than that. Then again it says, 'before she had this fit'. You never had fits my dear. I think.

Queen. (*Roaring*) Never. Never. Never. Sentence first. Verdict afterwards.

Alice. Stuff and nonsense.

Queen. Hold your tongue.

Alice. I won't.

Queen. Off with her head.

Alice. Who cares for you? You're nothing but a pack of cards.

They all gasp and rise.Alice is standing USC on the cube – pulls one of the cards from stand.
Sweeps down to King and Rabbit and hits them with the card.
Rabbit and King swirl to SR and exit.
Queen steps off cube and moves DSC/Knave enters DSL.
Alice hits Queen with card.
Alice hits K with card and both exit DSL.
Cook and Hatter enter DSR – Alice hits them with card and both exit DSL.
Duchess enters SR and crosses to Alice CS.
Duchess takes card from Alice and exits DSR.
Alice swirls to DSR, falls to ground and sleeps.

SCENE ELEVEN

Lights up. Alice is sitting beside Edith in the garden as in Scene One. Edith is asleep with her book.

Alice. Edith. Edith wake up.

Edith. What time is it? (*She consults her watch*) Heavens, it's almost half past six.

Alice. I've had such a curious dream, Edith.

Edith. Well, tell me later. We better move inside now. The bridge tournament is due to start.

Alice. No. Stay here. I want to tell you about it now.

Edith. I can't listen to you now. Mother wants me to help.

Alice. Go on then.

Edith. You'll be needed too. You'll have to do a recitation.

Alice. No one will want to hear a recitation. And besides, I don't want to do one.

Edith. Oh, come on Alice. You know you love performing.

Alice. I don't actually. I only do it because I'm told to.

Edith. Mother will tell you to.

Alice. And I shall tell her that I don't want to recite any more.

Edith. What's all this, Alice? Are you all right?

Alice. I'm fine, thank you, Edith. You go in and serve out the tea.

Edith. What are you going to do out here?

Alice. I'm going to remember. I'm going to think.

The cast assembles and sings.

> Thus grew the tale of Wonderland:
> Thus slowly, one by one,
> Its quaint events were hammered out –
> And now the tale is done,
> And home we steer, a merry crew,
> Beneath the setting sun.
> Alice! A childish story take,
> And, with a gentle hand,
> Lay it where childhood's dreams are twined
> In memory's mystic band,
> Like pilgrim's withered wreath of flowers
> Plucked in a far-off land.

End.

Notes from Mary Elizabeth Burke-Kennedy

I wrote *Alice in Wonderland* at a time when we had two little daughters who had spent their young lives trailing around theatres with us, watching rehearsals of Scandinavian or Russian plays which must have bored them senseless, although they were always too polite to say. So I wrote *Alice* for them; for them to go to and to enjoy and to be able to talk about afterwards with authority, for they knew what it was about.

I also wrote it for myself because I loved *Alice in Wonderland*. I loved it as a child because it made me laugh and because I felt I knew her confusion about being big one minute and little the next and because I recognized the nasty, bullying, adult beings it depicted, in all their glorious stupidity.

I was lucky to be working at the time, in a Studio in Focus, where I was the director, with a group of actors who were adventurous and eager to experiment on the stage. So *Alice* became The Focus Studio's first production and the group set about rehearsing the play and getting it on.

We were also lucky in having a dazzling creative team. John Mc Nulty, the artist, designed a set which was an adventure playground, with a swing, a slide, a rope ladder and all kinds of beautiful wooden structures that could be transformed by the cast as they worked with them.

The lighting design was by Declan Burke-Kennedy, who had lit all of Focus productions and established his own distinctive style. In this production, some of the effects came from on-stage lights, manoeuvred and changed by the actors themselves, a radical breaking of the suspension of disbelief, not just for the regular Focus audience, but for the new audience the production attracted.

The costumes were designed by Joan Bergin, the first costume design by the designer who has gone on to win countless Emmys and Iftas.

And the music was created by Roger Doyle, one of Ireland's most distinguished contemporary composers.

And last but not least, the visual magic was enhanced by Robert Lane's magnificent masks.

It was a break away from naturalism, from psychological realism and from the somewhat earnest atmosphere of Focus's work.

Everyone was being invited to play. The young audience members sitting near the front of the stage were issued with slates to become part of the jury in the trial scene. And no one enjoyed himself more than the boy who shouted aloud that a real mouse had fallen out of the theatre loft on to the table where the Mad Hatter and the March Hare were having their tea party, and was running over the head of the Dormouse, sleeping in her mask.

Alice marked a departure for me, a new direction that led me together with the Studio players to devise such work as *Legends*, *Curigh the Shapeshifter*, Gogol's *The Nose*, *The Parrot*, *Women in Arms* and ultimately the many productions with Storytellers Theatre Company. This comprises a body of work for adults and for children, work which has revelled, as *Alice in Wonderland* did, in the art of a good story and in the artifice of theatre.

The Day Of The Mayfly

A Short Play

by

Declan Burke-Kennedy

Cast:

Man

Woman

The Day of the Mayfly was first performed in April 1980 at the Focus Theatre in Dublin.

The cast was Tom Laidlaw and Mary Elizabeth Burke-Kennedy. It was directed by the author.

The action takes place in the main room of a lakeside fishing lodge in rural Ireland.

© *The Day of the Mayfly* is copyrighted by the author.

Carrigahorig
Nenagh
Co Tipperary
Ireland.
Dbbken2@gmail.com

SCENE ONE

The main room of an Irish lakeside cottage in early spring, 1980. Wintry afternoon lighting. Fishing rods nets and other angling paraphernalia adorn the walls. The exterior door is open and lake water laps gently against the shore. A bald coot calls and then a moor hen. There is the rustle of powerful wings on water as a swan takes off.

The man is taking a photo of the lake through the open door. The camera clicks once, is rolled forward and clicks again. We hear the swan's whoop-whoop-whoop fading into the distance.

Man. (*He is in his thirties and has a middle-class Dublin accent*) Gotcha, my beauties...

We hear a car pull up on gravel. The engine is switched off and a car door opens. Footsteps on the gravel as the driver opens the car boot and comes towards the house.

Man. At last. (*Calling out*) Welcome to my sanctuary, albeit a borrowed one. Are you exhausted?

Woman. (*Same age, same accent*) Pretty exhausted.

Man. Come on in. Let me give you a hand.

Woman. No problem. I can manage.

She enters, wearing a long fur coat, a matching fur hat and carrying an enormous supermarket bag which he takes from her and sets down on the kitchen counter beside his half-unpacked bag of groceries.

Woman. Have you been here long?

Man. Long enough to unpack a few things, turn on the water supply and take a picture or two.

Woman. It's chilly enough, isn't it?

Man. I'm surprised you feel the cold with all those furs on. (*He closes the door and embraces her*) Let me put my arms...

Woman. Wait! Give me a chance to thaw out.

Man. (*Playfully*) I just want to devour you. With those things on you look like you might devour me.

Woman. (*Moving away*) I just might. (*After a moment's hesitation she puts her car keys on the table. There is an awkward silence*) So this is it.

Man. Yes. Do you like it?

Woman. Yes, it's fine. (*Looking in direction of the audience*) And this is the famous lake. It's certainly very... fascinating.

Man. You can see the whole length of the lake from over here. See. Isn't it beautiful? Six miles of wooded islands and inlets. I dream about it so much I begin to wonder if it's real.

Woman. (*Pointedly*) And are you disappointed when you find it is?

Man. (*Admiring her*) On the contrary, I'm always surprised. Pleasantly surprised.

Woman. You know something? I think I could very easily grow to love you. (*They are both surprised and slightly embarrassed by her declaration*) I know I'm not meant to say such things. It's against the rules. (*He moves towards her but she moves away and changes the subject*) So, tell me everything. How did you manage?

Man. Manage?

Woman. To get away?

Man. Oh no trouble at all. I explained that I needed a break from my work.

Woman. (*Picking up the camera*) And what about all this?

Man. I've always enjoyed photographing the lake in winter. There's something private about it at this time of year.

Woman. I'd better keep out of range. (*She sets down the camera*)

Man. So. Tell me about you. How did you manage?

Woman. Oh, I'm officially at a trade fair in Düsseldorf, buying ideas and materials for autumn fashions.

Man. Autumn fashions? Isn't that a bit on the early side?

Woman. In the rag trade we've always to think at least two seasons ahead.

Man. Won't it seem strange when you arrive home with no samples?

Woman. They'll be at home when I get back, don't worry...

Man. You know, you're a very cunning lady. It's no wonder you've risen to the top.

Woman. (*Going to the window*) I'm tired of it all. I'd prefer your life any day...with all your impossible dreams. Six miles of wooded islands and inlets. Hmm! (*She seems to be mellowing*) You know...

Suddenly there is a hollow thunderous sound over their heads. She starts with fright.

My God! What's happening?

Man. (*Laughing, shouting above the roar*) It's only the water pump. I turned it on when I arrived. It must have been stuck or something.

Woman. Does this go on all the time?

Man. No. Only at select moments and intimate interludes. It makes less noise as the tank fills. (*The noise reduces but continues*) There, you see. It'll turn itself off in a minute or two.

Woman. (*Rummaging in her bag, agitated*) For a moment I thought it was Angela and a posse of her friends coming to lynch us. (*She lights a cigarette*) What have you done about her anyway?

Man. I thought we agreed to leave spouses behind.

Woman. She knows you're here?

Man. Of course.

Woman. I presume you took steps to ensure she won't barge in on top of us.

Man. Of course. I let the air out of her tyres.

Woman. Seriously.

Man. Then I broke her legs and took her chequebook.

Woman. I'm not up to any scenes you know. There has to be a stage in life when one leaves all that behind. I doubt if I could take even a mild altercation after that nightmare journey.

Man. She won't be around. I promise.

Woman. (*Still agitated*) It's just that I want you to relax. It's no good if you're all tense, listening for footsteps, peeping through curtains. It's no good for you that way.

Man. You're very thoughtful.

Woman. I wouldn't go that far, but I am concerned about you. You know what you're like when you start thinking of her?

Man. Well, that's why I...

Woman. I mean physically. You do remember, don't you?

Man. Do we have to go into all that again?

Woman. Well why not? Why make a big thing of it? It's quite common, I'm sure. I doubt if you're the first man who couldn't make it when he thought of his wife.

Man. That's not the whole story.

Woman. Why do you deny it? I'm only repeating what you told me yourself.

Man. Well let me tell you something else. That's not a common occurrence for me. It only happens when I'm with you.

Woman. I see. This looks like being a great weekend.

Man. What I mean is it only happens if I think of her when I'm with you. When I'm with her it doesn't happen. Especially when I think of you.

Woman. (*More pleased than shocked*) Really?

Man. Really and truly.

Woman. Well I'm glad that's out of the way. (*Pause*). You know it sounds to me like you've got a concentration problem. I mean, here we are, two hundred miles from suburbia, right in the heart of your dream world, and all you do is talk about your wife.

Man. But I...(*He sighs*) Oh, I give up.

Woman. Does that lake not look funny to you?

Man. Funny?

Woman. I mean, not quite right.

Man. How can a lake be not quite right?

Woman. It looks sort of swollen and puffy...like an allergy.

Man. I don't see that.

Woman. Are you sure it's safe?

Man. That depends on what you intend doing with it.

Woman. I mean to live near.

Man. Do you mean will it come barging in on top of us?

Woman. No. I mean vapours. Is it giving off vapours? Look at that mist. It could be poisonous.

Man. Where on earth did you get such an idea?

Woman. Something I read about pollution. And what about that water tank...?

Man. Come, come. I'm sure we'll be alright for two days. Let's get the things unpacked and get a good fire going. That might help you thaw out. (*She starts unpacking the groceries*)

Woman. The house is quite warm actually.

Man. (*Breaking twigs to start the fire*) They keep the central heating on all winter.

Woman. Do they use it much?

Man. They keep it on all winter.

Woman. I mean the house. It's kind of cute.

Man. Oh. No. Only in summer. Maybe a weekend or two for the mayfly.

Woman. Is that all? No wonder they've to keep the heating on.

Man. What do you mean?

Woman. I mean they wouldn't have to keep the heating on if they used the house more often.

Man. Oh?

Woman. An empty house gets cold because there's no body heat in it. Didn't you know that? I read recently that the nuclear family has contributed to the global energy crisis by increasing our per capita consumption of domestic heating fuels.

Man. You read the most amazing things.

Woman. It looks like somebody keeps an eye on the place. I mean no cobwebs. All that firewood. Is there a caretaker?

Man. There's a local man who looks after the garden and his wife does the odd bit of cleaning.

Woman. Do you know him?

Man. Sure I do.

Woman. What's he like?

Man. He's a big burly bloke with a twitch and a flaming orange beard. You should see him splitting logs.

Woman. You make him sound like a Nordic lake monster.

Man. That's a good description. He used to be a gillie. He knows every inch of the lake. I'm telling you, he wouldn't be long getting those furs off you. Maybe he'll come around this weekend and lend a hand.

Woman. You shouldn't joke about things like that.

Man. Well he may come to split a few logs. He usually does if he sees smoke and other signs of life about the place.

Woman. (*Agitated*) Are you serious?

Man. Sure.

Woman. (*In a near panic*) Well, don't just stand there. Put that fire out! (*She runs to the sink and fills a saucepan from the tap*)

Man. What are you doing?

Woman. I'm going to put out the fire so he won't see the smoke!

Man. (*Intercepting the saucepan*) Hold on. Calm down. You'll make twice as much smoke pouring water on the fire.

Woman. Well then, what'll we do?

Man. What do you mean?

Woman. What'll we do if he recognizes you? It's bound to get back to the owners and Angela and then...

Man. Please. Calm down. I haven't seen him for years. He wouldn't know me from Adam. I'll tell him I'm a circus manager and you're my performing bear.

Woman. I'm not worried for myself. It's you. You know what happens when you're all uptight. I don't want us to ruin everything for one silly little weekend.

Man. (*Angry*) What do you mean silly little weekend? We've been planning it and talking about it for weeks. Every time I said we should sort things out you said, Wait till the lake.

Woman. I know I did, but I thought we'd be completely alone. You never said anything about the woodcutter and his wife.

Man. Of course I didn't. I wasn't planning spending the weekend with the woodcutter and his wife. I tell you they won't come by. And even if they do, they won't know who we are or why we're here.

Woman. Any educationally sub-normal half-wit would know why we're here.

Man. I wish I'd never mentioned him.

Woman. But you did. And you know why? Because he was on your mind. You *are* worried. I know it. You can't hide anything from me.

Man. I wasn't worried until you got me started.

Woman. Then you admit you're worried.

Man. Yes I am. Suddenly I'm very worried. But not in the way you think.

Woman. Why don't you admit it? You're worried about us. You've no real faith in this relationship. You're worried that we might have blown it out of all proportion. I mean drifting drunkenly into bed after an office party is one thing. It's another to meet like this in the cold light of ...of calculated deception. This is pure unmitigated adultery and you're scared to death that you won't make it big enough to justify all the trouble and expense.

Man. If you want to discuss it that frankly, please stop pacing about, take off those furs and sit down.

Woman. I think we should have a drink first.

Man. Alright. Let's pour ourselves a drink and then sit down and discuss it all calmly....without furs. (*She takes off her coat and he drapes it over a chair*). That's better. Now. Where did you put the drinks box?

Woman. I must have left it in my car.

Man. Give me the keys.

Woman. No wait. I'll go. That would be safer. Can I have my coat please? (*She starts to put it on again*)

Man. O no! Not the coat again. What do you mean safer?

Woman. Just in case the gamekeeper comes by.

Man. Who?

Woman. The red-bearded skull splitter. (*She picks up her keys from the counter and leaves*)

Man. (*Speaking to himself*) This must be purgatory. Maybe some music will do the trick.

He fiddles with an old radio. There is a blast of French, which fades away. He taps the radio but it remains silent. We hear a car boot being closed.

Merde, alors! (*The woman enters*) Bring out the cognac. That's what we both need.

Woman. The box isn't there. It must be in your car. Maybe you brought it in already.

Man. I don't see it here. Are you sure you didn't bring it in?

Woman. I only brought in the groceries.

Man. Are you sure it's not in you car?

Woman. Positive. Are you sure it's not in yours?

Man. There's the bag of provisions I brought in my car. You said you'd take the booze in yours. Maybe...(*He rummages in her bag of groceries*) No, it's not here.

Woman. O no! (*Realizing*)

Man. What?

Woman. Do you remember I went back to the shop while you took the groceries to my car?

Man. Don't tell me.

Woman. I must have got flustered when the shop assistant said my husband had left his chequebook.

Man. Your husband?

Woman. You...she thought you were my husband.

Man. Don't tell me. I didn't. Did I?

Woman. You did. (*She goes to hand him his chequebook from her coat pocket, but then thinks better of her intention and holds on to it*).

Man. (*Downcast*) Don't tell me.

Woman. (*Annoyed*) Don't keep saying that. I've told you for Christ's sake.

Man. Thirty-six quid worth of booze! What a waste.

Woman. How far back is it?

Man. About fifty miles. You insisted we should shop miles away. At least fifty miles away.

Woman. (*Laughing*) Did I say that?

Man. Forty-six quid worth of booze. What a waste.

Woman. You're starting to repeat yourself again.

Man. So I am. Ah well, there's a pub only two miles back the road.

Woman. The local?

Man. Yes. I'll pop over and replace the lost liquor. Can I have my chequebook please?

Woman. (*Clutching her handbag*) But what about our discussion?

Man. It'll keep, don't worry.

Woman. And the woodcutter? The one with the twitch and the orange hair. He more than likely drinks in the local on a Saturday night.

Man. Oh no. I give up! (*He goes and sits apart*)

Woman. (*Following him*) Come, come. Don't tell me you can't spend a few hours with me unless your mind and senses have been steeped in alcohol. That's not very flattering is it? Let me massage your furrowed brow. (*She does and he relents gradually*)

Man. I wasn't thinking of me. It's you. You know how you are if you don't have a drink...oh that's very soothing. Shoulders. Great.

Woman. Well stop talking then and concentrate.

Man. Concentrate on what?

Woman. Anything. The sensation. You should take up yoga, you know. It would release you from the clutter in your mind.

Man. I'm not sure I'm the one...

Woman. Hush. Relax.

Man. Oh that's good. (*Passionately*) Come on. We've only got two days here. Why don't we...

Woman. Wait. Hold your horses. We haven't eaten yet. I bought some beautiful things for a curry. A hot one.

Man. But we've no wine or beer. I can't eat hot curry without beer or wine.

Woman. You'll survive this once. I thought this weekend was to be a voyage of discovery, a journey into the unknown...isn't that what you called it?

Man. That was in a different context. It was not meant to be a temperance outing.

Woman Shh! You're not concentrating. Look it's getting dark. The lake is like the glass floor of an enormous ballroom. Imagine we're dancing across it to the most beautiful music in the world. Does this radio work?

Man. If you kick it. (*He taps the radio and it obligingly provides an orchestral version of 'The Continental'...very lush...very seductive*)

Woman. Imagine we're gliding, in perfect harmony, with effortless grace.

Man. I hate dancing.

Woman. You wouldn't hate it with me. I would dance like Ginger Rogers and you would be magically transformed into Fred Astaire. (*The music continues*)

Man. You have a very nice body.

Woman. Not any longer.

Man. Yes you do. I'm a photographer. I know about these things (*Pause*). You also have an extraordinary imagination.

Woman. I read somewhere that dreams are like vapours from the body...unused body energies. What do you think?

Man. I've no idea. It's an interesting theory.

Woman. I was always told at school that I had too much imagination. I used to write fantasies in those days. I once got ten out of ten for a story on the evils of marital infidelity. I called it the disease of our time.

Man. Tell me about it.

Woman. All I remember was that a couple of runaway lovers found a hideout in the woods which promised secrecy and seclusion – until they were plagued by a scourge of tiny insects that ran up and down their bodies and caused them to abandon their den of iniquity in hideous agony. It was very symbolic. The nuns loved it.

Man. You must have been a hateful child. A smug, intellectual prig.

Woman. On the contrary I was very sensuous. You would have loved me. But I was only interested in pale, anaemic types who looked like they wouldn't survive a bad winter. Nordic lake monsters and gillies didn't turn me on at all.

Man. What else did you write about...besides your future career?

Woman. Oh, beautiful delicate things...like silver cobwebs at dawn and petals floating on streams. Beneath my stern façade I was a hopeless romantic. I haven't changed much, have I?

Man. Alas, I don't think so.

Woman. So what did you write about?

Man. Oh, nothing very significant really...people escaping from prisons, things like that. I never got ten out of ten. Except for catechism.

Woman. Really? Did you have exams in catechism?

Man. We had exams in everything, all the time. It was a way of keeping our minds off sex. Needless to say I was an academic failure. Though I always enjoyed learning things by heart, poems and catechism...for some reason.

Woman. Recite some catechism for me. I find it very soothing.

Man. Let me think. What is sanctifying grace? Sanctifying grace is the grace...sanctifying grace is the grace...I've forgotten. Wait, I remember this one: what are alcoholic drinks?

Woman. You would.

Man. Alcoholic drinks are drinks that contain alcohol...such as whiskey, porter, wine, brandy, rum, beer, gin, ale, hops and cider. Howzat?

Woman. Magnificent!

Man. It was the most popular question in the catechism. Whiskey, porter, wine, brandy, rum, beer, gin, ale...God, I'd love a drink. (*The music fades away*)

Woman. (*Angry*) Oh you're impossible. Maybe if I feed you, you'll calm down.

Man. Fifty-six quid worth of booze!

Woman. I think that lake is diseased. Look at the way it keeps changing colour.

Man. It's getting dark. No one would see me in this light.

Woman. (*Vehemently*) No. No. No.

Man. All right, don't shout. I thought you were (*imitating her*) beyond that kind of thing.

Woman. If you're going to go on and on about drink I'm getting in the car and driving home this minute.

Man. Wait.

Woman. I mean, what did we come here for anyway? To drink?

Man. No, not to drink. But you know how you are if you don't…

Woman. (*In a fury*) I know nothing. Absolutely nothing. We've been here for almost half an hour and all we've done is talk about drink and your wretched wife. I've had enough.

Man. That's not true. We talked about other things.

Woman. Such as?

Man. Such as the lake. Your compositions. The catechism.

Woman. Great! In the middle of a global energy crisis we drive two hundred miles in two cars, that's four hundred miles in all, eight hundred by the time we get back, and all we do is sit around talking about sanctifying grace and sixty-six pounds of lost alcohol.

Man. I need a drink. I really do.

Woman. It's enough to make me mad. I spend God knows how long trying to calm you down and at the mere mention of drink you erupt like a volcano. I suppose it'll be the same in bed!

Man. So that's what this is all about. Well let me tell you something. If you're happier with your macho lover boy…what's his name…why don't you stick with him and let's call it quits.

Woman. That's why I was brought here. To be told to stick with what's his name.

Man. I think I'll go for a walk. Can I have my chequebook?

Woman. (*Rummaging in her bag*) That's right. Off you go, into the great unknown. (*She tosses him the chequebook*). Typical. Leave me at the mercy of the woodcutter and his wife. Are you sure you shouldn't axe me to pieces yourself?

Man. I've got to get some air, to clear my head.

Woman. I hope it blows into the lake.

Man. Why don't you come with me? We don't really need to eat, do we?

Woman. And what else are we going to do with this stuff? Bring it home? Here dear. A souvenir from Düsseldorf. Two pounds of filet steak and a Spanish onion. (*She throws provisions at him as he exits, banging the door*).

Woman. Typical. Can't even light a fire properly. (*She paces about*) That's what's wrong with this place. No body heat. (*She stops and looks at the lake*) Godforsaken cesspool.

Lights fade and the gentle sounds of the lake increase in volume.

SCENE TWO

There is a blazing fire and the woman is reading. She laughs at something she reads.

There is a sound at the door. She drops the book and stands up.

Woman. (*Alarmed*) Who's there?

Man. (*Slurred*) Let me in. (*She opens the door and he staggers in. She closes the door*) Why did you take the key out of the lash? The latch, I mean. It's always left in.

Woman. (*Picking up the book and sitting*) I see you've managed to clear your head.

Man. It's a beautiful night. Intoxicating. You should have come with me.

Woman. I was having too good a time here.

Man. There was a great crowd in the pub. The craic was ninety. What are you reading? *The Illustrated Encyclopaedia of Freshwater Angling.* Very interesting.

Woman. I couldn't put it down.

Man. Could you not find anything else?

Woman. I've read everything else...while you were out.

Man. Why didn't you make a break for it. Whoosh!

Woman. Don't think the thought didn't cross my mind.

Man. You've made the place nice and warm. (*Pause*) Look what the cat brought in. (*He produces a bottle from inside his anorak*) Vintage port. Let's have a hot one to celebrate my return.

Woman. Did you meet the Nordic gamekeeper?

Man. I don't think I met anyone fitting that description. (*Pause*) Well, what's new around here?

Woman. What's new? Oh, a lot. I now know the favourite haunts of pike, perch and trout. And I'm a fund of knowledge on the mating habits of insects.

Man. Good. Time well spent.

Woman. It may interest you to know the mayfly performs a ritual dance before mating.

Man. Who?

Woman. The mayfly.

Man. I hate dancing.

Woman. So you keep saying. All in one day, they rise to the surface of the lake where they were hatched, fly into the air and perform their ritual dance. Then they select a mate, copulate on the wing, deposit their fertilized eggs on the water and die.

Man. Who?

Woman. The mayfly.

Man. It sounds like they cram a lot into one day.

Woman. They've no choice. It's their last.

Man. Hmm! I know the feeling. (*He yawns and stretches out on the sofa*) I think I'll call it a day. I feel like a spent gnat. (*He yawns*)

Woman. A spent what?

Man. Gnat. G-nat look that up in your Funk and Wagnall.

Woman. You'd better cover yourself with a blanket if you're going to sleep there. Tell me where they're kept and I'll get one.

Man. Try that chest beside the fire. It's a kind of emergency capsule. It contains flares, safety jackets, parachutes and the like. (*She takes a sleeping bag from the chest and spreads it over him*).

Man. I don't like this menacing calm. It makes me feel ill at ease.

Woman. Shhh. You look very shaky. Are you going to be alright there? (*He snores*) I was right when I was a kid. Marital infidelity isn't all it's cracked up to be.

Man. (*Sitting up wide awake*) You were dead right. The disease of our time.

Woman. Is that why you got drunk?

Man. Not at all. I got drunk because I drank too much (*Lies down again*).

Woman. Because you think I let you down.

Man. (*Up again*) You've let nothing down, that's the trouble. Not a damn thing. You're all furs and frigidity, like a seal on a pilgrimage. All you've done since you arrived here is stalk around sniffing vapours from the lake. This was meant to be a dirty weekend and so far it's been the most sterile, moral, upright event of the decade.

Woman. So that's how you see it?

Man. That's how it is. (*Lies down again*) Isn't it?

Woman. I see it differently.

Man. Well, go on. Don't keep me in suspense.

Woman. You're on edge – like a bear with a sore head, and you're trying to blame me for your own reluctance to take the bull by the horns.

Man. There are too many animals in this story.

Woman. Do you deny that you've been on edge since we arrived?

Man. (*Up again*) Of course I've been on edge. Do you have any idea of how I was looking forward to this weekend, trying to arrange everything so it wouldn't end up like a therapy session. Of course I was on edge. But I had it under control.

Woman. Until it turned out that we'd left a few bottles of drink behind.

Man. The drink is immaterial. Besides it was you who left it behind.

Woman. So what then?

Man. So what then yourself. (*Down again*) Why should I be analysed, massaged, interrogated? I'm not the one who thinks the lake has a disease.

Woman. There's really not much point talking to you when you're in this state.

Man. Alright. No more talking. (*Up again*) Here, take a swig. (*She declines the offer*) So here's to us: bottoms up, knickers off, mud in your eye and down the hatch! (*He drinks*) Now it's my turn to be truth and frankful – fruit and thankful…you know what I mean.

Woman. (*Laughing*) Sometimes that's not such a good idea.

Man. Ah ha! Getting worried, eh? Afraid you're in the spotlight, is that it?

Woman. I've nothing to hide.

Man. Of course you have. It's just that you haven't found it yet. You're sitting there clutching your furs waiting for me to find it for you.

Woman. Let me tell you something. I'm not going to sit here and be told how repressed and frigid I am, when I happen to know otherwise. (*She picks up her overnight bag and stamps out of the room in the direction of the bedroom.*)

Man. Typical. (*He calls out after her.*) Typical woman. All give and no take. (*Down again*) Or all take and no...what the hell. I'm too tired...too tired...

The radio comes on and blares out some French pop or rock 'n roll – maybe Françoise Hardy. He pulls the blanket over his head and groans. Lights come down slowly.

SCENE THREE

The cottage, not long after dawn. The woman is listening to the sounds of the lake, wearing a silk dressing gown or peignoir and a pair of leather riding boots, the man is sleeping fitfully. In the distance a church bell peals over and over.

Man. (*Suddenly, in his sleep*) Oh! Oh!

Woman. (*Gently*) Wake up, you're having a nightmare. How's the head? That bad. I'm not surprised. (*Intimately*) You needn't have got so desperate. I wanted you to come to bed with me.

Man. For all I knew those furs had fleas.

Woman. If you ever manage to get those eyes to focus again, you may notice some changes.

Man. Oh. You're swathed in silk. That's nice. But why are you wearing leather boots?

Woman. When you didn't put in an appearance this morning I decided to do some local research for myself.

Man. Why didn't you come and join me here?

Woman. What? In full view of the lake? You can't be serious. Why are there no curtains in this room?

Man. Because it's a house policy: you either do it in front of the lake or you don't do it at all. Listen. Church bells. (*Quoting*) *The holy hush of ancient sacrifice.*

Woman. What?

Man. (*Slowly remembering*)

> Complacencies of the peignoir, and late
> Coffee and oranges in a sunny chair
> And the green freedom of a cockatoo
> Upon a rug... mingle to dissipate
> The holy hush of ancient sacrifice.

Woman. What's all that about?

Man. What does it matter?

Woman. Don't be sulky. I just wanted time to thaw out, that's all.

Man. (*Quoting*)

> She dreams a little and she feels the dark
> Encroachment of that old catastrophe
> As a calm darkens among water lights.

Woman. Where did you pick that up?

Man. I can't remember any more. Wait (*He quotes*)

> The day is like wide water without sound
> Stilled for the passing of her dreaming feet.

Woman. It's beautiful.

Man. (*Dismissively*) It's called Sunday Morning. It's all about you listening to church bells across the lake and longing for your childhood innocence.

Woman. (*Changing the subject*) Well? Did you have pleasant dreams in your turbulent sleep?

Man. I don't remember. Something about escaping from prison as far as I recall. It's my recurring dream.

Woman. I'd have that looked into if I were you. Fruit juice or coffee?

Man. Both please. (*Quoting*)

> Coffee and oranges in a sunny chair.

I've so many toxins in my system at this stage that I'd better not stop now. I didn't notice those flowers last night.

Woman. You wouldn't have even if they'd been there. I went down to the lake to take part in the the dawn chorus this morning. Wonderful.

Man. Ah! The boots.

Woman. It's a hive of activity at that hour. Terns diving for moths on the water, spiders' webs all through the grass and reeds, tree creepers looking for insects in the trees, birds diving for fish, fish rising for flies. It's not exactly a very friendly neighbourhood.

Man. No petals floating on streams?

Woman. No. Nothing as tame as that.

Man. That sounds like an advance on last night. I suppose anything would be.

Woman. So what do you plan to do today?

Man. If that mist lifts it might be a good day for suicide.

Woman. What about your sailing expedition?

Man. Sailing in February?

Woman. (*Suggestively*) I can hoist a halyard you know.

Man. I don't doubt it. So you waited up for me last night. That's nice.

Woman. We can still make up for lost time.

Man. Right now my head's lifting off. Let's have some more coffee first.

Woman. I must be losing my touch. I used to be able to seduce men at will...metaphorically speaking of course. Now, I have to queue up behind coffee and port and sleep. Not to mention the real obstacle for both of us.

Man. What's that?

Woman. Angela, of course. What else?

Man. I thought we agreed to leave spouses behind.

Woman. Yes, but somehow or other we both managed to smuggle Angela along.

Man. Probably in place of the lost booze box. Well, don't you think we could send her packing at this stage?

Woman. I see. You love her too much to talk about her in these circumstances, but not enough to avoid these circumstances in the first place.

Man. I've never believed it was possible to measure love.

Woman. Some men remain faithful to their wives.

Man. A threatened species. Like Bavarian sheepdogs.

Woman. It must mean something.

Man. There are still people who believe the earth is flat. What does that prove?

Woman. I've no idea.

Man. Neither do I. (*She pours coffee*) Fidelity is something I associate with not very enterprising woolly animals and fundamentalist church-goers.

Woman. (*With sudden impatience*) Then why are you torturing yourself over your wife? What is it that's gnawing at you and coming between us? Why have you to soak yourself in alcohol before you can rise above your obsession with her? Why do you think that poem sprang into your mind? What the hell is going on?

Man. Hey, steady on. You don't believe in leaving space for answers, do you?

Woman. Why don't you admit it? You're still in love with Angela.

Man. Alright. I'm still in love with Angela.

Woman. And the guilt you feel is *not* because you're carrying on behind her back. It's because you've never been able to satisfy her.

Man. Hey, that's a sudden leap.

Woman. Sometimes that's necessary.

Man. Alright. Do I get general absolution or do I have to itemize every gruelling moment of failure?

Woman. (*Eating, mouth full of toast*) You've no idea how good this makes me feel.

Man. (*Ironically*) But think how we're deceiving Angela. And what's his name.

Woman. (*Responding*) It disturbs me profoundly.

Man. I mean they must assume by now that we're in the throes of intimacy.

Woman. Exciting pillow talk.

Man. Multiple lakeside orgasms.

Woman. Scenes of unspeakable lust.

Man. I'd hate to disappoint them.

Woman. Don't feel guilty about it. They're probably doing equally badly somewhere else. He's probably in Milan or Stockholm...at some fictional medical conference...with an ambitious radiographer or theatre nurse.

Man. Riddled with recrimination, no doubt.

Woman. No doubt. Or more likely he's over there in one of the chalets on the other side of the lake.

Man. Do you think so? My God this place is going downhill.

Woman. The transparent lies I'll have to put up with when I get home.

Man. I can imagine.

Woman. And nothing I say will convince him that all we've been doing is studying the mating habits of insects.

Man. Well don't try to convince him. Let him think what he will.

Woman. I suppose you're right. I shouldn't try to shatter his beliefs. I mean what would we put in their place?

Man. (*At window*) Do you really think he could be over there?

Woman. It's quite possible.

Man. You could have travelled down in the same car. Imagine!

Woman. We could have all come in the same car. Imagine that! For all we know Angela might be over there with him.

Man. (*Shocked*) You shouldn't joke about things like that.

Woman. Well she was a nurse, wasn't she?

Man. (*Playing with the possibility*) Yes, but...don't be absurd.

Woman. They're probably training a telescope on us this very minute.

Man. (*Sudden release*) Well then. What's all the fuss about?

Woman. That's what I say.

Man. Let me hold you in my arms.

Church bells sound again across the lake as they embrace.

Woman. Shh. Listen. The stillness.

Man. Do you think they're listening too?

Woman. Who?

Man. Angela and what's his name.

Woman. I'm sure of it.

Man. How long have they been seeing each other, would you say?

Woman. I don't know. Maybe as long as us.

Man. I bet they don't have half as good a time...

Woman. How could they?

Man. The little self-righteous hypocrite. I bet she thinks she's pulled a fast one on me.

Woman. Him too. Little do they know.

Man. You can trust no one nowadays.

Woman. Not a soul.

Man. I find it distressing that trust is breaking down.

Woman. Long live the church bells.

Man. Long live Angela and what's his name. The hypocrites. The bloody hypocrites.

Lights down as they embrace and go offstage arm-in-arm towards the bedroom.

End

Notes from Mary Elizabeth Burke-Kennedy

The Day of the Mayfly was commissioned as part of a lunchtime season of new Irish one-act plays, which launched the second half of the Focus Theatre season of 1980.

The play was inspired by Declan's fascination for and love of Lough Sheelin, in county Cavan, where he had spent much of his youth watching the moods of the lake and waiting for the arrival of the short-lived mayfly, which signalled the start of the fishing season.

He wanted to write a play about the lake, and especially about the pollution, which threatened it seriously at that time.

But somewhere an ungovernable sense of mischief intruded and this worthy enterprise was shelved. *The Day of the Mayfly* emerged from its sombre chrysalis and took flight as a light-hearted comedy.

Instead of focusing on recalcitrant pig farmers, the play turns the spotlight on a pair of upwardly mobile, 1980s city dwellers, a photographer and a fashion-store buyer, who have come to conduct their affaire at a fishing lodge on the lake.

While neither of them is given a name, (they are always Man and Woman), we come to know them intimately as the eerie splendour of the autumnal lake strips away their attempts at sophistication and seems to threaten the consummation of their tryst. While the Man can quote at length from Wallace Stevens and the Woman can dictate what everyone will be wearing two seasons from now, they are less sure-footed when confronted with priming water pumps, lighting fires and surveying their isolation.

The play relishes their discomfort and their insecurities and its observations on adultery, Irish-style, are both delightfully funny and surprisingly affecting.

Talking Through His Hat

by

Michael Harding

Michael Harding
Timpaun
Lough Allen
Carrick on Shannon
086 1712587
Hardingmichael@mac.com
Agent's address:
Jonathan Williams
Glenageary
Co Dublin

SCENE ONE

Swift addresses his company.

You may not believe what has happened.

Just now.

I have fled, from my own dining table.

A table at which I was not altogether happy.

Although Miss Bleasedale did not make me unhappy. She is hardly sixteen, and plump, and extremely modest.

But it was quite a commotion. They all fled at the one moment. Everybody to the coaches at the door like rats from a galley; I to the limited security of this room. I say limited, for Squire O'Carolan is still out there, in the drawing room, playing the harp.

Today was my birthday. I think. Pressed to be sociable I agreed for once to spend the evening in company. The Bishop of Clogher. He's ninety-one. Mister Clyde from the Dublin newspaper. A nice man. Which is to say a man of nasty ideas. Mrs Winters, the English woman, whose husband died so tragically in the bath, and last but not least, Charlotte Bleasedale, her niece.

I was watching Miss Bleasedale. And Mrs Winters was watching me.

Then she moved: I am not aware of your work, Dr Swift. I believe you write pamphlets.

Those were the first words from her mouth.

Talk about getting me on the wrong foot.

Madame, the entire world knows Jonathan Swift. Only yesterday I believe it was said that to observe the Dean of Saint Patrick's preach was to observe the collapse of an empire.

Whatever do you mean sir?

What do I mean? Well, Samuel Johnson once met me on the street, Madame, took off his hat with a bow of surly recognition, scanned me from heat to foot, and immediately passed over to the other side of the street. Does that give you the picture, Mrs Winters?

He disliked you perhaps?

Good God Madame, the entire world dislikes me.

I dislike myself. Did you see that elm tree on the right as you came in? Withered at the top.

That is me Madame. I shall rot from the top down.

I am not quite following you sir, but why should the great Doctor Johnson dislike your company?

Perhaps, Madame, because like you, he is English.

And after that altercation, my guests began to resemble mourners, in a mortuary. And they gazed at me as if I might be the corpse, and they were disappointed in me, to have died on them.

The Bishop took me aside.

Now look here Swift. Your problem is to be incautious with the truth.

You lack discretion. Try to be jolly. A little frivolity. A little manners.

Me? Manners? Well, I walked across the room, to where Mrs Winters stood at the mantelpiece.

Madame, I said, my good lord the Bishop has just admonished me for being blunt, and I do apologize. But believe me, I have almost exhausted myself in seeking to improve the general standard of manners and conversation in this kingdom.

Miss Bleasedale was grinning at me like a Cheshire cat. Unfortunately, Tom Clyde, a large slithery fellow, listing to one side, was grinning at Miss Bleasedale like a larger cat.

In fact, at that moment, we were all together...grinning. And I knew to my horror that this grinning would ultimately flower into full blown laughter.

There is a natural involuntary distortion of the muscles, which is the anatomical cause of laughter. But there is a deeper, more profound cause. A foundation on which all laughter is constructed. That is good taste.

When like-minded people assemble, sniff each other, approve of each other, there is a certain flush of delight which issues in grinning, and flowers in laughter. So if we were to judge by the laughter this evening, we might say that everything was founded upon good taste. We all behaved well. At that very moment, before we sat to supper, we were all behaving as refined ladies and gentlemen of the kingdom ought to behave. We were all grinning.

Except for Turlough O'Carolan of course. His puss rarely radiates a grin. He enjoys more the grimace of the afflicted. And he arrived a little later, unexpected, half drunk, and he was not seen as good taste. To my other guests he is a Papist risen so high in society that we simply must have him at the table, yet are constantly appalled, by his crudity, his poor manners.

The point I am coming to is that the society of refined ladies and gentlemen requires only one thing – teeth. Good teeth, well displayed. And the true management of every feature and almost of every limb.

Some peculiar graceful motion on the eyes, or nose or mouth, or forehead, or chin, or suitable toss of the head, with certain offices assigned to each hand, and in ladies, the whole exercise of the fan. And different postures of the body. The several kinds and gradations of laughter, which the ladies must daily practice by the looking glass, and consult upon them with their waiting maids.

Yes. I have often wished that certain male and female instructors would set up schools for the instruction of young ladies like Miss Bleasedale, and then we could all go to dinner gesticulating and masticating in perfect harmony.

Shoulders back, girls, heads up. Trotty trotty trotty – that sort of thing.

Shoulders back, Miss Bleasedale, head up.

Trotty trotty trotty, one two three. Trotty trotty trotty, one two three.

Mister Clyde. What are you staring at?

Ah do sit down Doctor Swift, or we worry that you will exhaust yourself before the evening has begun.

My left ear lobe was now between the thumb and forefinger of his lordship the Bishop. And in a low voice, he was saying, Dean Swift, oblige me by possessing yourself with a calmer spirit. You are out of sorts. Look to your company. We are here for a pleasant evening.

A pleasant evening? Mrs Winters admiring Tom Clyde's new coat, which he bought on Cuffe Street? You call that a pleasant evening!

Why Tom, you are high in the fashion.

Ah well, it is better to be out of the world than out of the fashion. And then he turns to Miss Charlotte. And she blushed. Oh, what lovely red cheeks you have Miss. And I hear, you two ladies are always quarrelling. I fear it is your fault, Mrs Winters, for I can assure you, she is very good humoured.

Aye, so is the devil when he's pleased.

And they both fell about the place laughing.

SCENE TWO

They're all gone now. Except that frog's fart from Ballyfarnon.

Turlough. It's late. Very late. What shall I do with him? I have no servant. Turlough.

I dismissed my servant. He was a young slightly fellow, and oftentimes whenever a pretty mistress was at my table, he would run his nose full in her cheek, or if his breath was good, he did breathe full in her face; and betimes with very good consequences. Although it is not for that misdemeanour that he was dismissed.

The cause was simply that he broke all my earthen drinking vessels below stairs, and thought one copper pot would do as well as all. So he used this one pot to boil milk, heat porridge, hold small beer or in case of necessity, serve for a chamber pot; he applied it indifferently to all these uses; but never washed or scoured it, for fear of taking off the tin. So I had to let him go.

For fear of falling down dead of the plague.

Now I fend for myself. And I am good in daylight. The night is a black smoke...

Turlough. Turlough. Ahhh. I wager he is sleeping.

O'Carolan is an entertainment of sorts. Takes the wine with me, though he prefers the whisky, and is a fair cantankerous nature when disturbed. Specially if you suggest there is a better musician in the kingdom than he. And he is Irish. Old Irish. Old savage Irish. Old Irish savage.

–But you are Irish too, born in Dublin, schooled down in Kilkenny.

–My arse . I am no more an Irishman than a man born of English parents at the Hudson is a Mohawk.

I lay my opinion before the world with a grave simplicity and a perfect neatness. That is English.

–But you talk like an Irishman .

–Don't ridicule me sir.

I dread ridicule, and that is English in me too.

–So why didn't ye stop in London.

–I don't know Turlough. You know I devoured books as a young man. In London. Extraordinary libraries. And the King actually taught me to cut asparagus in the Dutch fashion.

–Oh London is a very Dutch town.

–I had a salary of twenty pounds. Dinner at the upper servants table. Yes, I wore the cassock. I bent the knee. But I saw the men who had governed the great world. Saw them.

–So I'm asking ye, why did ye leave them.

–I don't know.

Perhaps because they were such men underneath those enormous periwigs.

–Ah, now you're mocking me.

–Forgive me. In truth you know why I left. I left because I was in the employ of an English gentleman.

–Ah ha. Ye niver leked the English gentleman.

–Mr O'Carolan sir; the English gentleman made me eat humble pie for ten years.

Gathering learning, yes, but swallowing scorn, and submitting with a stealthy rage to my misfortune. But when it got too hot, politically speaking , the English gentleman could retire to his retreat at Moor Park; and let the King's party and the Prince of Orange's party battle it out among themselves.

–Sly bastard.

–The English gentleman reveres the sovereign (and no man perhaps ever testified to his loyalty by so elegant a bow); he admires the Prince of Orange; but there is one person whose ease and comfort he loves more than all the princes in Christendom, and that valuable member of society is himself. To see him, between his study-chair and his tulip-beds, clipping his apricots and pruning his essays, – watching to see which way the wind blows, so he can go with it.

The English gentleman would perpetually quote Latin and the ancient classics apropos of his gardens and his Dutch statues and the Assyrian kings. Apropos of beans, he would mention Pythagoras's precept to abstain from beans, and that this precept probably meant that wise men should abstain from public affairs. The truth is that beans made him fart like an officer's horse.

–Did ye find any improvement in the fragrance of the Irish gentleman.

–Well of course the Irish gentleman looks in the mirror. He sees a fool. He never sees himself. And he is more religious. He does stand in the turning of a street, and calls to those ladies who pass to favour him with a handsome kick on the arse.

And why. Well, to prove that he is a Christian gentleman. In this he is comforted by what he had undergone for the public good. I have seen him down on his knees, up with his eyes, as he falls to prayer. Prayer.

76

Among the poor. In public. But the poor who understand his pranks are sure to get as far enough out of his way for indeed he can of a sudden with one hand, out with his gear and piss full in their eyes, and with the other hand all to – bespatter them with mud.

I suppose you could say, he is truly a walking lantern of enlightenment.

Very good Turlough. Yes. But may I finish my paragraph? The Irish gentleman. He does catch a burning candle, and swallows it, with an agility wonderful to conceive; and by this procedure, maintains a perpetual flame in his belly, which issuing in a glowing steam from both his eyes as well as his nostrils and his mouth, makes his head appear in a dark night like the skull of an ass, wherein a roguish boy hath conveyed a farthing candle, to terrify the world. And despite all that, here I am in Dublin. God help me.

–So here ye are and here you'll stay, let all the asses folly the hay.

–Don't mock me Turlough. It is our misfortune, Turlough, that the English consider even the Irish Protestants to be Papists. And though we are Catholic, we are in a sad predicament, twixt the savages in the countryside who see us as English, and the English who see us as savages.

–What am I supposed to do about that ?

–Why don't ye write a book ?

–Damn you. No. But I shall tell you what is to be done in Ireland.

In Dublin. Sit down and mind your own business.

SCENE THREE

That's what I said to Sheridan. Sit down and mind your own business, I say to myself.

Expect no more from an Irish man than what that animal is capable of. Think and deal with everybody in Dublin, as though he were a villain – without telling him so. And smile at everybody, while trusting nobody. In short, sit down and mind your own business.

He returns to the table.

More salt Mrs Winters? More claret Mister Clyde? How is your duck my lord Bishop?

Are you enjoying the tongue Miss Bleasedale?

In short, sit down and mind your own business.

A pity I did not listen to my own advice this evening.

I make no doubt Bishop, that with Berkeley, you still believe in God. And your hope is in heaven. But do tell us, do you still believe in hell? Do you?

–The question hardly merits a reply.

–No seriously Bishop.

You see you and I think we know where hell is.

The teagues believe they know where hell is.

And dissenters are certain positive of the address.

–Then we are all agreed on the matter

–No. My lord. I am asking you. Where do you think hell is? Might hell be where the damned are walking? Is it far away, or is it at home?

Is it here, or there? There or here?

–You're talking through your hat again, Doctor Swift.

–Oh. Well then I shall go and ask the musician.

And I went to the door. And called in a loud voice. Commanded O Carolan to stop the music, and attend me.

O Carolan of the wispy fairy music approached.

Now look here sir. You will please to resolve a theological puzzle for us. They say that music is like brandy on the road to hell. And you are a musician. So you will please to tell us where hell is.

He did not like being summoned. And I saw his black empty eyes twitching, as they do when he gets irritated and I was afraid he might throw a bottle at Mrs Winters, or beat the Bejaysus out of Mr Clyde, or simply take the Bishop up by his silky neck and swallow him.

So I said, politely, Mister O'Carolan, sir, esteemed friend, I hope you are not angry with me now.

–Too much talk, too much talk from you clergymen. I am just a poor player. I have no truck with religion. Backgammon is my game.

That is all he said. And left me there.

Standing in the doorway. And he returned to the harp, and played a mazurka I think, so that I was undone. I could see them, in their buckles, and square-toed shoes, and lace ruffles and ambrosial wigs...I could see them, sneering at me.

–I am a poor player. I have no truck with religion. Backgammon is my game.

Well I have had truck with religion, sir, and lived to regret it. For we have just about enough religion in Ireland to hate each other, but not enough to love.

His dark eye sockets as empty as the word god itself, and then he returns to his instrument and assaults us with mazurkas, and them to be played not even in our presence, but out there, from afar, as if we poor beasts in the mud could not rise ourselves to be equal to a ballad singer from Ballyfarnon.

What to do then?

SCENE FOUR

Well I turned to the dinner table.

I do apologize, my lord Bishop. Do forgive me, Mrs Winters.

Sit down and mind your own business.

I did. For a minute.

Does anyone wish to use the jacks. A general evacuation would do us all so much good. And then we could return to the table, and eat more, and continue to tear one another, and howl and grin and chatter.

Mrs Winters appeared particularly puce in the face, as if she might have ingested something disagreeable. Ate too much bird perhaps. So I said that there existed a cure for ailments caused by over eating.

–What is that she wondered.

–Well Madame, 'tis a mixture of the patient's piss, and shit, forcibly put down the patient's throat. Oh yes...and I do freely recommend it to you Mrs Winters, for the general good, as an admirable specific against all diseases produced by repletion.

Well the Bishop, like a lark from its boggy nest, rose up off his lardy arse, and declared

–You have said too much this evening, Doctor Swift. You said too much yesterday. You said too much this morning. You said too much this evening. You speak too much nonsense. Indeed, you write far too much nonsense.

Do I? Well we shall see about that.

It is a melancholy object to those of us who walk through this town, when we see beggars of the female sex, followed by three, four, or six children, all in rags.

Whoever could find out a fair, cheap and easy method of making these children useful members of the commonwealth, would deserve so well of the public as to have his statue set up, for a preserver of the nation. A young healthy baby well nursed, is at a year old a most delicious, nourishing and wholesome food, whether stewed, roasted, baked, or boiled. And I make no doubt that it will equally serve in a casserole.

Always advising the mother to let them suck plentifully in the last month, so as to render them plump and fat for a good table. A baby will make two dishes at an entertainment for friends; and when the family dines alone, the fore or hind quarter of the baby will make a reasonable dish, and seasoned with a little pepper or salt will be very good boiled on the fourth day, especially in winter. Those who are more thrifty may flay the carcass; the skin of which artificially dressed, will make admirable gloves for ladies, and summer boots for fine gentlemen. And I rather recommend buying the children alive and dressing them hot from the knife, as we do roasting pigs.

I was coming to the point. I now had a dish in my hands. A silver dish, covered with a silver lid.

Excuse me Mrs Winters, Mr Clyde, allow me to squeeze in there between you. Thank you.

I placed it upon the table.

Some cold meat before ye go home, says I, the night is such a storm, and it will mop up the alcohol. Swim in the claret, with the fish.

Couldn't eat another morsel, says the Bishop.

Oh but says I, you won't refuse this delightful tender young buck. And as I lifted the lid, Miss Bleasedale fainted. And Tom Clyde tried to explain that it was only a rabbit on the platter. That was the end of the dinner party.

I would have liked Miss Bleasedale to remain.

Companion me by the fireside, for tea, and buns. She would have made a pretty nurse.

Indeed. And she was comely dressed. By Jove, what would I do for just a lock of her hair.

Such treasure. Lace. And brocades. Ringlets. Amulets. Strings and straps.

But observe me now, in a dirty smock, the arm pits well besmeared with months of sweat, observe me approach the perfumed girl.

In truth, no comb could rake the dirt so closely fixt behind me ears. The sweat, the dandruff, the powder lead and hair upon me shoulders.

Before beginning I took a forehead cloth with oil to smooth his wrinkles. I have ointments now, they say are good for scabby chops and each morning I fills a filthy basin with the scouring of me hands, and the scrapings of me teeth and gums. So now in candlelight I doth approach the lady fair of lilly hue, pale and blushing be the fire. Approach, tip toe tip toe, closer and closer;

Will I, won't I, woo her, do her, win her with me airs and graces.

An old man spits and spews with excitement for the task, me face a nasty compound of all hues, blue and purple, pink and white. She's there upon the mat, before the fire, her shoes undone. And like a great rhinoceros I bellows out me vowels – anything my dearie, my lilly poopie doopie dolly wolly, for a lock of your hair –

And I casts me handkerchief at her feet. A gesture I hoped was taken as gallant.

But oh Bejasus it did turn her bowel, when Charlotte sniffed the snuff, on me snotty towel. She pulled her legs up underneath her petticoats and cast the handkerchief at me feet.

Me nose was itching. I took a tweezers to the spot. Could not find it. So from the other pocket I draws forth a glass that can sight disclose the smallest worm in any nose. And faithfully I direct me nail to squeeze it out from head to tail –

Aghast, the maiden screeches; Doctor Swift, what are you doing?

I sought to reassure her. Do not fear, my dear, for catch it nicely by the head, it must come out alive or dead.

I ought to die now. I lose my teeth and hair, I have no distinction of taste, but eat and drink whatever I am given. And when I look upon other old people I consider it the most mortifying sight I ever beheld, and the women more horrible than the men.

Now me head hurts. And me ear hurts. And I hear no music.

SCENE FIVE

Turlough! Turlough! I wager he is sleeping eternally. And he has no candle. Of course he needs no candle. I said to him once – how does it feel to live in a dark room? And he replied

–Which of us d'ye think lives in the dark?

Turlough. Turlough. Turlough.

–Ahhh. Do you dream Doctor Swift? Do flitting shades intrude and cause your mind delusions? Hah?

–Yes.

–Well tell us this and tell us no more.

Does God send the dream? Or does it rise from hell?

–I don't know. Perhaps they are merely productions of the brain. But I make no doubt Turlough that you will not be long dead before your magical qualities are made manifest.

Some pitiful creature seeking a cure will find out your grave, dig up the corpse, and take out the skull, and use it as a cup. Pour goats milk into it, or virgins' piss, or waters from a holy well, and raise the bony beaker to his lips.

And no doubt he shall be cured. And your skull preserved. So that the diseased masses of the nation may come and drink magical libations from the skull of poetry. The bowl of music.

The cup of girls' laughter.

And my numskull. Perhaps mine too ought to be dug up. But not for cures. For this is a hat of reason. My house of logic. A curiosity. To be examined by medical students – or cast in the bottom drawer of a scientific laboratory.

So be it. And let the day perish wherein I was born and the night in which it was said, there is a man child conceived. Let that day be darkness, let not God regard it from above, neither let the light shine upon it. Because it shut not up the doors of my mother's womb nor hid sorrow from your eyes.

Why died I not from the womb? Why did you not give up the ghost when you came out of the belly?

I could have slept with kings and counsellors and infants that never saw the light.

Now my flesh is clothed with worms and clods of dust, my skin is broken and become loathsome. Am I a sea, or a whale that thou settest a watch over me?

That thou scarest me with dreams and terrify me with visions so that my soul chooseth strangling and death rather than life.

How long will thou not depart from me nor let me alone till I swallow down my spittle. I have sinned. And why dost thou not pardon my transgression and cure me.

For now shall I sleep in the dust and thou shalt seek me in the morning but I shall not be.

Curtain

A Note From Michael Harding

One of the advantages of working with the Focus Theatre over the years is that it provided me with a platform in Dublin to present my work.

In 1991 my play *Misogynist*, a controversial interrogation of the male psyche, was presented at the Abbey Theatre in the Dublin Theatre Festival, and the reaction from various sectors of the media was so vitriolic that it was taken off after three weeks. However, in collaboration with the great actor Tom Hickey, a lifetime associate of the Focus, we reproduced the show in a slimmer version for smaller venues and toured Ireland the following year delighting audiences up and down the country. What we then needed was a Dublin venue with the courage to present a show that one year earlier had been so brutally attacked. The Focus bravely stepped in. The play was again reviewed, this time favourably, and went on to further success in London and at the Edinburgh Festival.

Without the Focus as a venue in Dublin with acknowledged standards of excellence, the rest would not have been possible. We needed a venue to stand by the play and the Focus did as much.

That was the beginning of my relationship with the theatre. Ten years later I had evolved my work in theatre and was operating as a writer/performer. The first and pivotal production was *Talking Through His Hat*. It was directed by Cabrini Cahill, a wonderful director who had become my mentor at the time and who was the person who gave me courage to cross the threshold of the greenroom and walk out into the glare of the public stage as a performer, for which gift I will be always in her debt. We rehearsed and presented the work at the Dunamaise Theatre in Portlaoise under her company's title – Shake The Spear. But once again we needed a Dublin venue to take over the show and the Focus again stepped in. Initially we ran for two weeks during the Fringe Festival and after it was nominated for Best Performance in the Fringe Festival and gained rave reviews, we returned the following April for a four-week run. The Focus didn't give birth to the play but it was the midwife that allowed it grow and nourished it into being a performance that went on to tour Ireland for many years, and also played in Newfoundland and Paris.

Pinching For My Soul

A Play For Stage In Two Acts

by

Elizabeth Moynihan

Setting:

A department store

A bed/sitting room in post 'Celtic Tiger' boom Dublin.

Cast:

Chike. 30's-40's African/Irish heritage, security guard born in south London.

Brona. 40's-50's. Upper-middle class Dublin. Beautiful. Perfectly groomed.

Shania. 19. Working class, inner city Dublin junkie. Ravaged by drug abuse.

SCENE ONE

Lights come up on Chike, Brona and Shania. Following dialogue is spoken by Brona and Shania. Chike mouths and writes the words on his iphone app.

Chike. Burglarize

Brona. Carry off

Shania. Lift

Chike. Defraud

Brona. Embezzle

Shania. Hold up!

Chike. Snatch

Brona. Pilfer

Shania. Run off with

Chike. Pillage

BRONA. Walk off with

Shania. Steal.

Words build and are repeated.

Shania	brona
filch	purloin
hide	appropriate,
lift	conceal,
swipe	enclose,
take	steal

Chike. Pinchers!

Abruptly the lights change. The security guard is picked out by a special 'he is in work' mode. He speaks quickly.

Chike. High street, yeah? Kensington High Street. TK Max. Liked it there, I did. Sorry I moved 'ere. Dublin's a bit well...small, really, dead...dying. More of a town now than a city. Innit? Grafton Street looks like it's moved to the wrong side of O'Connell bridge. 'To Let' signs everywhere 'n that. S'alright tho', for the moment. *Hold up!*

(On his radio) 'Come in, Phelim. Copy. I just clocked her. Separates, yeah? Them dreads ain't real, neither. She was in last week. Not worth it mate. Junkie...don't miss a thing bruv'! Safe.

As the other characters speak. Chike writes using his note book app on his iphone.

Brona. Kensington, yes! High street, London. Weekend jaunts in the good old days when the Tiger roared. Liked to make my way back on foot to my hotel. Not far. Olympia, handy. Sounds grand, doesn't it? Grecian? It isn't. Dull really. Lots of men in cheap suits talking on iphones. Still...

A beat.

Brona. To be honest, I prefer shopping in Dublin. You know exactly where to find things. Yes...London, Paris, New York have the novelty factor. But we have everything nicely arranged in our bijoux city haven't we? I find it quite nerve-wracking shopping abroad. And our city needs my business, never more so.

Shania. Dat ting... De whatd'yamacall it? Yeah! Dat walkie-talkie ting. Always yakking on it to his mates.

Durrrrt! Blink and ya'll miss me.

Brona. I don't want to miss a thing on a city break. Never get me on a tube. Awful. You can actually see the air you breathe. Filthy...even try to avoid the bus. No, I prefer to walk everywhere. Taking it all in? Ah! Knightsbridge. Love to snake through the crowd. Past the covered women like flocks of black birds; twittering in Arabic but talking at such a high volume, I want to cover my ears. Loud! And guttural, like Irish, in a way. The sound coming out like some invisible ventriloquist is pulling the strings, 'cause you can't see their lips move. Can't see their lips at all. Covered up...completely. Not even their eyes exposed. Or their hands. Hands? Indecent, provocative? Hands? Are they...?

Chike. Characters all around me. Provoking me. I lagged that little junkie a year ago, sure of it. Doing her little, mad dance, look? Putting stuff in her coat and then putting it back on the shelves. 'Aving a laugh at my expense. Really? You won't be laughing when you is banged up again, my darling.

Chike takes out his iphone and writes this idea into his notebook app.

Brona. An African woman laughing, yes...all in white. Nipples visible through the T-shirt material of her dress. Walking behind the covered ones. No – swinging like a gate opening and closing. So utterly beautiful and exposed. I am a little turned on, you could say. How odd...well no doubt you think it's odd. Mmm. Do you? In here it's nothing out of the ordinary. The woman in the room next but one pulls out her hair and eyelashes. Hardly a rib of hair left on her head. Now that's odd!!

Shania. Turned on, yeah! Dat's what it's like, I tell yah! ! First time, dat's how it was. Rushin' tru your veins. Me sitting dere, him sitting dere. He's out of it, couldn't give a shite, no. I'm all jumpy, jumpy. Eight sleeping tablets in me and not a wink in two days. Baby cryin' in the night an all. Ah! Fuck dis I says to meself. Here give us a bang off dat. An' he does. No cock compares, I tell ya. Ohhhhhhh! Noooo!...

A beat.

Shania. But now I'm just chasing...chasing what?
Dat...dat...dat...dunno...first high, I suppose.

It comes to him finally...almost to himself. Writes something down on his iphone notebook.

Chike. Yeah!

Brona gets a hot flush.

Brona. Good Lord! Menopause. I suppose. That could explain it. Or maybe it's the fact that it's been such a long time since I've felt arms, his arms, here.

She turns to her husband as if he is standing beside her.

Brona. Intimacy.

A beat.

Intimacy? He repeats what I say. Only slightly sarcastic. And I sort of feel a blush rising in my cheeks and I'm well embarrassed... 'Yes!' I say again. 'I need intimacy.' Of course he's still there looking at me.

Gripping her hips, with arms crossed in front of her.

Brona. Well, there's the children, of course, but that's not the same, is it? I mean, not the same as the feel of him? Expression of ecstasy on that almond of a face. No...not the same. Seems like a lifetime since you lay underneath me. Arms splayed out like the crucified Christ. Me on top of you, watching, watching till you come. Colour so high I think you're having a heart attack...but no, you're not, are you?

A beat.

Brona. Now I look at your back mostly.

Turns to the fourth wall.

Oh! Okay, you're thinking: 'That's why, that's why. Are you? I mean, there has to be a reason. Doesn't there? All neurosis, personality disorders, all manner of the crazies have to have a reason. Underlying factors...well, no...

No...not necessarily.

Chike puts away his notebook. Catching some random shoplifter.

Chike. Hey! I seen ya switching price tags on them candlesticks. I should just lag you now. I should...no point. Can't touch ya till you put

89

the merchandise in your bag. Even then I chase ya down the street, you won't resist when I grab ya. You'll go all quiet and apologetic and then I always feel like a right dick.

Shania. Stupid but...

Chike. So you think you is in control now do ya! Well that ain't how it works.

He speaks into his radio as Shania speaks over him.

Shania. I am still chasing it. But can't never gerrit back. Oh! Dey do warn ya so dey do but that's fuck all good to me when it's three days 'n no sleep. D'ya get me?

Chike. Nerve of that bitch...right under my...you testing me? You testing me? No way I'm falling for that. I catch ya doing something worth my time this week, for sure. She ain't getting me on the 'tag-switching'. No fuckin' chance...nahhh! I'll wait till my girl is servin'.

Sounds coming through on the radio. Phelim tries to take the piss out of how he speaks.

Chike. I copy that, over. I am there.

A beat.

One more person takes the piss out of my accent, I tell ya! I have to listen to these boys on da radio yeah? Imitating the way I speak. Sounds Aussie when they try and do it. I don't sound like no Aussie. So I tells 'em. I am a Paddy like you lot. Tired of tellin' this lot my Mum's from Raheny. It's getting silly now...

Brona. How silly! Because my husband turns his back on me in bed, it's somehow the cause or gives me a reason, a need? To get his attention? Attention! What attention?

Chike speaks into the radio.

Chike. Come in Phelim. Yeah! I've clocked that couple in household. In last Monday, no Tuesday. Remember them? Can you keep an eye? She's in a pink shirt and he's, well, in a grey short jacket. Bomber style. Too much hair gel. See 'em? I've got to keep an eye on my junkie. She's sniffing around accessories.

Brona. Honestly, I mean (*sighs*) I like to shop. That's it. Some people drink. I shop. I particularly like 'Diva'. Nice staff. Everything under one roof. Although he stares...a lot (*referring to the security guard*) quite rude, isn't it? To stare? But I don't say anything. He might take offence, well he is black and everything. More importantly I don't want to cause a scene...and well never a good idea to defecate on one's own doorstep. And I simply couldn't do without the food hall...adore it. Clodagh, his

PA, sent me a very nice hamper. Food here is inedible...and I have said it! Oh! Yes on several occasions. It fell on deaf ears of course!

Shania. Oh! I know it's a mug's game doing gear but I just needed a night's sleep don't ya know? And now, well...

Shania nods out momentarily.

Brona. Can't remember the last time I was in that food hall...months, probably. No! In fact it's about eight weeks now that I come to think of it. A small lapse in concentration on my part. Which I explained. He of course didn't believe me. Sent me into Coventry for a week. He didn't actually send me to Coventry. No. It's an expression. He basically didn't say a single word to me for seven whole days. 'The humiliation', etc., etc., etc... 'His position, department of foreign affairs', and all that. Ended up in the papers.' I should clarify, that bottle of montrachet, well...I hadn't planned to...the phone went and I got distracted. I was on the street before I realized...

Comes to with a jerk.

Shania. Oh! Yeah...dare y'are, little list. I'm organized dat way? Ya get me! Okay, now. Shoes patent high heels, size 3. Wha'? Oh! Me Ma has me shoppin' for midgets now? Dresses black, sizes 16 to 26. No size 26 in here, ma. Have to go to de fatty shop on Henry Street for dem...okay, now what else? A foot spa, two clocks, and 'Prison Break' – the box set.

Chike. Grown to like 'er ! She ain't no sket. Killiney, for sure or maybe Dalkey, think I seen her on the telly?...my tutor says I must use what I have in my line of vision.

Speaks the word 'groundwork' into a tape recorder.

A beat.

Shania. Me nose running like a tap. Withdrawals. The good thing about being on gear: ya never get colds or flu or nuttin'. I swear to ya...the gear do be low grade the odd time. Cut to bits...more baby laxative in it than heroin. Oh! Shut up! Call comin' in. 'Ma? Yeah, is dat you? Your number didn't come up. You withholdin' your ID again. Thought I showed ya how to turn off dat function.'

Chike. Inspiration is all around. 'Must – keep – eyes – open – all – the –time'. So the stories in my head can take shape. Started doing it as a kid. Sitting on Dollyer strand. Too cold and windy to go in the water, but Mum keeps us there till teatime anyway. 'Cause, well, it's summer holidays and that. We're, like sittin' there, in a row till six on the dot. Me, Mum and my Nan. Huddling in our towels on the rocks. Nan bitching 'bout the tourists leaving rubbish all over the sand. 'Brit's no class'. Blah, blah...this is where Mum kicks off. What are you talkin' about in God's name. 'They invented it.' Then the back-and-forth before the bus home. Nan going on about the Black 'n' Tans and the atrocities they committed in 1921 and the 800 years of oppression. It grows by a century each time. I'm sure it was only 500 hundred years first time she mentioned it. Mum telling her to shut it, 'cause like England is where we live, innit. Me tuning out so I could just go to that place in my head away from the argument and ancient wars before my time. That place where I imagine the lives of others. Back then it was adventures on islands surrounded by waters teeming with sharks and mutant creatures born from nuclear incidents.

Shania. 100 euro! Wha'! Robbers, dey are. Bleedin' robbers! Plastic an' all! *Look (looks at the sole)* Vegan??? Wha'

A beat.

Brona speaks emphatically as if standing up for herself.

Brona. And that is how it happened.

Quite embarrassing really. 'Exhausted, you're exhausted', he tells me when he finally decides to speak. I am, oh, I am! I say. 'Little spell at a health farm in Mayo and a right good think is the best all round,' he says. 'To hell or to Connaught.' I mumble. He looks blankly at me. So from now on I realize I need a system: decoy tactics, if you like.

Chike. Or I wonder what that Foxrock fanny's like at home.

Nods towards someone in the distance.

Chike. I am not thinking nothing filthy mind.

He sees her in front of him.

Chike. Nah! I don't think about you like that. I mean, you ain't hot. You're old innit. But man you smell peng. When you walk past you leave a little trail of scented air, soaked in the essence of you. It wafts around my face and nostrils...exotic, mystical almost. A little of you left behind in the wake of bland punters going about their daily routines and whatever, but you don't have no routine. Do ya? Coming in different times and days. Innit? Innit? Always mixin' it up to keep my attention. But that's cool 'cause I have your Chanel caressing my senses giving me ideas for the page. I imagine you at home maybe. And there you is ; cooking a steak in your kitchen, or a roast. Or doing some gardening. Sitting, reading, or whatever posh fannies do in their spare time. Lunch, innit?

He laughs.

Shania. Love an ice-cream, I would. But I've only one hit left so need to get a bleedin move on. Can't move cause of that spanner of a security guard. On me like a fly on — *(spits in his direction, suddenly feral.)* Shite! Should 'a brought me little jar of filters. Me plan B I do call that little jar. 'Cause I cook 'em up when I can't get gear. Squirt a few drops from the spike before I bang up. Keep it in me bag when I'm out and get sick or can't score. Muppet! Look at him laughin' like a fuckin' hyena, to his mates on da radio. And that accent 'o his...go through ya, it would...

Chike. 'Go ahead there. I've clocked that one, copy!' Copy!

Brona. So when I fill my pockets with smaller items they don't see me. A lipstick, or a little bottle of nail varnish from toiletries. That feeling, rush, I get is the same as taking something like say...an evening dress from the designer floor. The size or cost doesn't matter. It can be something small, anything.

Shania. Have to dump me loot in the changin' room. I'll move to the food hall once I'm sorted. Love dat 'food hall'. It's great here, ya can nick pants and Pernod under da same roof. Brillo pad! And da toilets are lovely and clean. Charge ya, but not if ya go in the disabled when no one's lookin'. I won't be disturbed there...nip in and bang me last one up; Dutch courage like...fuck! Where is it?

She searches her pockets for the wrap of heroin but can't find it. Looks up sees the security camera.

Shania. Eyes, eyes on me all de time. Look. Those eyes. Eyes everywhere.

Brona looks up at the camera.

Shania points to the camera.

Shania. I...see...you...seein'...me!

Chike. Cctv named it that 'cause it see see's everything.

No denyin' the playback, is there?

Shania puts her ipod in her ears as the withdrawals kick in.

Shania; okay, yeah! Okay! Think it's time to kick this shit again.

Brona. I stroke it in my pocket, while I walk the aisles pretending to look for something...white truffle oil, or something like that. I love asking the shelf-fillers for things I know they don't have. They dread to see me coming. That makes me laugh...a lot. Then I like to treat myself to lunch in 'The Sky'.

Shania gets another stabbing pain.

Shania. Oh! Jaysus. Oh! Holy Christ...

Brona. No, not the actual sky! It's the name of the restaurant on the top floor of 'Diva'. Their seafood platter is very good value. Have several glasses of Pinot. Like a nice crisp glass of white wine with seafood, essential. Flirt a little too overtly with the waiter. Very handsome, in a low rent sort of way. I ask if he is mediterranean, and he says 'yes'. I say, 'Italian, I'll bet'. 'No, Lebanese', he says. I say 'aren't they Arabic'? He seems to take offence at this and doesn't come back to the table after that. I feel the wine making me woozy – I've always been a lightweight when it comes to alcohol. I think I might actually be allergic to the fermented grape. It's quite common you know. More common than you might think. Unfortunately people are often misdiagnosed as being alcoholic when in fact they are just suffering an allergic reaction.

Shania. That security guard hasn't taken his eyes off me in the last hour. But I looks nice today so he didn't notice me come in. I do blend when I make an effort.

The withdrawals kick in again and Shania represses a groan.

Chike. Class ain't something you can fake. You are either is or you're ain't. It's not the clothes or the accent. It's the way you move. The volume you speak at, the *way* you wear your clothes. The lack of grey in your face. Innit?

Chike writes this down.

Brona. Could have done with a latte, but the waiter is avoiding eye contact. Obviously still offended by the Arab comment. It's nearly four so I think I'll skip it, need some fresh air. Can't find where in the hell my cloakroom ticket is. Tip my bag out onto the table, have a proper search. A very helpful woman sitting in the next booth helps me rescue my make-up from under the seat. There it is rolling in every direction and I am embarrassed that my mascara is a rather cheap brand. I want to explain to the helpful woman that I have sensitive eyes and although Dior is by far the better brand, I may as well wear barbed wire on my lashes. So embarrassing when that happens isn't it? 'Cause, well, make-up is so personal. Isn't it? I feel like I am going to be sick crouched underneath the table, which strikes me as somewhat inelegant. Anyway, she calls the waiter, the Lebanese waiter, to the table and tells him my situation. He asks me to come with him to the cloakroom. So I do.

The girl convulses again in pain.

Shania. Okay, yeah!
It's time...

Brona. We get to the cloakroom and the waiter offers to search for it. Suggesting I come in and help...help? I guess I am still being punished for the Arab remark. I am beginning to see everything in soft focus now. Edges blurred by the wine – like the guy made of peppermint in the ad. for...well, mints with a soft centre. And that is exactly how I feel; like a mint with a soft chewy centre. I can feel the Lebanese waiter's breath on my ear. Or maybe I was having a hot flush? Then...slam! My head hits the wall. If it wasn't for the Pinot, I'd call out for someone. But his hands were on me and his tongue was prising my teeth open. Darting, darting in and out through my lips and I couldn't seem to...not let him.

Shania. Go home 'cause I can't find me last wrap 'n can't score in town neither. Pains in me stomach are like giving birth to a grown man, guts churning. No taxi will stop so I hop a bus. Den the sneezing starts. One sneeze after another den another and again on and on. People starin', I don't care. 'What are youse lookin' at, haven't ya never seen someone strung out before'. Drag meself off da bus. I feel every bit of me insides. Blood pumpin' round me heart. I can feel me muscles stretching like rubber bands ready to snap in two. I can even feel inside me bones. D'ya know that way? The marrow all spongy. Manage to score from a dealer on the floor below me. Never fuckin' there when I'm desperate. But today he is 'cause his dog got run over on the weekend and he hasn't left the flat since. Gutted he is. Poor little Minnie, Jack Russell. That little dog always looked embarrassed, he did. I mean we don't know do we? Maybe dogs do feel embarrassed. I mean Minnie looked like she was. It's like she could tell the gear was being cut and I was gonna be back at the end a the day to score again. Poor little embarrassed Minnie, is in doggy heaven now. I bang up there 'cause I'm in a bad way, an' I mean bad. Did I say that already? Drop into me Ma's with de foot spa, after. She rips into me 'cause I did give the dealer the rest of the stuff on the list. To knock a bit off what I owe. 'Ah, now here', I says. I says, 'Wake up, you – I'm not on the rob to keep youse in style, so I amn't.' Then me sister starts cryin' an going on about me on gear an all. 'n I feel guilty but not showin' it like. Can't, 'cause I'm nodding out and can't look up never mind look guilty. Ah! She do wrap me around her little finger, she does. Then Ma says 'If your poor Father was alive you wouldn't be in this state.' 'n what am I going to tell Chrissie in the pub tonight with nuttin' on the list got? Huh? Tell me that?' I don't know Ma', I says. Laughing like, 'cause I do feel so chilled now. Me veins pumping the gear around me heart and lungs. 'n I says 'Ma!'

Here, tell Chrissie I got robbed".

She laughs hysterically at her own joke.

Brona. My heartbeat's deafeningly loud. He grabs my shoulders turning me around to face the wall. I don't cry out. All my senses feel like the volume has been turned down. I can't respond either way. For instance, I can feel his hand up under my dress, his fingers going inside...of me. But it doesn't feel like it's me. It's as if I am watching from the door of the cloakroom. I'm tasting my tears, they're running into my mouth and I'm thinking, Oh! I must be crying. Tears never usually taste this salty. Still I make no sound. No sound except for my head knocking against the empty hangers. They begin to jangle on the rails. Like bells sounding...what? My reaching the edge of all that is left of my reason? Finally a sound does come from my mouth. 'Please' I say. 'Pleaseeeeeee'. (*This sound turns into a repressed scream.*)

Chike. Pleased with myself, I am. That's me on target for the week. One of my pinchers got banged up today. She came in early that day and left to score probably. Then made the mistake of coming in again before closing. I spotted her in household. With twenty previous it's custodial this time. I think a pint is in order, celebrate. Not easy making friends if you don't go to the pub. Or maybe it's the accent. Don't sound Irish, but I bleedin' am. Carry around me Irish passport just to prove it. The other lads joke 'n that. 'Black 'n Irish. Not a bastard too are ya?' I fuckin' give up. Economic migration mate I tell them. Ever heard of it? These ignorant people. Haven't a clue what I'm talking about 'n it ain't the accent. Never read Joyce or Beckett. I have. I know our literary heritage, man. It's what sets us apart. What do you fuckin' know? Nuffin'!

Brona. Nothing, I feel nothing, oddly. Phone my husband to pick me up, regret it. His face like storm clouds when he arrives. Goes on and on at me. 'Drunk in the afternoon, letting the side down, what if the press see you in this state' etc. Etc. I'm hardly Cheryl Cole. I say. He has no idea who I am talking about not ever having seen The X Factor. Would anyone care? I almost yell. He's furious at this point. I tune him out, he sounds a bit like a hum or a radio on in the background. I look past him to a couple standing at the bus stop. 20's maybe, early 20's. He keeps pulling her back gently and kissing her, with a kind of verve and passion not appropriate for the setting, I feel. Well, really, we're in the street. I try to focus on what my husband is saying, but I can't pull my gaze away from the kissing couple. The motion of his hands – the boy at the bus stop, not my husband – and how he gathers the girl's hair while he kisses her transfixes me. The boy's hands gathering and dropping fistfuls of her hair makes me want to yell at my husband buzzing in the background: 'Shut up, will you, for Christ sake just shut up!' for the second time today I am silent when I ought not to be. I imagine the smell of the girl's shampoo and how it might stay on the boy's palms, mixing with the salt and sweat of his hands. Maybe comforting him on the walk away from her. They kiss one last time, before the bus pulls away. Not at all how I was kissed by the waiter in 'Sky'.

Lights resume a blue state. We see the woman all in white. Sitting a little spaced out, centre stage. The girl listens to her ipod on stage right. The guard talks on the walkie talkie as he walks the playing area.

Shania. I'm sick of all dis. Getting samey now. No, I'm serious! And I get caught pinching one time in…well loads…shouldn't have gone back into town the second time. I was too wasted. That muppet clocked me.

Chike. Game over!

Shania. Then the muppet hands me over to the manager. The usual shite: taken upstairs to the office – half the time they don't bother to get the filth. Just threaten all sorts. This time the manager tells the muppet he'll take it from here. Then he says gimme a blowjob 'n we'll forget about it. I'm thinking to meself no harm in sucking his cock if it keeps me outa the Joy? But then the dirty double-crossing cunt calls the filth the minute he zips up his pants.

Chike. Lonely now and then. Hard to listen to these guys when the highlight of their conversation is anecdotes from 'securityguard.com.' In the pub they are banging on about a boy who was killed in the States. Guards admitted in a taped interview the kid they were chasing ran under a security van. 'He didn't steal nuffin' but his pants were sagging where his underwear was showing and that's not allowed.' A security guard confronted the boy about his pants being low and asked him several times to pull them up. The 15-year-old refused, so one guard chased him on foot and another in a golf cart. So then the kid runs to the edge of the main road and right in the path of a truck carrying livestock. The guard who was watching it all from a security tower said chasing after the teen was a violation of the company's policy. The teenager's grandmother says no dollar amount will bring her grandson back. They sued the company for 20 million dollars. It reminded me of that pincher who died on me just outside casuals...

Shania. I am looking at custodial this time for sure.

Brona. Over breakfast next day I think I might have been forgiven, as he seems to want to confide in me. You know, all cloak and dagger tones across the kitchen table. 'We might be seeing a new captain, if you get my drift.' Drift? Oh! Shut up, I think to myself while I butter his toast... It's all up for grabs, he tells me. 'All up for grabs.' oh!, I say...and he goes on though I haven't encouraged it. 'Unfit' the headlines scream on the front page he insists on reading out. 'Drunken captain in charge of a leaky vessel. Oh! Another nautical analogy. I say aloud and wish I hadn't. The health farm in Mayo is mooted again. Health farm? Is that what they are calling it now?

Chike. Might just fuck off back to London. It's turning into a ghost town, here. Shop fronts boarded up. A feeling in the air of defeat. Hold up! I should save that (*speaks into his iphone*). 'It's turning into a ghost town, here. Shop fronts boarded up. A feeling in the air of defeat'.

Brona. 'Might just keep her off site while the leadership challenge is going on' I overhear him say minutes later on the phone to the Tánaiste. Then an awkward cough, as I walk by his study door.

Chike. If I go back I won't write. Too many distractions. No way I could deal with living at home again neither. No! London's a step backwards. In Dublin, my life is writing. Here, my need and my purpose are all bound up in one. I am just another black guy standing around a department store policing the natives and no one gives a shit what I do outside of this (*indicates his uniform*). Whether I write porn or fairy tales makes no difference to them. But that's' cool 'cause I have you (*holds his hand in front of his face*) this close. You might fool that...

Points to cctv.

But you don't fool that!

Points two fingers to his eyes. A call comes in on the radio. An Irish voice trying to be ghetto, "Hey bro clocking off time". Chike doesn't take the bait.

Brona. Sometimes I dream I'm disabled. That I've lost the use of my legs. I wake up and realize it isn't true. Well, there are tears. Soaking the front of my nightie. Big heaving great sobs. I catch my reflection in the mirror. My face is contorted in the silver half-light before dawn. You'd think I'd be relieved, wouldn't you? To be able to get around on two healthy legs.

A beat.

Well I'm not. I'm disappointed...no, really. You see it's exhausting sometimes. Getting through each day. I want to just stop. Sit still. I try, but my mind keeps racing and there is no...peace. None. Now if I could just get run over or lose the use of my limbs. Then I could give up with dignity. I'd have a reason, wouldn't I? To wallow. I mean, I would have to stay put, hmmm? Then maybe my thoughts would be still too...Instead, I wake up to this...to you and having to explain my thoughts everyday in this circle of insanity. And none of you are terribly well really. That is why you are here I suppose. Dead eyed, bearded boys, little girls so thin I can see right through them, like parchment. And I feel more unwell than before he put me here. So please 'just for today' don't wake me, please? Today I think I'll just sleep.

Shania. Woke up this mornin' thinkin' this might be me last morning and it's the same 'aul ding-dong in de flats on either side o' me. On one side they're fuckin each other's brains out, and the other side are fuckin each other out of it. At 7 in the morning (every morning!) Her goin' 'oh! Oh! Oh! No, no, no no. Don't, don't, don't!' Scream. Ah! Don't do that not that pleaseeee. Scream! Den de other one goin' 'fuck off you, ya whoremaster.' Him back at her, going 'slag, bitch, cunt!' I tell ya, it's like being stuck between City and United. And City are winnin'.

Brona. Hot flushes on and off in the night. My legs jumping around under the duvet like they belong to someone else. I pull the covers back and watch them for a bit...doing their jerky little dance. And there's me dreaming I couldn't use them at all. Very odd. He used to get up and go to the spare room. Needed his sleep. I couldn't blame him what with all the carry-on in Kildare Street... 'Et tu Brute', I heard him yell in his sleep.

Shania. Mad! All kinds a carry on, day and night, don't need the telly 'cause I've 'Corrie' on one side, and 'EastEnders' on the other. I won't miss this I tell ya. Most mornin's I do bang up, nod out for a bit, then up to me Ma's in time for Jeremy Kyle. A bit of peace...but when I get there this morning she won't let me past the door. Oh! She don't mind taking the money for the stuff I feck though, oh no! Let me in Ma, I'm yelling now. Get away from this door you! I don't want her seeing you in that state anymore. Well me sister, she do see it all over the flats: needles, and vomit all up and down the stairs. So it's normal. But those junkies are dirty bastards. I mean, ye can be clean about it. Bang up somewhere else. Puke up on your own doorstep. In your own toilet. Not on the bleedin' stairs, for me family to walk in. Durt birds the lot of yis. There's me shoutin' thru' the letter box 'Ah! Ma please. Jeremy Kyle is startin'! Nuttin', she won't budge. She's like that, but.

Brona. It's like I'm looking at my life through gauze. Everything blurred, the children, him on visiting days. Staring back. I often think, if that disabled dream were real then I could be utterly depressed and sad at the awful blow that fate has dealt me. There I'd be: my broken body wheelchair bound. There is a certain dignity in that, isn't there? A breakdown on the other hand is just so...ordinary. At times it's like you're...invisible. Well, women my age are. Aren't they? Even the beautiful ones.

Shania. Many's the time she kicked me out to go on da rob. 'Do you wanna go back on the lorries?' Ah! Ma ya know I bleedin' don't. Her waitin' every night with her hand out and I had to give her 40 euro didn't I? Didn't give a shite if I couldn't face it. 'cause I'd been roughed up or bottles shoved up me, all sorts a stuff you wouldn't want...or, I was just wantin' to sit in and be a bit sad you know that way. But she wouldn't have it. If you wanna do gear then you better bleedin' earn it. Now gerrup off the only thing you have worth selling and sell it!

Fx of other guards telling jokes on the two way radio.

Chike. When things are slow the boys like to wind me up on the radio. Pisses me off no end. 'cause like I'm thinking of different conversations that my characters might have. Or I'll be thinking about different ways to describe light on water say or the colour of the streets at dusk. They're just a bunch of wind up merchants. Everything is a joke to them.

A beat.

We had a pincher die on us few months back. Some of 'em even joked about that. I was covering 'casuals' that day. Clocked him several times over the week but this morning I was distracted. Three rejection letters in the post that morning and I was blue I tell ya. So my mind was driftin' when Phelim's yelling code red into the radio. I know the drill. Code red means all security on that floor to the main entrance. So I belts it from 'casuals' through 'cosmetics'. I close in on the pincher and he starts waving a blood-filled syringe in my face. Then the training kicks in yeah? He falls pretty easy. Phelim radios it in while I restrain him till the feds come. My arm is across his chest. I can feel his heart pumping as fast as mine. Making a click, click, click sound under my hand. My other hand goes to his neck as he lifts his head and opens his mouth.

Shania. D'ya like it?

She indicates her dress.

Keepin' it. I am...suits me.

More emphatically

Suits me, it does. Love it. The colour, yah see? I always could wear yellow. Now not a lot of people can. 'Cause it can drain ya. My sister can't wear yellow at all! Makes her look sick, it does. But it always suited me. Funny dat, isn't it? Two in de same family, but! Wanted to look nice for me day in court.

Chike. I keep him there, pinned to the ground. My knee is bang on his chest now as he's resisting. Pushing hard against me, hard, hard. Then he bites, like an animal; biting and spitting, like he ain't human. A dog maybe, or a badger. Yeah! They'd give you a nasty bite. But I have him. So he don't make contact. And his spit smells of shit. Never smelt nothing like it. I want to gag. But the adrenalin keeps me from hurling all over him and the two other lads. And I hear a siren in the distance and I'm thinkin' 'fuck, I hope that's them now'. But it fades away, and I don't know how much longer I can hold him. Then he starts to turn a funny colour. Not blue like you expect, no...red, deep red, then a strange grey. I hear what I think is a snore. And for a second, I think he's dropped off...the little fucker. Having a nap, are ya? I'm like screaming into his face now. Right in his face. 'I'll wake you up, you bastard'. He don't.

A beat.

Dead.

He's dead.

SCENE TWO

Chike is in his uniform centre stage. Flanked by Shania and Brona. He loosens his tie.

Chike. That pincher dying like that rattled the boys. Yeah..

He trails off as the enormity of what has happened sinks in.

Chike. It weren't no one's fault. I mean. That pincher was on the way out anyway. 'Known to the feds', it said in the papers. I got called upstairs. Questions an all that. Phelim looking at the ground. So then I get it. I'm being made to take the rap. Is this how it's rolling? I'm hauled over the coals for weeks. I clear the canteen like a bad smell. My brief says to stay put 'cause there ain't nuffin' they can do. I'll quit when I am ready. You ain't pushin' me out on this. Nah! Nah dat!

Shania enters in a new disguise.

Shania. Released on Monday. I only served three months 'cause I was on remand for 5.

A beat.

Shania. Thought I'd try being a redhead, fresh start like. Noel loved me as a redhead. 'Christmassy', he'd say. Loved Christmas, he did. His birthday is Christmas Day, y'see. Dat's why his ma named him 'Noel'. It means 'Christmas' in another language. Don't ya know. I never liked the name 'Noel'. Something old-man-ish about it. Be worser if he was called 'Jesus'. 'Cause if you were called 'Jesus', you wouldn't know if people were swearin' at ya or sayin' hello!

As if calling out to someone on the street

Shania. 'Jaysus'.

A beat.

Shania. Lots of little boys called 'Jesus' in Spain, but ...

A beat.

Swear to God!

Chike. *Hahahahah! Funny!*

Brona. That is why I am here. I know. I am not well...and what with him having to deal with 'the Captain's' radio debacle the other morning and the press outside the door day and night. Of course it's best all round that I come here for a rest till the election at least.

Shania. Enjoyed me little holiday. Me little skank holiday, I do call it. All clean on the inside. Nothing like a spell in the Joy to sort ya. Lots of skank in there, but I never touch it when I'm banged up. I do get me head down and get clean. That's why the gear feels really pure last few days, I'm not used to it. I had a little taster to celebrate me release like, so now I'm a little bit strung out you could say...tried the methadone programme one time but it's not worth a shite, 'n they don't gimme enough of it so I do feel sick mostly. Then I can't go on the rob. No use...but I do wanna come off it, so I do...

A beat.

Shania is distracted by the glitter of the jewellery displayed.

Shania. That's dead easy to stuff in me jacket. And most of it's not tagged. Too small. That fuckin' eejit never even catches me at it. Look at him! Full of his self. I know he'd ride me if he got a chance. I wouldn't touch it if he paid double. Thinks he's all that so he does! Look at him, pumped on those drugs they do use to make 'em muscly. Hah!

For the first time we see Chike react to Shania. He opens up his note book app and begins to write.

Chike. Don't fuck with me.

Chike reads the following as he writes:

'She laughs and starts to convulse a little as the withdrawals kick in. Then she puts in her ipod and switches it on. Katy Perry fills the air'…

Yeah! I loves you, I do, little ipod. It blasts out of me head, the pains in me veins where I can't use the spike no more, the pain in me heart and the *doubt!* Kicks it right out of me head. No…More like a little hoover, it is. Sucking up all the bad feelin's and sad feelin's, and that just makes everything okay.

Chike. Weird how blood looks blue under the skin. I noticed that the veins that weren't burnt out from smack on that pincher's arms were so blue. Hold up!

Radio alerts him to the girl in a red wig. Acting suspiciously in 'footwear'.

Chike. On it! She knows it too. Hate red hair on a woman. Married a red head, Carla. She was 'long' I tell ya! I shouldn't gas 'cause she got me writing. I don't miss her or nothing, too controlling ya get me? All up in my business. Never could relax. Phoning, texting 20-30 times a day. 'Cause I was seeing Rhonda for a year before I left her. I was a torn man. Long time. Hated lying to her 'bout where I was, why I smelt of someone else when I got home an' all that. But Rhonda…whoa! I couldn't resist. That…something. She tied me up good and proper. I had no choice. I just wanted to smell that smell of her. Mess up that make-up. I'd, like, write little poems to impress her. Never showed 'em. When I'd see her sweating on the pillow after we'd been banging…well. Seeing those little shiny beads of sweat gathering all along her hairline…I'd just feel this rush of, like…I dunno…inspiration to tell her how much she meant to me. But I wouldn't…one time, yeah, I wrote three poems in a row. I can't remember how they went. No, hold on! Em…

> 'walls runs with a mist
> Your tears and mine.
> Time lapses between
> Desire and my despair
> Are we strangers?
> The two of us.

You the stronger.
Indifference flows as freely
As blood through veins.
De dum de dum...de
Dum'.

Fuck! Nah!! It's gone. I can't remember no more of it. Must dig 'em out
though. Got stacks of notebooks filled. I'm done with all that shit now.
Only poets making money are dead.

Call comes in on the radio.

Shania. Noel died when I was in the Joy. I was at his funeral in
handcuffs. Fuckin' stupid! What was I gonna do – leg it at me fella's
funeral!? The screw was good about it though. Kept sayin', 'Sorry about
the cuffs' in her mucker accent. I start laughin' like a mad bitch.
Everyone staring at me they were. But I was dead sad inside – only on
the outside I was laughing me arse off at how mental it was. Me chained
to that *'culchie'* while my Noel is put in the ground. I remember looking
at him in his coffin before they closed the lid like. And I was shittin' me
self at the idea of seein' him dead. But the screw held me hand and said,
D'ya want me to look first? You shut your eyes an' I'll look an' then I'll
tell ya if Noel looks okay.' So that's what we did. I looked away and she
looked first. 'He looks like he's asleep', she says to me. Why do people
always say that about the dead? They do fuckin' not look like they're
sleepin'. So I opens my eyes and she pulls on the cuff to bring me closer
and I look in. Slowly like. 'Cause I am brickin' it. There he is laid out in
his old karate uniform 'cause he was national champion when he was
14. And when we would talk about our funerals he always said he
wanted to be buried in his karate uniform and I said I wanted to be
buried in the nude the way I came in.

A beat.

Poor Noel looked nuttin' like his self. Nuttin' at all. 'Cept for his hair.
His beautiful hair. I lent in and kissed it 'cause it was the only bit of him
that I could recognize. It was shiny and thick and lovely like he just had
it blow dried. Do they do that in the funeral home d'ya think? 'Cause he
did have a bit of make-up on his face and I thought maybe they did his
hair as well. Though the make-up looked dead weird. But his hair was
gorgeous, so it was. And I did feel better about seein' him then. Hands
were joined like he was sayin' his prayers. And then I did cry 'cause I
didn't think his hands looked how I remember Noel's hands to be. No,
they were all puffed up like two big rice krispies. And he didn't look like
he was sleepin' he looked ....dead. Yeah...dead.

Chike. No I remember the end of it now.

In your eye you
Hold me to a promise

To try to be as none before
This...this...wish I have...

A beat.

Chike. Shit no it's gone again.

Shania. His poor da. Never got over it. Noel was the baby, see. Five out of seven were on gear. Only Jolene and Chrystal left. Sad. Noel 'n me talkin' for ages on the phone the night before he went. Him laughing his arse off 'cause some cunt in a Merc nearly ran him over at the zebra crossing by the phone box. So Noel goes up to the door, and yer man in the car nearly shat his self. Presses a button an' all the doors lock at the same time. So Noel makes a big, mad, scary face. Like he's gonna smash the window or something. Yer man pulls off like he's on 'Top Gear'. Vroooom! Last thing Noel said to me that night, still laughin' when he said it. He goes 'that pig in the Merc nearly snuffed me out tonight, babe'. The thing is next day he was...

Dead.

Dead

And so I just kept laughin' like Noel was laughing with me there beside his coffin. Two of us breakin' our shite. When really they were puttin' Noel in the ground.

Chike. Yeah! I copy that. I see her. Yeah! She just stuffed it down her front. She's got her coat stuffed wiv bras and pants. I can see the straps danglin' out the bottom of that puffa jacket. I'm moving in now. She is heading out of lingerie to...

He scans the distance. Then shouts.

Side door, side door. Go! Go! Go! She's out the door. Go!!

Chike. Went to his funeral. Thought I should. His woman was at the graveside. Laughing like...nearly fell into the grave 'cause she is laughing so hard and fallin' all around. She's cuffed to this screw and she has to pull her back from the edge or the two of em'll go ass over tit. Then some old guy leans over and slaps her across the face. I think it was the dead pincher's dad. It did the trick and everyone else just stares ahead and the priest just continues saying 'Hail Mary's like everything is all normal. Then the screw walks her away and puts her in the back of a squad car taking her back to the 'Joy' I suppose.

Chike. I knew her too! The redhead in the joke shop wig.

Shania. Me Ma says to me, 'Ah! Now here. You are going nowhere with this lark. And two stints inside? You should think of doing something else.' Well Ma, says I, if you come up with a career change you think might suit me let me know will ya? Course I'd prefer a job in a shop selling clothes, but...Noel thought I had real style and I could 'a. He was right. I miss him bad at times and it's a stabbin' pain in me heart like I am gonna die but I go out to Dollyer strand and lie in the dunes looking at the sky and I get to thinking how birds are kinda lazy really, aren't they? Especially seagulls. I mean all they do is piss about up there in the sky. Half the time they don't even fly they just float letting the wind carry them. Lazy little shites. It's a bird's life I want next time around, and not the dog's life I've been given.

Brona. This bathroom sharing business is untenable. The other patients are just not very clean. It's a real eye-opener to be honest, having to live like this.

Chike attempts to clean dust from his uniform and hands.

Chike. That little sket I chased this morning dumped her loot in a skip outside the store. Then the builders dropped a load of bonding down on top of it. Useless! I had to bring it all back in anyway...evidence. What a fucking joke. Most of the ones I get in here are junkies or homeless. But I see all sorts. Women with their prams stuffed full of meat: shoes, household stuff. There's all kinds a stunts they pull to pilfer stuff. One time this woman returned a microwave. But only the box —and she got her money back. When we opened it, it had a brick inside wrapped in newspaper. The boxes were checked after that, I tell ya. So I goes up to the office with the stuff from the skip and the manager has the pincher there in the office. Her make-up's all messed up and she looks small and lost and so young and I'm thinking in one part of my head what a brilliant character study for Shania and then the other part of me is angry at the waste. You was someone's little girl once. Were you ever loved? Held? Tucked up in bed and read a story to? Now you're sucking cock to get out of a thieving charge. Manager don't think I know but I clock the damp at his crotch and her lipstick all fucked up.

Brona. No privacy whatsoever and they expect you to get well under these circumstances. I can't bring myself to use the toilet when I'm out shopping. In here I am sharing with some very unwell people, hygiene is not their priority, let me tell you. You never know what you will pick up in a strange bathroom. Though I have to say...M & S loos are very clean...and B.T.'s, of course. 'Cause they have an attendant. Hands you little individual towels, and there's decent fragrance, not the cheap kinds named after celebrities. Oh! And mints, should you need one. But I won't go anywhere else. Try to go in the disabled toilet, if I'm desperate. Footfall, you see. I mean, it doesn't get used as much, does it?

Chike. I just got a new laptop. Brilliant. I can write on my lunch break. Something to look forward to. Puts a little comma on my day. I come up with ideas, then put 'em all down here at lunch. Mostly I use the app on my iphone when stuff comes to me on the floor. Y'get me?

Shania. I'm drifting too...lovely...laying on me back in the dunes. Watching the clouds. White fat ones. Bits of God's beard floating across that big, blue dish of sky.

Shania drifts off to sleep,

Brona. I don't know how much longer you can keep me here. Because now it feels like I am being held prisoner. You'd think I'd been the one doing drugs. They never would have gotten to her in time if I hadn't pointed out to the attendant that the disabled toilet seemed to be engaged for an inordinately long time. I mean half an hour at least. I was there when that black security guard broke the door in. We found her contorted on the toilet. A little scrap of a girl twisted up in a yellow dress. Ice cream coloured sick all down the front of it. Blooded arm, a syringe still stuck in her vein. No blood in her face. Finally the sound came.

The woman lets out an almost silent scream and then builds to a volume. Shania wakes with a jolt as her phone rings.

Shania. Yeah. Can ya hear me? Huh? Ma? *I have.* I've been in town all day on da rob, yeah! I swear ta God I have. Ah! You're breaking up. Phone ya later, right.'

She ends the call.

Brona. He visited today and I tell him I just can't get the picture of that little girl out of my head. Did she die? I ask him. 'Two words, Brona' he says. 'Economic crisis'. All he wants to talk about is the election disaster and the mop-up operation. And the fact that he Googled 'oniomania' and how 'text book' my case is. I mean, really, he's paying 3,000 a week for this place and we could have just Googled the problem! I am so relieved that it's not something more sinister. Like a brain tumour or something. 'Cause you read about that sort of thing don't you? People behaving totally out of character only to find there is a medical explanation for it. He's relieved too. I can tell.

Chike. If it weren't for the writing I wouldn't be so stressed about cutbacks. On the shop floor I find stories and poetry in the drudgery. Stuff grabs my attention...sad or weird it doesn't matter...like that pincher dying. 'Cept it's the way he died. Seeing it up close. The life in him slippin' out of him, under my hand. Or when his arm goes to hit me and I can see all the burnt out veins and the track marks like a map leading to his tattoo that said 'Babe 4 ever.' I feel...dunno. Sorry for him, I suppose. Don't get me wrong, scumbags most of 'em, but seeing that tattoo I think well...he ain't just a junkie pincher, is he? I mean he must 'ave a girlfriend or a mum, and that.

Shania. I do keep me phone in me hand and away from me head. See.

A beat.

Chike. On the food hall today worrying about the rumours of cutbacks. I'm lookin' at babies stuck in the front of trolleys. Little heads and hands turning, pullin', takin' it all in. Soakin' it all up. Learning. And then I get to thinking you could grow up 'n end up like any one of these junkies...pinchin' for a fix. When you see how chubby – perfect they are at that age – well then it all kicks off and I am called upstairs and the axe falls; 'last in first out'. But that ain't it. I am getting the chop cause of that pincher. They's taking me for a fool. But I can't hear nothing the manager is saying to me 'cause a call comes in and all I hear is...

Phelim's voice comes over the radio.

'Code red, the disabled toilet.'

Lights fade on him. Coming up on Shania as she touches the bluetooth device in her ear.

Shania. Stops you getting cancer, it does. I do spend an awful lotta time on the phone. And I seen this programme about a woman who got cancer in her brain like, from talking too much on her mobile. Yeah! Mobile phones could give me brain cancer. Jaysus, no way I wanna die of that. Now if I could die how I wanted, I'd go for...drowning. Now, a lot a people'd hate it, but I'd plan it.

Chike. And so there we are, Phelim, me and another dead junkie, the door of the toilet hanging off its hinges. My posh pincher screaming the place down. Her hands have blood on them from the junkie's arm and I am afraid to touch her but then I do. Have to, to calm her and she just folds like paper, collapsing at my ankles. Her grip is tight and I can't move. She lets out a scream so long and loud and I just end up saying shhhhh! Over and over shhhhh! Till she loosens her grip I stare into her hollow pools and she whispers, 'Fear gorm'. What love, I don't understand? 'Blue she says. You're blue.' 'n I think, man she has lost it. Her little hand sliding down my arm, I just manage to break her fall as the ambulance pulls up outside the store.

Shania. The sun shining on my face, salty air leaving a crust on my face and collecting with sand at the corners of my mouth, my feet dip, dip, dip dip them in the water yeah!! Ahhh! Cold! Hard, cold. Seaweed, curling round my legs. Mermaids purses between my toes. Oil slicks from outboard engines make mini rainbows on top of the water. I run my fingers through them, breaking them up. Warmer now. Legs not hurting no more. I slip, slip again. Then I just slide under the water slowly, slowly. Slippin' under the waves. Gentle like. Me yellow dress all floaty. The way everything is under the sea. Even rocks and stones look all floaty down here. The salt water gets in my eyes and mouth and I feel myself inhale it instead of air. Can you breathe water? No I don't think you can. When you breathe water it's called drowning! I'd take one last look at the sky through the water and the clouds racing mad over it. I close me eyes like I'm noddin' out and drift away, away.

Lights fade and a special picks Chike out. He is no longer in his uniform. He sits with the laptop open.

Chike. So that was it. I walked out of the job. No point in staying to see out my notice or fight it even. That second junkie's death was the final straw. It's always a bit sad when someone dies even if you don't know 'em. Just seeing them like that. Emptied of their soul. Even when I have to kill a character off or hit delete on a line I get a bit sad like it's someone I know or a member of my family. But then I get a buzz too 'cause it's a world I am in control of. My world. I can bend time, fall in love, kill any one I want...

A beat.

Chike. At times it gets messy. When the two worlds collide? That real life plot-twist sent everything tumbling, tumbling towards what? This I suppose; real life and fiction all messed up in here. (*Indicates his head*) Not good. Now I ain't got a job. Without it, I ain't got no source. No chance anyone will hire me with that dead pincher on my record. I mean I know it weren't my fault but that dirty, doubt stain says otherwise. I just need to start fresh somewhere else. Away from Dublin. Fill that hole created when I have to kill one of my characters. Find the excitement again in a new plot. Not easy though. Decision made man. I ain't going back on it. Shania is in her watery grave. Too late for you now my twisted, broken, little angel...

Chike goes to his laptop and opens it up. Brona's voice coming through the laptop. Distorted nightmarish sounds. Chike is terrified of the tricks his mind has begun to play on him.

Chike. No! No! You are in my head. Not real. You exist only in words. Words! Words! Words. Whoa! Man are you losing it? No, no, you can't let this happen...this is not happening. It's just your mind. Your mind playing tricks. Have a drink...yeah! That's it or go for a walk or maybe read. Only not what you just wrote. No...need a break from that. From your own thoughts maybe. Cause that's the problem, it's your own thoughts not anyone else. Not Brona. Not possible. It's not her. She isn't real.

You created her, remember. So you decide what she says. And you can destroy her whenever you decide.

Chike frantically opens his laptop. Goes to the file 'my novel' then hits the delete button.

Chike. Delete, delete, delete!

Shania. (*Her voice now comes through the speakers*) You can hit that delete button all you like but only a blunt instrument shoved up your nose and jiggled around your frontal lobe for a bit will get rid of either of us.

Chike. Least I have one, unlike yours burnt out from heroin.

Brona voice over. Cheap!

Shania's voice over. 'Write crap, re-write, write better?'

Chike. I think you'll find the quote is 'Fail, fail again, fail better'.

There is a cacophony of sound-distorted dialogue of Brona and Shania's voices. Chike is terrified. Then a silence, he begins to cry...

Chike. Okay! Okay! Please, please please. You have to leave me alone now. Shhhhhh! Just shhhhhh! Quiet...empty...quiet...that's what I need...still. I want my thoughts to be still. 'Pinching for my soul'...maybe.

Chike opens his laptop. Tentatively. Continues typing words on the screen as the lights fade.

End.

Notes from Elizabeth Moynihan

Describing a rehearsal period is like expounding on the merits of a new lover. It feels indiscreet and uncomfortable. I am often asked questions about my process and why or how I write what I write and really I would be happier if I could just let the work speak and never be drawn on any aspect of it. I live for what I do but I don't want to talk about it and yet it seems for the purpose of this book I must. Every waking hour if not eating or sleeping, is consumed more or less with thoughts of how and where and when I will work on a current piece or planning the next. My life in theatre and helping to create theatre is a privilege and a joy most of the time but like any love it is often painful, sometimes disappointing and always a mystery. The handing over of anything born out of one's deepest, at times darkest thoughts seems unnatural and I feel gawky and inarticulate, but my work by its very nature is not mine to keep and my thoughts around it, I am told, are of interest to some...maybe...I think...Who knows...Here goes.

I had a rough first draft of *Pinching* which I sent to Joe Devlin soon after I finished it. About six months later Joe said he was putting together a programme of 'Experimental Theatre'. It was very much a new departure for me and I wasn't sure that I fit the bill. But I agreed to the offer and followed the usual process of handing the work to a director who then casts it whereupon it becomes the temporary property of the actors trusted to bring it to its rightful place...The empty space and the audience.

Sometimes the experience is rich and exciting, sometimes painful. In the early years of writing plays I thought it was a given that the writer would be shown an 'Open Door Policy' to the rehearsal room, only to have a director tell me in no uncertain terms during a rehearsal of an early work that I was not welcome. I was deeply shocked and worried that my play would not resemble the work I had struggled and fretted over for so many hours, days, prior to handing it over to the cast and director, or worse, it may be adulterated beyond recognition. What if they made cuts to lines that were as precious as new born babies to me? I put a call in to a fellow playwright and friend Richard who suggested for future reference to 'Get it in writing that you will be there at your own discretion'. I did! Thankfully no such contract was ever needed at Focus Theatre. There it is a truly collaborative process from start to finish. At Focus the writer is respected as much as the actor. A consideration not always afforded at other companies.

When Joe Devlin asked to stage *Pinching for my Soul* I knew the very person we would engage as a director who would respect and honour the delicate sensibilities of the writer as well as the cast, giving us equal opportunity to rise to our best and allay any fears of being shown the door.

As a teenager I went through phases of reading everything by a particular author; F.Scott FitzGerald, Anthony Burgess, the Brontes. I was going through a John Fowles phase in my late teens when something resonated with me that would influence my work 25 years later.

I tended to inhabit the world of the novel I was reading. Full of teenage trouble and angst. I wanted to isolate myself, and County Cork in the 1970s was hardly a hot bed of opportunity to test my darker self so I became a nerd instead. Completely immersing myself in the world the novelist had created to the point where I got depressed when it came to reading the last page. A creeping sense of loss would wash over me. The idea that the characters in the novel would have to be left behind like some brief holiday romance was heartbreaking to me. It was a death and I mourned the characters leaving my life as I would a friend. Then I experienced an epiphany moment while reading a chapter of *The Magus*. The author suddenly spoke to the reader (myself in this instance) from the page, threatening to destroy any given character if he so chose. Warning me that he was the ultimate creator of the character I had begun a virtual relationship with. As the author he was the only one who could destroy that character, in turn destroying the world his words had convinced me were real. I was devastated. That day was a sort of birth, an awakening. Novels lost their mystique and power.

I began my drama training shortly after that. I doubt the two events were born out of each other but it is far too long ago to remember exactly what did lead me to my first drama class. Perhaps John Fowles had opened a door in my imagination and in threatening to shut that door I was moved to seek out another medium where I could create and explore character myself. The writer as a character became the focus of my curiosity. I was interested in the person behind the work and not so much the work itself. I no longer trusted the writer to take the characters where I wanted them to go. Unwittingly I had sown the first seeds of a desire to write.

Pinching for my Soul began as a one man show where the actor playing the security guard also played the politician's wife Brona and the junkie Shania. I decided that although the character of Chike is a novelist and essentially uses the two shop lifters as inspiration for the characters in the novel he is writing, it might be more interesting to have the three characters visible on the stage. I have never been a fan of the one person show. It is characters relating on stage that fascinates me most. Deirdre O'Connell talked about relationships between characters all the time. She said there was nothing more exciting than seeing characters relating. 'You don't even need words. If it is truthful and the actors are fully present in the moment then an audience will be captivated.' In studio she set exercises to explore this and that is why I write so many pauses and beats in my scripts. I want my characters to just be for a moment.

Sadly the doors are now closed on that theatre space. Never was there so magical a black box. That space was charged with an artistic energy you felt as you walked through the door. How lucky am I to have had the privilege to tread that stage and to have my work performed both by the studio members and non-Focus actors alike that summer. 19 years ago I walked down the lane an actor and as the doors on Focus Theatre closed I walked up that lane as a writer. A circle completed. It didn't lessen the sadness that engulfed me on that last night, knowing it really was my last night engaging with that space and it with me..

Hollywood Valhalla

by

Aidan Harney

Cast

Rock Hudson: late 50's, a slender man, close to death
Toby: Rock's fitness instructor, late 20's.

1985

A general living area in The Castle, the residence of the former film star Rock Hudson. Both the property and its owner are tatty and in decline.

TOBY, buffed and glistening, is sitting in a hard chair, watching football on T.V., performing bicep curls. He lights a cigarette, the setting on the lighter switched to full, shooting up an impressive flame. He smokes and pumps iron.

Enter ROCK. He pads around the room, seemingly in a vague search for something, before eventually coming to a stop. Upon Rock entering, Toby quickly extinguishes his cigarette, hides the butt and fans the smoke away. Rock dithers then speaks.

Rock. I can't sleep.

A pause.

My mind...

Toby. (*Lifting weight*) Six.

Rock. Things I thought were gone, tumbling back.

Toby. Seven.

Rock. Marine guy, Momma brought home one time.

Toby. Eight.

Rock. *That*, and I don't even recall what I had for breakfast.

Toby. Ten! (*Dropping his barbell*) You didn't eat breakfast.

Rock. I need rest but I'm so Gawd-awful restless. Why is it that – ?

Toby. You do look tremendously lousy.

Rock. I haven't slept. I get a few pages in, close my eyes, I see her and this cocky marine she must have thought was the answer to all her...I must have been only about...Maybe it's the book I'm reading.

Toby. Hey, I'm watchin' the game here, okay?

A pause.

How many pills you on?

Rock. Nothing that should make things so vivid. Bring people back.

Toby. I'll get you nitrazepam. Then you'll sleep.

Rock. Maybe I'll go walk round the gardens. Smell the...

He goes to the window. Toby's gaze follows him. Toby flicks the sound off on the T.V.

Toby. You wanna go out?

Rock. Naw.

A beat.

My whole life, I never thought of him 'til twenty minutes ago.

Toby. You're a walking crock. *Who?*

Rock. This marine guy. Pa wouldn't come home. (*Toby flicks the sound on again.*) We eventually found him living rough, selling doughnuts. Bus home, she meets this uniformed guy with this crazy lookin' scar right across his –

Toby. This is all in your dream?

Rock. I can't sleep, I told ya! I'm awake and these things are comin' at me. Faces. *People.*

Toby. You gonna sit or you gonna keep pacing?

Rock. Mm. (*distant*) Bet your old man was pretty solid, huh? I'm guessin' he didn't just, flake out.

Toby. Child o' Woodstock, you're lookin' at, Mr H. (*flicks off sound*) My mom smoked so much weed, she was never quite sure who my Daddy was. You look all caved in or something.

Rock. I'm tired. 'n' when I try to rest, these – Sellin' doughnuts, he was, when we found him. With this, lost look in his eyes, you know?

Toby. (*Flicks sound back on again*) Too much Scotch is your thing. I told you, lay off the juice. That is one dull game. Come on guys! (*Flicks T.V. off altogether*) Right, I'm headin' for home.

Rock. Home?

Toby. Yes. A place I go to sometimes. *My* home.

A beat.

Rock. Oh man, this place, when I was your – . Champagne. Pool parties. The barbecue never stopped. And if Tony, old Tony on security, if he was alive, he'd run Marc Christian right out o' that cabin and tell him to just keep on marchin'.

Toby. He would now, eh?

Rock. Sure. Man was a diamond. Not one scoop, not one photograph, not so much as a...Now. Now! That bastard camped on *my* property.

Toby. He's a loser. The guys a letch. What the fuck did you see in a guy like that? Hootchin' around out there. That's blackmail, you know. Playing his funky records. What's his game anyway?

Rock. You tell me. I – . Like Fort Knox, old Tony had this place. Anyone tried to scale the walls, Tony'd break their legs, throw 'em back over. If he was around today –

Toby. He'd be sitting behind bars. Times have changed, Mr H. You know, we so much as touch your little long-term, live-in, lover, you'll find a big, juicy lawsuit in your mailbox quicker 'n you can say 'Sayonara'.

Rock. Mm. Least I'd have mail.

Toby. Sayonara. Go and sleep. Better still, go eat, *then* go sleep. You look like shit. You have to eat, man.

Rock. Toby, before you – , would you ask one of the house staff to get me a blanket? It's – don't you feel it's damn cold in here?

Toby. What house staff?

Rock. Tom or Max or, any one of the boys.

Toby. No, you loon, *what* house staff? There ain't no house staff left.

A beat.

There's me, there's your ex skulking around out back, yeah, and, that's it.

Rock. So, where did they...?

Toby. Duh, you fired 'em! Fired everybody.

Rock. *Fired?*

Toby. That's why the whole place is fuckin' empty. You cleared 'em all out.

Rock. Oh, man...

Toby. You gotta rest. I'll see you in a few hours, okay?

Toby makes a beeline for the door.

Rock. 'S' *cold.*

Toby stops dead in his tracks; throws down his training bag and doubles back to Rock. He goes to a closet, pulls out a warm blanket and throws it to Rock.

Toby. There, ya happy? Now eat!

They glare at each other.

Rock. How much mail *did* arrive today?

Toby. What's that?

Rock. Mail, today, how much?

Toby. How the fuck do I – ? One or two – on the counter there.

Rock. And they are?

Toby. What, you want me to see if you got any lawsuits?

Rock. I just want to see if –

Toby. There. The *Times*. And this one.

Rock. (*Waving the two pieces of mail*) See?

Toby. What do I see?

Rock. (*Drifting.*) Everything's...Nobody writes.

Toby. Who do you expect to write? Get with the times man. Fax. Everybody's faxing these days.

Rock is clearly dejected

What, not getting a bundle of fan mail at 59 is now a disgrace?

Rock. I didn't say – . I was thinking more...Here, can you, I can't even see these without my – . Can you – ?

Toby. Gimme. (*Opens envelope and scans the enclosed*) You still feeling sorry for yourself?

Rock. What is it? Give it to me.

Toby. You still feeling sorry for yourself?

Rock. *What?* Read it, don't –

Toby. Dear Mr Hudson. (*Dramatic pause to savour the moment*)

Rock. *Read!*

Toby. Further to our conversation with your agent...man this is – , we hereby enclose *shooting scripts, contractual terms* and *running order* for your participation, as feature guest star, in the next series of the television drama... *Dynasty*!

Rock. What the – gimme that!

Toby. 'Oh everything's drifting, nobody ever writes.'

Rock. Give me that, show me.

Dynasty?

Toby. Jerk. *See.*

Rock. Well fuck me pink.

Toby. Oh, that cheer you up a bit?

Rock. How? I mean I didn't even realize – ?

Toby. Contract, Confidentiality clause. Oh, here we go. Sounds like you're going to upset the whole apple cart. (*Laughing*) 'Villainous millionaire horse-breeder, Daniel Reece.'

Rock. When is this?

Toby. Right away, boss. So snap out of this 'vampire about the house' thing. We need to get you spruced up and ready for action again.

Rock. I swore they had Dickey Chamberlain.

Toby. Evidently not. They want you, grumpy guts. Right back in the limelight again. 'On the lot'. That is what you want, isn't it?

Rock. I...I...

Toby. And check out the big fat fee.

Rock. *No*, it's...this is fucking excellent.

Rock extends his arms. Toby diverts a hug into a manly handshake.

I appreciate everything you do for me, Toby. You do know that.

Toby. Fuck you, man. You're forgetting basic biology. You don't eat, you die. Literally, and on camera.

Rock. A true friend. Ever since the day we met. (*The start of a well-rehearsed routine. Noel Cowardesque*) Our eyes clicked across a crowded health club. What was it called – ?

Toby. (*Luke-warm*) Yeah, yeah. The Sports Connection.

Rock. That's it! The Sports Connection. I asked you to come back to The Castle here. To be my fitness guru.

Toby. You practically pushed me into that cab. (*Warming to the game*) I needed the job though.

Rock. And for the first time since I had it installed, the gymnasium actually got used.

Toby. Too right it did. No pain, no gain.

Rock. I told you you were handsome.

Toby. I told you I was engaged.

Rock. I said that made you even more handsome.

Toby. I told you 'Go jump'.

Rock. You broke my heart, Speed. But I'll settle for your loyal friendship any day.

Toby. You're weird, man. But, thank you, Mr Hudson, for saying that.

Rock. Not at all. It's true. Your ass *is* very cute.

Toby. Ha, ha. Look now, Liberace, I gotta split. You gonna be okay?

Rock. Go, you go. I'm gonna be just superb, with *this*.

Toby. I'll take this (*the newspaper*) so.

Hang on. What's that in your eye?

Rock. Which eye? Nothing.

Toby. No there is.

Rock. Where?

Toby. There, look.

Rock. What? Get off me.

Toby. I thought so. It's a twinkle!

Rock. There's the door. Go through it. And fuckin' close it.

Toby conducts an orchestra to the 'Dynasty' theme tune, weaving footsteps around Rock.

Toby. Starring rusty-old Rock Hudson.

Rock. Hey, less of the 'rusty' please. And a lot less of the 'old', okay?

(*Throw away*) Go home to your wife before she forgets what you look like.

Toby. Eat, okay? You ever see a skinny millionaire horse breeder? Think John Wayne and eat!

Exit Toby. Rock sits in a chair, begins to read.

Lighting change. Morning.

Rock has slept in the chair, script pages around his feet and on his lap. Enter Toby. He moves around the room, fixes a sandwich, before speaking, loudly.

Toby. So. You been there all night?

Rock. (*Waking suddenly, his chin shoots up off his chest.*) Who's that? Wh-where...?

A beat.

Toby. You're a fuckin' asshole, you know that, don't you?

Rock. Uh, 'Good morning' to you too, Sport.

Toby. You're a fuckin' asshole. Here.

Rock. Thank you.

Toby. I want that eaten.

Rock takes a half-hearted bite, chews laboriously and eventually swallows.

Rock. What's got you this morning?

Toby. What's that?

Rock. The little welcome speech.

Toby. It's nothing, okay?

A beat.

Rock. This is good. *What?*

Toby. *Later*, you just, feed yourself.

Rock. Okay but...

Toby. Look, I haven't rehearsed this so –

Rock. Oh, spit it out, Toby. If it's –

Toby. Yesterday's piece in the press (*he has the clipping*).

A beat.

Rock. *Times* didn't exactly get my good profile.

Toby. Your statement says 'anorexia'.

A beat.

Mr Hudson, I majored in Food Science.
I've doubled your protein.
You're under a hundred and ninety!

A beat.

Mr H? I'm –

Rock. Don't be so nosy, Sport. Okay.

Toby. I just wanna know what's –

Rock. Don't be pushy with this. It doesn't suit you.

Toby. I oughta know what's going on.

Rock. Don't fuckin' dig now, Sport. Just –

Toby. I knew you'd be like this. I'm only asking cause we usually –

Rock. Push me and I'll fuckin' fire you. Don't dig.

Toby. *What?* Why would you say – ?

Rock. Push me and I'll fire you. Don't think I'm afraid to.

Toby. And you think I'm afraid?

Rock. You'll be back a nobody. See then how brave you are. Don't push me on this one.

Toby. Don't threaten me, boss. *Hey*. I wanna know what's going on.

Rock. Don't 'Hey' when I tell you not to nose in where you're not –

Toby. Don't tell me not to – . When I read something like this. I wanna –

Rock. I will fuckin' fire you and have you removed from... Look, just leave it when I...

Toby. I read *this* in the newspaper. There's something not right here, I wanna know...

Rock. I will fire you.

Toby. Don't you think I know you well enough to...I frickin' feed you. If there's something up, I...

Rock. Okay, you're pushin' me now.

Toby. I want an answer, boss.

Rock. Fine. Answer is, you're fuckin' fired.

Toby. I'm fired.

Rock. You are fired.

Toby. So I'm fired?

Rock. Yup.

Toby. Just like everyone else you've pushed away from you.

Rock. You can leave now. You're fired. And I don't want this sandwich.

Toby. I ain't fuckin' fired.

Rock. You are, fired. And take this.

Toby. You can't fuckin' fire me.

Rock. I just did. So get the fuck outta here. Take your...

Toby. Eat the fuckin' sandwich, will you!?

Rock. You, are, fired. Go. You're gone.

Toby. What is this? You mean this?

Rock. I mean it.

Toby. No you don't. Gimme the fuckin' sandwich so.

Rock. I just said it.

Toby. You don't mean it.

Rock. I just said it, didn't I?

Toby. Gimme the – . What is this?

A beat.

You don't mean this?

Rock. I told you. Don't push me.

Toby. I'm sorry. I didn't mean to.

Rock. I told ya.

Toby. I know, I know. Look, I'm sorry.
I didn't mean to...

Rock. I warned you, didn't I?

Toby. But...Man, I need this. I...

Rock. Too late.

Toby. You're kiddin' me, right?

Rock. I said you're fired.

Toby. Yeah but. Mr H. This is...
You're kiddin' me, right?

A double beat.

Rock. When I say, don't push me, in future, don't push me.

Toby. Jeeze.

Rock. Now come here.

An awkward hug.

Toby. Jeeze, you frightened me.

Rock. You're an asshole.

Toby. You're the asshole.

Rock. Hey, don't push me.

Toby. What, you gonna fire me?

Rock. That's it! You're fired!

Strained laughter.

Toby. Fuck you!

Rock. Now you really are fired!!!

Toby. Eat the fuckin' sandwich!!!!!

Nervous laughter spirals down into silence. Toby crumbles up the paper clipping and throws it away dejectedly, wounded from battle. Rock realizes the futility of their war.

Rock. (*Pointing*) The framed photo, by the bureau.

Toby. The tuxedo one?

Rock. Bring it here, would you, Toby? (*Toby does*) Good old Ron and Nancy. Did I ever tell you, she has an absolutely filthy sense of humour?

Toby. No! Nancy Reagan?

Rock. Vile, I'm telling you. And she farts when she walks up the stairs. (*They enjoy this*) Like a little ship leaving port – bummm. All these state functions, she's walking around totally po-faced, droppin' her little newks – muummmm. "Must be the dog. Out, boy. Out!" (*Laughter*)

She is some gal.

Toby. You two sure hit it off.

Rock. Yeah. We connected in a way that –

Old Ron's a bit stuffy. This was taken in The White House, see.

Toby. Classy. Chandeliers, eh.

Rock. Presidential dinner.

Toby. Autographed. Nice.

Rock. Nancy slipped this little note, I remember, between the glass and the – , said: 'Why don't you use *Erase*...on that big blemish on your neck?' See.

Toby. Yeah, why not? Looks like a little bug there.

Rock places the blanket over Toby's shoulders.

Rock. I was never one for make-up. Went to see my dermatologist instead. He did, a test. Biopsy.

Skin cancer.

Toby. Okay?

A beat.

Rock. You got any cigarettes?

Toby. Uh...

Rock. Sport, I know you smoke.

Toby. Maybe *this* ain't the best time to be smokin'.

Rock. Y'sound like my...

They size each other up.

I ever tell you I was married once?

Toby. *No!*

Rock. Loved me near as much as my Momma. Which was damn close to *adoration*.

Phyllis. Very sweet and very innocent.
My God, Phyllis. Another ghost.

Toby. You two were actually married?

Rock. Woman had, when I met her, more let downs than the Russian ballet. Huck Finn here comes to Hollywood. Direct from Winnetka, Chicago, Illinois.

Toby. I never knew you were an Illinois boy.

Rock. Gosh yes. Roy Fitzgerald from Chicago, Illinois.

Toby. Roy Fitzgerald. Well ain't that a revelation and some.

Rock. You better believe it. Damned crooked eye tooth and all. An' Phyllis is such a god damn pain in the ass she goes and falls in love with me.

Toby. Oh sure. And you didn't in any way encourage this *infatuation*. Didn't she detect you were – ?

Rock. I didn't give a damn what she detected. Milk and Cookies, they called us. Two kids, dancin' every dance hall. We got married. Off to...where was it, we honeymooned? And *Life* magazine. And a ten page full-colour special on the two of us. Rock and the little wifey at home. And Phyllis cookin' and darnin' socks. And me choppin' wood. Like something off a Kodak box. Until, it started...from the inside...I started – *I grew a beard.*
I refused to wash. Was gone for days then. My great descent into, I don't know what, or where.
What do I do then, Speed, only give her hepatitis. Completely crush her. This woman who loved me so...Like I wanted to punish her.
Day she came home from hospital, she looked at me, held me a long time, said she had to leave but that she forgave me. Such, grace. Something I couldn't even do for myself. She *forgave* me. That was the last time I ever saw her. 'Til just a moment ago, when she seemed to...

Toby. Here now. Give me that. (*Takes picture to replace it*). Aren't you gonna finish that (*sandwich*)? Seriously. You should finish it.

Rock. Kid, I want to tell you the truth.

Stillness.

Toby. I want you to tell me the truth, boss.

Rock. That little mark on my neck was the sign I wasn't going to get away scot free after all.
I have 'grid', Toby.

Long beat.

Toby. You're saying what exactly, Mr H.?

Rock. G.R.I.D. They call it 'Gay-Related...'

AIDS. I have Acquired Immune -

Toby. You don't have to spell it out?

Toby hastily goes to light a cigarette but his lighter won't spark. He tosses it away, irritated, nerves jangled.

I – it occurred to me you might have some sort of liver or, or –I even, I said it to Christine, I said I knew you weren't well, but...

Rock. 'S' pretty big. I know.
Pretty scary.

Toby. *Grid.*

Rock. Sport. I know this is just about the worst...

Toby. Why didn't you tell me before?

Rock. I –

Toby. I mean, you tell me everything.

Rock. I really thought that if I said anything...

Toby. Well clearly you didn't think, boss, because...

Rock. I wanted to tell you, I did, I was worried you'd...react...

Toby. What the hell do you expect me to do? *Oh my God.* I don't even know you're sick. I don't even know you were married. You have, you have, a disease which, which is about as..., and my wife is leaving me. You do know that? You do realize, I've just found out this week that Christine wants a divorce?

Rock. Kid, you didn't...The worst thing you can do now is....

Toby. This makes a really bad scenario monumentally fucking serious.

Rock. Look, I didn't even know you guys were...

Toby. No, because *apparently* I'm married to my job. She says.

A beat.

I hope you're fuckin' happy now! Because, with this, we are *all* fuckin' fucked. Holy Jesus Christ, we are fucked.

Rock. The main thing is not to panic.

Toby. Oh my God, we are so *fucked.*

Rock. No one else has to know!

Toby. This is the sky falling in. This is...I have to go. I have to go. I need to get to Christine! I have to go. She is my wife!!!

Toby exits. Rock *picks up one of the series scripts and calmly places it on the table.*

Rock. That went well.

Rock places the blanket around him and sits in his armchair. Lighting change. Times passes. Enter Toby.

Toby. You sleep?

Rock. Not much, I have to say. You?

Toby. Good. No, I...

A beat.

Rock. (*Simultaneously*) Toby, I think...

Toby. (*Simultaneously*) Boss, can I just...

Rock. Go on. You go.

Toby. No, just, I'm sorry, for the way I...I didn't mean...

Rock. It's a pretty big fuckin' deal.

Toby. Man, I just wish you had...

Rock. I'm just glad, now, you know.

A beat.

Toby. I have to ask, 'cause my mind is just...Do you know, does *anyone* know, what are the chances, you know, that I, or ...? I mean could I...

Rock. *No*, of course. Doctor says absolutely none. Zero. *Zero.*

Toby. Zero, huh.

Rock. *Absolutely* no chance, he says. Intravenous drug use. Blood transfusion. That's absolutely it.

Toby. So...your heart by-pass was how, you think...?

Rock. That, or from being with one hell of a lot of cute guys.

Toby. Hm. George. Does he...?

Rock. My oldest friend, George. George knows, yes.

Toby. And Mark. Your agent, Mark, I mean, not...

Rock. Yes, Mark knows too, but not the bastard out back. He had already threatened to go to 'The Enquirer' 'bout us so I reckoned best not...

Toby. You should have told me, Mr Hudson.

Rock. Yes, absolutely, yes. I should have but I, I took a decision to *protect* certain people so...

Toby. Jeeze. If I'd realized.

Rock. Keeping you in the dark means you've remained exquisite company, Toby. I didn't want to lose that. I don't want pity, Sport. You know me. From you 'specially.

Toby. Damn, so it wasn't my protein shakes?

Rock. It was not your protein shakes. They are still wonderful, I assure you.

A beat.

Toby. Hey, you are gonna whip this thing, right? I mean...

Rock. Well, all I can say is...Our time in Paris, yes?

Toby. Yeah.

Rock. Dr Dominique Dormant. Frowns a lot, has dandruff. He had developed a serum, it's not a cure now. He felt it might delay...

Toby. So those bruises on your arm were...?

Rock. Infusions.

Toby. Not, then, a clumsy French chauffeur, closing the door on your arm, like you said.

Rock. No. I may have, slightly...Et maintenant, la vérité, mon chéri.

Toby. You're such a dick, Mr Hudson. You know I don't speak French. I would have liked to know, so I could have...

Rock. What, my bright boy? We'll have all the time in the world for reality. I wanted to have *fun*. We did have fun, didn't we?

Toby. Yeah. Lotta good fun is now though.
Hell, I really don't know what to say. I mean, *you*, how are you...? Are you in any sort of pain or, or...?

Rock. Not with the morphine.

Toby. *You're on....!* What? Oh my Lord. So...jeeze. So, what do we do?

Rock. I do not know. I always did want to play a happy-go-lucky golden oldie opposite Liz and Doris or...Now, I'm not so sure I'll even...Not so sure about this Dynasty part.

Toby. No! You can lick this thing. Sure!

Open-heart was meant to knock you for six months, you were up and around in a week, right. Strong as a buffalo, they said. Now look, we, we double your calorie intake, maybe some bulking tablets, vitamin tonics, get the weight back up again. You cut out the Scotch, okay, and them cigarettes too, you hear me? Bad for you. My best guess is you'll be as right as rain in no time. Right? Mr H? *Okay?*

Rock. Even the finest fitness instructor ever to come out of Tampa, Florida, may not be able to lick this one, Toby.

Toby. I don't want to *hear* you talkin' that way, boss. You start that kind of talk or that kind of talk gets out – jeeze, think of the image that it would...

Rock. *Image!* (*He laughs*) I've spent my whole life trying to protect this image. They won't be dressing this one up. Every inch of this body is going to betray me. Look at me. Once this breaks it's sledgehammer headline time. Fuck. My *image* is going to be...

Toby. Not just *your* image.

Rock. Whose?

Toby...

Rock. That bastard deserves everything he gets. He's like a hawk, hovering out there, waiting for me to...

Toby. I ain't concerned about him.

Rock. Who else needs to...?

A beat.

You? You mean you?

Toby. I *had* a real, nice wife. Now she's gone. With our *dog*. She's talking. People are talking.

Rock. So I'll buy you a puppy.

Toby. Don't be...I'm *young*. I'm building up a pretty good callanetics business with some pretty good clients but my car and my clothes, my *house* are all bought with a loan that I have to pay for on the strength of my own good...

Rock. I don't see how me being *ill* will have any -

Toby. AIDS, Mr H! Just the sound of it is enough for most people to frickin' freak.

Rock. *And?*

Toby. You know fine well, 'And'. I'm gonna speak frankly here now, okay?

Rock. Oh shit. *Now* he's going to speak frankly…

Toby. I am going to…I don't know how long you've known and I don't even want to know, but if you, *deteriorate* from this, right, you know what I'm saying. You do and your 'ex-lover' out back will sue your estate for every dime you ever earned. *Then*, who the fuck do you think will be called as star fuckin' witness number one to defend you? When he says you also put *his* little life on the line?

Beat. Calm descends again.

Rock. (*Almost a mumble*) He doesn't have it.

Toby. Do you *know* that? How can you be sure he…

Rock. *Yes*, he doesn't have it, okay? That has all been…Look, I'll be gone. You just said it. Don't defend me if you don't want to.

Toby. Exactly, you'll be gone.

Rock. Don't be…(*Very angry*) You have a business, kid, 'cause you have spring-boarded off of *my* name. If I hadn't hired you, you'd still be sweating it out at The…The…

Toby. Sports Connection!

Rock. Agh! You don't have the faintest idea what you're talking about, Toby, so just leave if you're too…

Toby. *Nobody* has the faintest what we're talking about here. Sharing a hot-tub? Breathing recycled air on a private jet? Hell, using the same kitchen cutlery? Sorry now for being paranoid but every article in every paper I read has a different take on this thing. Grid. AIDS. The new plague.

If I'm a little fuckin' *terrified*, apologies for not being Mother-shittin'-Teresa right now.

Tony goes to Rock *and grips him by the shoulders. The horror is out in the open and they share a moment of raw fear.*

(*Trying to be brave*) We can beat this. Fuck it, we can beat this. Come on. *Yeah*?

Rock. If the shoe was on the other foot…You know how big a coward I am. You don't have to be here.

Toby. I'm doing this for *me*. And you're gonna do this for me too.

Rock. I should have fuckin' fired you.

Toby. Just my luck. The only fucking member of staff left.

Rock. Why's that, you think?

A beat.

Toby. After *everything*. Everything you've achieved.

Rock. What? Read some lines into a lens. Is that what you call an accomplishment, kiddo?

Toby. Damn sure it is, the way you did it.

Rock. What I would have given, to just, just...hold hands, with a guy. Open, walk down the sand. Buy a popsicle. A connection. All my flicks, I might as well a'been selling doughnuts on the street corner. Hell, I'm as ridiculous now as my old man was when he...

Toby. Now hang on a sec...

Rock. Rock Hudson's not even my real name.

I'm Roy Fitzgerald.

And now look at me.

Toby. I will not even acknowledge that kind of...

You as Tony Wilson in 'Seconds', yeah? You were robbed you didn't get an Oscar for that performance. Man.

Rock. So *you're* the one went to see that movie!

Toby. Haw, haw. I love that movie.

A beat.

Rock. My face is so, changed. (*Purring*) You really reckon you could make me ready for another close up, Mr de Mille?

Toby. I have no fuckin' idea who Mr de Mille is, but I promise I'll do everything I can. You look good, man.

Rock. I know how I look. Yesterday's *Times,* you said it. But what choice do I have? This is all I can do.

Toby. It's a gift of a part, Mr Hudson. I wouldn't say it if I didn't think...We just need to pep you up's all.

Rock. So we...?

Toby. So we...We start with you learning them lines. And I, I will start by cooking us up a power lunch like never before. And then, we will, just friggin' see where we friggin' go from there. That's all we can do for now, I reckon. Sound like a plan?

Rock. It is if you say so.

Toby. Then go! I say so. Go, go.

Rock *exits. Lighting change. Time passes. Rock enters, towelling his wet hair. He is continuing to decline. Toby is reading the newspaper. He fetches some drugs.*

Rock. My little, mobile drug store. How are you?

Toby. Yours are on the left.

Rock. Plenty of cocaine in here, I hope.

Toby. Cyanide.

Rock. Hu-ho.

Toby. So, what voltage are you running on this morning?

Rock. This morning has been a good morning, nurse Toby. I have only vomited four times, thanks ever so much for asking. I feel better now I see you though. (*Slaps his behind*)

Toby. Come on. Squeeze my hand.

Rock. Your what?

Toby. *Hand.*
Not much breakfast was eaten, I see.

Rock. I ate as much as I could but...

Toby. Squeeze hard now. I told you I want it finished no matter what.

Rock. I can eat at the studio.

Toby. Studio-lot food? I want to see you at least down one glass of milk and two bananas before you leave The Castle today, okay?

Rock. If it will make you happy, my little meringue, I'll eat the tray and all.

Toby. You can give me my hand back now. Thank you. Let me see your eyes.

Toby examines his pupils.

Rock. Any news from your little woman?

Toby. Nope.

Rock. Doggie?

Toby. Nope. Gone, I told ya.

Rock. Wanna talk about it?

Toby. Nope.

Rock. Anything interesting in the newspaper?

Toby. Nope.

A beat.

It's all Live Aid. Philadelphia to London. It's pretty impressive. Eyes are good.

Rock. How are we for time if I lie down for a while?

Toby. You're not on 'til later but you'll need to rehearse, I suspect.

Toby reads the paper.

Rock. Something up, kid?

A beat.

Toby. Aw. She, aw, she moved on. Out.

Rock. On, out. What does that mean?

Toby. We're definitely finished. She says.

Rock. W-what's finished? What happened?

Toby. Um, well, I went home. She was back, packing. I went to, hug her, see if... She sat down, other end of the table. I looked at her. She *smiled*. And then she *laughed*. And then she became very serious – like a cloud was after...And, she tells me; she announces she's met someone else. Before any of this happened. *Steve*. An oboe player. She's moving in with him. Taking the dog and the golf-clubs and she, she'd rather now I didn't have any contact with her. That's it. Steve, the fuckin' oboe player.

Rock. Oh, Speed. She said that?

Toby. That's what she said.

Rock. Well fuck her, son. She doesn't deserve you anyway.

Toby. She's the only girl I've ever wanted. Since the day we met. And I was good to her. That's the scary thing, boss. I worked hard for her, you know that.

Rock. I sure do.

Toby. So we could have *things*. If she was *alone* that was because I was always workin'. *Here*. What's a man supposed to do?

Rock. You were too good to her.

Toby. I know the last few months have been *patchy* and she was a bit *off* lately, in bed and all, you know, but this... a fucking oboe player.

Rock. Fuck him. It won't last.

Toby. I wasn't *artsy* enough.

Rock. That's not it.

Toby. She's always been into this mad pop-art shit. And there's me – just pumpin' irons. She's so, *talented*. Gawd.

Rock. You've been loyal and good to that woman. Don't talk yourself down.

Toby. I loved her, you know.

Rock. I know. You gave her everything.

Toby. She changed my fuckin' life.

Rock. Wow. She did?

Toby. We clicked, you know.

Rock. Sounds special.

Toby. I was totally lost, like literally, I mean lost, plus lost in life really and anyhow, I was running late for this class with a bunch of Jewish housewives on Upper West Side, all wanted to get their butts toned for their husbands – so they hire me and a crummy studio near The Hudson. Couldn't find the place anywhere. Real late, running past this little gallery, Christine is in the window, hanging some of her final year work. I'm just like, Fuck. So quirky and so...So I go in, under the guise of asking directions. And we chat, and her eyes. Wow! And her little hat, a beret thing, and she's like, 'Come by later for the opening.' Now what the fuck do I know about art? There's a canvas. Waw, throw some paint on it. Wow, man, it's fucking art! No it's not, it's a canvas you just splashed some paint on. But, we clicked, you know. We actually did. One of those, things, right? She laughed when I told her about the Jewish housewives. She even touched my arm.

A beat.

She never changed. All the time I've known her, (*laughter that builds to breathlessness*) she has worn, get this, *impossibly* blue eyeshadow, impossibly blue turtlenecks, impossibly blue, dangly, earrings and even impossibly blue lipstick!

Rock. (*Laughing too, childish, schoolboy snorts now*) Blue lipstick?

Toby. 'Dilemma blue' it's called.

Rock. (*As if hearing the most hilarious joke ever*) Dilemma blue!

Toby. (*In fits of giddy, childish, belly-aching laughter*) This blue conundrum. And she comes home seven months ago, she's wearing red, glitter shoes. (*Rock really enjoys this, exploding with nervous fun.*) Fuck. I know!!!
I shoulda known, right?

Rock. Unless she was casting for Dorothy in the Wizard of Oz.

Toby. She was bangin' the Tin Man, is what.

The laughing stops. They both dry their eyes. Seriousness returns again gradually and Toby is smitten.

Man, she was so...We had it special.

Rock. You had love. Real love.

Toby. Yeah. She's...

Rock. (*Rock gently taps Toby's hand twice.*) Her and *Steve* will end up hating each other. It's always the way. Come on, an oboe player.

Toby. Jeeze. Friggin' kills me to think of her with..., that's the worst bit...her and some...But what can I do?

Rock. Why don't you put a fuckin' hit out on him?

Toby. You think I could hire a guy who'd...?

Rock. *Easy.* Joke.

Toby. Oh.
You never do know, do you?

Rock. The magic of first love.

A beat.

For me, it was such a long time ago, I can hardly even remember his name.

Rock freezes, as a distant echo from the past rings in his ears and a vision materializes.

Toby. Mr H? Mr Hudson, you okay?

Rock. It was night time. Real blowy, up in a little shale-filled vantage point, up in the hills in L.A. Lights – a million glowing embers just waiting to be fanned. He was beautiful. Beautiful skin, dark, and he was so skinny. Hungry. We were all hungry. And afraid. But excited. So I gave him my hand. And we scootched down out o' the breeze. His hand went to the back of my head, touching my hair. Looking right down on the drive-in in the valley. *Clarke Gable* lookin' right back up at us. And I knew then that's what I wanted. My voice to be boomin' out 'cross the valley. But I knew too I wanted so much to be with this beautiful guy.

We'd become very close lovers. But I knew we couldn't. I knew I had to choose. Juan Cardona. That was his name. *Juan.* 40 years ago.

Toby. That's nice.

Rock. Better believe it was nice.

Toby. Yeah, even though it's two guys, like, I can kinda see how...You tell it nice.

Rock. A guy as butch as you has never had cock. Is that what you're saying, Toby? *Come on.*

Toby. Only my own, boss, I told you.

Rock. I know you frat boys.

Toby. Yeah, you wish.

Rock. Such a pity this eighties generation is so *defined*.

Toby. Fuck you. You got married. You weren't exactly waving a rainbow flag.

Rock. Of course not but it made it so much more *interesting*, you see. A comedy of the sexes. He might be married too but the trick was not to ruin it for everyone. Why ruin a perfectly good marriage over a perfectly innocent fuck?

Toby. Very convenient.

Rock. It's nothing to be ashamed of. It's part of one's formation. It's something that will always *stand* to you.

Toby. You're a crazy, fucked-up, old dude. Stayin' with people's where it gets tricky in life.

Rock. Hark, the oracle speaks. The fucking Caucasian Confucius.

Toby. Fuck you.

Rock. I happen to think staying is ever so noble too, Toby. It's just, lots of guys go limp at the thought of actually hanging round Rock Hudson after the deed is done, if you get me.

Toby. I know what goes on, man. No need to...Who the fuck's Confus-ious anyway?

Rock. (*Laughing – a twinkle in his eye*) See that's why I love you, Toby.

Toby. What, I never heard of the guy and you expect me to...

Rock. Alright, alright, alright. Script reading. Come on. Before my car gets here. You can fit me in or is your booming fitness business too busy?

Toby. I can practice with you, sure.

Rock. Excellent. Sit over here, Toby. I don't bite.

Toby. Crazy, man. I don't get paid enough for this...

Rock. They will have the, um...?

Toby. Yes, they'll have the dummy cards again.

A look is exchanged.

Cue cards.

Rock. Now, glasses, where are we?

Toby. I think you'll find they are on your fuckin' head.

Rock. Oh yes. Bright boy, eh? *Now*, I survived that horrible plane scenario yesterday, didn't I?

Toby. You most certainly did.

Rock. My accountant will be ever so grateful for that.

Toby. Ha, ha. Come on. Page five, Blake pulls you both out of the nosedive at the last second. And, next scene, no sooner are you on the ground than you, over to page six, trick his wife Krystle into going horse riding with you.

Rock. From the top of six then. You'll oblige as Krystle again?

Toby. Go on.

Rock. You do her so well. Oh, and would you read the directions again? These stories get so fuzzy for me. I-I keep adding bits of my own...Gets most confusing.

Toby. Come on. Where are we so? 'Daniel and Krystle gallop into a clearing. Krystle pulls her horse to a halt and turns to him.'

"KRYSTLE: Daniel I want to go back to the farm please. We've come so far. I need to be getting back.'"

Rock. (*As Daniel Reece, with sweeping arm gestures and gravel in the voice*) 'Look around you Krystle. All this can be yours. My company can afford to plant this acreage with daisies if that's what will make you happy.'

Toby. (*As Krystle*) 'You're so terribly misguided, Daniel. You're out of touch. I love Blake. I always have and I always will. He has many fine attributes.'

Rock. 'So does a cocker spaniel, but I wouldn't want to marry one.'

Toby. 'My husband is a fine man. I'm not so sure about your morals though, Mr Reece.'

Rock. 'Krystle, why do you always think the worst of me?'

Toby. 'Believe me, Daniel. It's not that hard.'

Rock. 'If I don't get my way, I can get very angry. I wouldn't want to have to crush your husband's business just because his wife wouldn't give me just one kiss.'

Toby. 'Let me make myself clear. I belong to my husband in the boardroom...and in the bedroom.'

Rock. 'Bought and paid for, Krystle?'

Rock's eyes are on Toby now.

Toby. 'I've never had to pay for it, Daniel. Have you?' (*Directions*) 'Krystle pulls her horse's reins to get away from Daniel. Her horse bucks nervously and she is flung to the ground.'

It's you Mr Hudson.

Rock. Oh, oh yes. 'Krystle! My Krystle!'

Toby. 'Daniel dismounts and rushes to Krystle who lies on the grass. He leans over her. She is uninjured. He pushes the hair back from her face (*Toby turns the page*) and they...kiss passionately?

He exchanges a quizzical look with Rock.

Rock. Is that what it says?

Toby. Yes. 'They kiss passionately.'

Rock. Oh.

Toby. This *is* today's script?

Rock. Yes.

Toby. Boss, you're shooting this before noon today. Hadn't you read this?

Rock. I-I did but it all gets so − . You mean the kiss?

Toby. Yes. 'They kiss *passionately.*'

Rock. What? Should I ask for a re-write?

Toby. I seriously doubt you can! The whole scene builds to...You told me you'd talk to them about any type of physical...

Rock. I did! I said nothing steamy.

Toby. It's not exactly steamy but...

Rock. But I should ask for a re-write then.

Toby. Jeeze. I mean you've had this script, didn't you...?

Rock. It goes out of mind as fast as I read it. I'm on *dummy* cards, for God's sake. Look, sooner or later they're going to want me to…What do you want me to do?

Toby. 'They kiss passionately.'

Rock. Look, I'll have a word with Rick. He's a reasonable guy plus he's a Queen too. If it has to be changed, I mean…it *has* to be changed.

Toby. Could it be, tender, maybe? They kiss tenderly.

Rock. And do the kiss?

Toby. I don't know. It'd barely be a touch. It'd be over and done with, like that. Then everybody's happy. I-I'd just do it. You have to just do it; just, just barely.

Rock. I can't go around kissing people when I know I…

Toby. For a split second. It's just – . Just, the smallest touch, would be all.

The security buzzer goes.

Now that's your car. Holy crap!

Rock. I'm going to cancel today.

Toby. No one's cancelling anything. You *have* to do this or the crew will really start…

Rock. I can't.

Toby. (*Seizing his arm*) Mr Hudson, you're doing this.

Rock. Toby, let go of me. That hurts.

I am not going on set with Linda, who has become a very…

Toby. We agreed.

Rock. Ow.

Toby. We had a deal.

Rock. Ow. You're twisting my…

Toby. Look at me.

FX: *Security buzzer*

Rock. Let go of me, that hurts.

Toby. Look at me!

Rock. I forgot the scene.

Toby. You get in the car. You go to the lot. You do the Gawd-damn scene, okay?

Rock. ...

Toby. You hear me?

Rock. Ow. Yes. I hear you now stop bending my...

Toby. You just go do this. I'm..., you're not even thinking straight.

Rock. You're actually hurting me.

Toby. I will hurt you, man. I really will. Just do this now.

Rock. This is fuckin' madness. How are you so...? What's happening here?

Toby. Look. 'He pushes the hair back from her face and they ...'

Toby steels himself and moves forwards, touching his lips off Rock's.

Rock. They kiss tenderly.

Security buzzer persists.

I gotta go.

(*Rock exits. Toby ponders then dabs his lips with his forearm. He seems very sad. Exit Toby. Time passes. Lights up now on The Castle where Rock is in decline.*)

Toby. Mr Hudson? Mr Hudson?

Rock. *Gawd*? Are you calling me, Lord?

Toby. It's me, asshole.

Rock. Mr President? *Ron?* Is that...?

Oh *Toby*.

Toby. What the hell happened?

Rock. I believe I collapsed on the set of Dynasty and thus caused a great deal of drama.

Toby. I know you...Place is surrounded by news crews, police...People are gathering...

Rock. What are they saying?

Toby. The clinic in Paris, they found out.
How do you feel?

Rock. Wretched. How do I look?

Toby. You look..., you look good. You look okay.

Rock. I slept. My mind feels, clearer.

Toby. Well, that's good.

Rock. Oh my poor boy. Look at you. Petrified.

Toby. I am not. It's just, things are getting stormier.

Rock. I did warn you. You still can run.

Toby. Button it. I'm here, okay.

A beat.

Rock. Every aspect of this, from the minute I got Nancy's note. Doctors, nurses, politicians – even you, my wonderful friend. *Fear.* When I woke, my mind felt so *bright*. And, it occurred to me...maybe there's a reason for all this. We have the attention of the world.

Toby. There are a lot of cameras. It's kinda scary.

Rock. I got to thinking, how many other guys are there just like me now.
All their mothers. I saw the way the paramedics looked at me.

Toby. Nobody knows. Everyone's paranoid that they'll...

Rock. I thought this morning, how can I help get rid of all this *fear*? Huh?

Toby takes out his cigarettes.

Toby. This is not the time for heroics. You need...

Rock declines the cigarettes with a wave of his hand.

Rock. I haven't done one heroic thing my whole blasted life.

A beat.

Toby. What?

Rock. Maybe this is a chance?

Toby. *What?*

Rock. I don't know.

Toby. You want to throw open the window and tell it to the world? Is that it?

Rock. Sure might make some difference.

Toby. Oh, yeah. Great idea!
Boss, just to be clear, and I don't want to put it too plainly here, but you *acknowledge* this to anybody and the seven press corps of every shade of doom, out there, are going to fuck you sideways into a tail spin.

Rock. They will get my medical records.

Toby. For now they don't *know* jack shit, okay.

Rock. You just said they know about Paris.

Toby. George is covering that. You don't need to...

Rock. There are other ways they'll find out.

Toby. Hold on a second...

Rock. If 'the squatter' out there sues for power of attorney, *when I die*, it's gonna go...

Toby. Hang on now, just for one...

Rock. If *I* put it in a statement, maybe we can then control it.

Toby. *Control* it? Are you...? You must be losing your total fuckin'...Have you looked outside today? Maybe go for a little walk in the garden and breathe in some reality. *They are camped outside.* How are you going to *control* anything? A sad, old man in his robe, wandering his garden, looking like a bag of bones? Are you going to *control* what they say about that? About every aspect of your life?

Rock. I know they'll paint me as a...

Toby. All any of us will be remembered for, will be *this*. You're on every news channel. With your anorexia bullshit. Try the truth and you won't be long experiencing, real up-close-and-personal, just how much acid mainstream American can, can *void* over one individual. Is that what you want? To be regally, Rightwing fucked over?

Rock. I don't know what I want. *You have to help me!*

Toby. I am. Jeeze. That's why I'm *here*. Because I don't want every fan you ever had – *gone*.

Rock. Who says I won't *gain* a few?

Toby. – ?

Rock. I know. The legacy of the first big-time faggot to die from this thing.

Toby. That's going to be some legacy.

Rock. I want to be out. I want to be out. I wanna be free.

Toby. You want to be – , I'll freewheel you out there right now, feather boa in one hand and a tub of Vaseline in the other. Is that what you want? Away we go. Big tah-dah to the world!

Rock. Agh.

Toby. People are *writing* – telegrams, faxes, flowers, cards – they're all downstairs. I don't even bring them all up. People who have *loved* you for 40 years, wishing you well, hoping you'll get better.

Rock. Yeah?

Toby. *Yes.*

Rock. That's all I ever lived by. Fan mail.

Toby. I know that. *See?*

Rock. So why do I feel now like I have to do something?

A beat.

Toby. Oh boy. You are one stubborn-ass bitch. Oh boy.

Rock. Why so frightened, Toby?

Toby. You *know* what has me...

Rock. No, come on, Sport. *Really*, what has you this terrified?

Toby. Because this is, this is...I'm seriously concerned here, Mr Hudson.

Rock. But I told you I'd be leaving you lots of treasure. So it can't really be finance. Come on. What has you so spooked, Toby? Speak to me.

Toby. I don't know what you're trying to...?

Rock. You go any further into that closet, you're gonna hit Narnia. Is that it? Say hello to Mr and Mrs Beaver for me. How's that for size, Toby?

Toby. How 'bout your fucking morphine is making you see the whole world as pink. I know you'd like that, Boss, and I know you would've liked a piece of this ass, but I told you then and I'm tellin' you now, with me, you were always barking up the wrong tree. Okay, how's that?

Rock. My straight fitness instructor. Even had a wife to prove it.

Toby. Fuckin' A.

Rock. She can testify how good you were in the sack. There you go. So what's eatin' you, Sport? I can't get it.

Toby. I dunno. You tell me. You seem to have all the answers all of a sudden.

Rock. If I didn't know better, I'd say...
I'd say you are going to miss me.

A beat.

Toby. You should know me better than that.

A beat.

Rock. 'Cause I'm gonna miss you.

A beat.

Is that it?

Toby. I don't follow what you...

Rock. I know the fear.

Toby. I don't know what you're talking about.

Rock. When your first love leaves you.

Toby. This has nothing to do with Chris...

Rock. I know that very feeling.
When you've buried your Momma.
And you never had a Pa.
And the only man you ever grew to trust; grew to *respect* in a way,
maybe; he fucks you over too.
And you *are* alone.
I know the fear. At night. In the dark. The silence and the fucking
loneliness. *I've been there.*
And you have been so good to me. And I have let you down now, just
like I was let down.
But I want to go out with dignity, Speed.
So when you think back on me – I want *you* to see, I did at least *one*,
just one thing that restored my self-esteem. And had meaning.

Yeah?

A beat.

Toby. I guess it's too late to ask for a pay rise?

Rock. You are so damned handsome, Sport.

Toby. I am so damned dead here.

*Beat. Suddenly, a beam of white light explodes onto Mr Hudson and
the roar of a chopper fills the room. He shouts with terror and pulls
the blankets up to his neck. A news crew has flown a helicopter low
enough and close enough to try and get exclusive footage. Toby races
to the window and pulls the curtains closed. We hear the chopper fly
off.*

Toby. Fuck! Fuckers. Get out of here. You can't do this. Get out of here.
Jeeze, can you believe that! Jesus Christ! They can't do that. I'm gonna
call the cops.

Rock. It's happening! Things are moving!

Toby. They can't get away with that.

Rock. Time is rolling in. Time to act.

Toby. I'm calling the police.

Rock. No. Let's do it my way now, okay?

Toby. Tell me.

Rock. I'll say, I have the disease. The rest will spin whatever way it spins. *I* have to say it.

Toby. You so don't have to.

Rock. My father ended his days selling doughnuts on a street corner. I do. It's the final thing I can do. For *me*.

Toby. After everything you...
It's gotta be your decision.

Rock. It's what I want to do.

Toby. Well okay then. I'll call George, have him take a statement.

Rock. It's short. 'Mr Rock Hudson has Acquired Immune Deficiency Syndrome. Rock Hudson has AIDS.' That's all I need to say.
You're not gonna run off on me now?

Toby. Well, you'll need *someone* to hold the door open, right?

Rock. What door?

Toby. Why, that big old closet you've been in all your life. This is gonna be one hell of a coming out party. I wouldn't miss this for the world, boss.

Lighting change.

Toby. Knock, knock. Hey, big guy. Look, I'm sorry man, she ain't coming but...

Rock. Oh, Phyllis can't come?

Toby. Who's Phyllis?

Rock. ...

Toby. *Nancy* . You asked me to try one last...Nancy Reagan?
She said it wouldn't be 'politically correct'. *But*...

Rock. Nancy said that? Oh Nancy. Tut tut. *Nancy.*

A beat.

You see the papers?

Toby. I got 'em, yeah. But look, don't worry 'bout the headlines...

Rock. *No.* I was wrong. I was wrong. So much for my big *gesture*. They want me to friggin' rot in hell. Jeeze, the, the...They don't mince how they print it. It was a bad idea to...

Toby. Hey don't let them get to you. Put 'em away now.

Rock. You were right. I was wrong. This is not how I wanted things to...Oh boy.

Toby. Hey, hey-hey-hey-hey. Come on. No. Don't, buddy. Don't let them.

Rock. I'm okay. I just got a shock when I read them and no one was here but the nurses, you know. The way they look at me now it's like...

Toby. Hey, it's okay. I'm here now. Okay?

Rock. I know. I know. Man. And how are you? I see they've named you.

Toby. I guess I'm finding out who my real friends are. Nice picture of me though, don't you think?

Rock. Hah! Only person I knew could weather this storm, see. One hell of a solid guy.

Toby. You reckon?

Rock. Where do you get that from?

Toby. I told you. Moma smoked a whole hell of a lot o' weed. Someone had to do the fuckin' dishes.

Rock enjoys a chuckle.

Rock. It's been good, Speed.

Toby. I sure do like working for you, Mr Hudson.

Rock. How come you don't want anything from me?

Toby. How come you think I have to?

Rock. Well, everyone I've ever known...

Toby. Everyone?

Rock. 'Cept you.

Toby. How 'bout your guy in the Hollywood hills?

Rock. Yeah. Him too.

Toby. First love.

Rock. Yeah.

Slight pause.

My only maybe.

Slight pause.

Strange.

Rock *strokes Toby's cheek.* Toby *reaches out and they grip, fiercely, each other's hands – as if in a strange arm-wrestle. They break.*

Toby. But hey! But hey, I gotta tell ya. Don't mind what the papers say. Listen. Radio. Radio on the way over. Reagan. Ron Reagan, right. Said this morning, to the nation, he is gonna find money for new AIDS research.

Rock. He did? He said that?

Toby. Not only did the President *say* the word AIDS in public, he's talking about forty million up front. And a new bill to go to Congress by Fall. That's what I wanted to tell you. It's in every living room in every country in the world.

A beat.

Rock. Well thank you, Speed. Nancy. *Nancy.* I knew it, girl. Now, that comforts me a great deal. (*Slight pause*) And now, take this. (*He hands him an envelope*) I'm letting you go, kid.

Toby. What? What do you mean? This is the time when...

Rock. (*Pause*) I don't want you here when I'm...

Toby. But I want to be here, if I can...

Rock. Your services are no longer required. Take the golden handshake. Forget about me.

Toby. Mr Hudson, there's no way I'm gonna ever...

Rock. I don't wanna hear, what you want and what you don't want. I said you're fired!
So go.

A beat.

Well, get outta here.

A beat.

Go on, go.

Toby. Mr Hudson. I understand why you...And I respect that you...I just wanna say...

Rock. (*Long pause*) You don't have to, kid.
I know.
And I do too.

Toby. I'm gonna call you tomorrow. Okay? So pick up. 'Fact, I'm gonna call you every day, man. We're gonna still talk every day, okay?
So, goodbye, boss.

Rock. Goodbye, Toby. And well done. And, Toby...thank you.

Exit Toby. Lighting change. **FX** *– we hear the wind blowing and a distant coyote call. There is now a blood red moon in the sky which casts a glow above and around the death-bed of Rock Hudson. This glow hovers, then fades to black.*

CURTAIN

Notes from Aidan Harney

The office job I took when I first moved 'up' from the country to Dublin in 1996 was in a mews building right next door to the dinky Focus Theatre, which I'd never even heard of. The reverberations of rehearsals seeped through the walls and I was fascinated; distracted. I ventured in and immediately fell under a spell. Lunchtime theatre beautifully countervailed the desk job and might well explain why I stayed so long in that particular role. The Focus became my oasis; the place where I loosened the tie and contemplated this wonderful other world of theatre.

In 2006 then, when I was contacted by artistic director, Joe Devlin, it somehow struck me as a moment I'd been unconsciously working towards. Joe wished to discuss the possibility of a full production of the contemporary comedy 'Being Miss Ross' I'd contributed to the inaugural Dublin Gay Theatre Festival the year before. We agreed that the audience reaction had been so positive that 'Miss Ross' deserved to go further. However, with a cast of nine and complex staging requirements we also agreed that funding the project would be a real challenge.

Joe asked to read my previous work (especially any scripts with fewer characters!) and when we met again in the foyer of Brooks Hotel, the seed of *Hollywood Valhalla* was planted. We discussed a sort of book-end to the 2002 piece I'd penned for Rough Magic about the young life of Rock Hudson in Hollywood. We wanted to use the film star's end-of-life as a lens for exploring themes of love, loss, betrayal and redemption.

And so the research process began. Then there was a series of meetings in coffee docks and hotel foyers as Joe and I unpacked the carnival which was the final days of the closeted film star. Nothing happened fast. Joe was patient in his mentoring and guidance. His questioning was challenging. We didn't find easy answers but we both felt Hudson's story was calling out to be told. And maybe this slow pace of progress was just as well because it was only with the economic collapse of 2008 that the play found form and a renewed context. The fall of an icon resonated with the fall of a system.

With a coterie of notable figures (Nancy Reagan, Liz Taylor etc) moving in and out of the final tableaux of Hudson's life, our play could have become a soap. Instead, the real-life character who stepped forth from the shadows to meet us was Toby, Hudson's fitness instructor. He had been loyal to his employer to the last, despite the furore which ensued when news of Hudson's AIDS illness broke. Once we found young Toby, all other characters fell away and we had a two-hander. The play found form. The voices spoke.

In 2009, The Focus staged a series of new writing to a full-house at The Mill Theatre and *Hollywood Valhalla* got its first airing. Singer Anne Bushnell, whom I didn't know at the time, happened to be seated beside me and gripped my arm throughout the final scenes. I think both Joe and I knew from that reading that the play had really touched the audience; certainly, for me, much more than I had anticipated.

Two difficulties remained however. In a post bank bail-out era, finding funding was an issue. Even more of a challenge though was the question of who could possibly play Rock Hudson. PurpleHeart's Stewart Roche had embodied the character of Toby so wonderfully that he was instantly our only choice for that part. Our 'Rock' eluded us.

In 2010, the issue of funding was resolved when a generous donor read the script and then called to say she wanted to write a cheque to ensure it went on. A closed reading of the play followed, for the Board of The Focus and invited guests. That night we found our lead in the form of actor Patrick Joseph Byrnes who read in such a way that he traversed the pitfalls of playing Rock Hudson, the Hollywood star, to become something else entirely: a vulnerable everyman who bares his soul. An extraordinary ordinary.

Rehearsing with Patrick and Stewart, under Joe's guidance and direction, was a wonderful time. For a writer, a letting-go process has to happen in order to allow the transformation from page to stage to take place. It is a hallmark of the great gift that Joe Devlin has that he created an environment of such trust and camaraderie that, as the saying goes, the play became the thing.

It was thrilling to see scenes I had lived with for so long in my mind coming alive in ways I had never envisioned. I think we surprised each other with some of the warm humour and the pure tenderness that was found. The truth of the piece, Joe kept reminding us, was that the play was one which required great heart. Both actors were incredibly generous in the level of passion they put into the process. The Focus Theatre in winter was not a luxurious place to rehearse.

And so in January 2012, close to six years after the spark of an initial idea, the play was ready to open as part of Bewley's lunchtime theatre. I was working in Eastern Europe at the time. The airport I was due to fly out from became snowbound and I learned, over the tannoy system, that I wouldn't be getting home as planned. I had a rush of anxiety and disappointment that, after all the effort, I was now going to miss the opening show. That quickly gave way to calm. There was nothing I could do.

Reading news and reviews, from afar, of the play which I had yet to see was a strange experience. I got a flurry of text messages following John McKeown's review in the *Irish Independent*: 'Mesmerizing...sharp and self-assured...the most entertaining, dramatically satisfying two-hander I've witnessed for some time.' The next day Emer O'Kelly in the *Sunday Independent* wrote: 'It's quite an achievement...whimsical, courageous, dignified.' Joe summed up the audience response in a text message to me: 'It's a hit!'

Reflecting on the success of the play, I think it worked so well because of the strength of the shared vision and the commitment of all involved. There were several times over the years when the process faltered. I thank Joe Devlin for his faith in me and the story. Joe's dedication to the play got it over the line and into the light where it connected with audiences in a way that was magnificent and magical.

To have *Hollywood Valhalla* so beautifully staged and now published is a double blessing. It feels like a play that was just meant to be...but without The Focus Theatre it may never have happened.

The New York Monologues

by

Mike Poblete

Anotherwriter@gmail.com
Http://mikepoblete.wordpress.com

Characters

Franklin, 17. A student at Stuyvesant High School during the attacks, he is bitter toward what a post-9/11 New York and America have developed into.

Reporter, 30s. After spending over a decade on the sidelines, she is finally getting her big break.

Hooker, 20s. Perhaps five years into her trade, she has seen ups and downs and knows how to take it all in stride.

Robbie Tennerman, 41. Going through a difficult family time, Robbie is focused on his job, at which he is great.

Mortician, 40s. A nice working class guy who has to suppress his untimely good fortune.

Lieutenant Freddy Gonzalez, 27. A rookie during the attacks, his friend officer Luis Ramirez died a hero.

Guide, 25. After a few hundred tours going by the ground zero pit he hits his breaking point with a specific group of tourists.

Minister, 40s. The Church and Christianity in general has seen better times. He finally has an audience again and will not waste the opportunity.

Paula Bryer, 30s. A business woman, Paula has proven herself as a lawyer and is used to having her own way.

Deli owner, late 30s or early 40s. An intelligent Indian immigrant, he has found solace in his profession, though certain ignorance is still intolerable.

Coach, 40s. After a rough season he has put the time into this team and nothing will stand in his way of a win.

Homeless, late 30s. Every day is the same, but this one day things just have to be said.

Kid, 6. Precocious and imaginative, the kid never gets to play with her older siblings so her adventures with her stuffed animal are all the more detailed.

Franklin, 67. As a grandfather in 2051 Franklin speaks to a high school history class about 9/11 the way he remembers it.

Settings

A psychiatrist's office

A TV news desk

An apartment

An office in the World Trade Center

A bar

A TV studio

A double decker tour bus

A church

An airport

A deli

A soccer field

The Q train

A child's play room

A high school history class in 2051

Franklin, 17, *is sitting at a desk writing. He finishes and stands holding the piece of paper.*

Franklin. I'd like to start by saying this is stupid.

He takes a deep breath and starts reading.

Nine-eleven sucked balls. I just started at Stuyvesant a few days earlier. I didn't really want to go, my friends were at Murrow, two stops away. I had an hour on the subway each way.

Stuyvesant had an air of superiority. During orientation they told us we would have to work hard right away to get into a good college. I didn't even know if I wanted to go to college. They have an Olympic size swimming pool...

He looks up from his paper.

What does a high school need with that? They had a robotics club, I remember thinking that was pretty cool.

He skims over irrelevant information until he gets to 9/11.

Okay, so...it was a Tuesday. I had class at 8:30, AB Calculus. It was around about twenty minutes in when we felt something, but with all the construction we didn't really notice. Ten minutes later Mr Teitel came on the loudspeaker and said a plane had hit one of the twin towers.

He is interrupted.

How did I feel? I don't know, it's just something that just happened. Can I keep going?

He continues reading.

At that point no one was paying attention. Mr Dandeklein was trying to go on about sine curves when we heard the second plane hit. So we turned on the TV.

He looks up from his paper.

It's a public school, how are they rich enough to have tvs in every room?

He continues reading.

And there it was, chaos and confusion. Teitel came on the loudspeaker and said we all had to stay in the building. Everyone was guessing what was going on, if people were dead or what. No one was really upset, we assumed they would have made us leave if things were that bad. Then one of the buildings fell, it was like an earthquake. The TV went dead, that's when people started getting scared.

We evacuated. I saw people walking uptown from the financial district, covered in dirt. A few were bloody. One of the teachers was on a radio and told us the subway was out. One of the girls in my homeroom lived in the village and brought a few of us over there. We sat around talking.

He looks up from his paper.

This doesn't come back to my parents, right? This kid Kevin had a bowl of weed on him. I had never smoked before but we all hit it. I got really high, kind of sick and laid down on the couch. I woke up a while later, other people were asleep or gone and I just got out. It took a few hours but I eventually got home. My parents were so glad to see me they didn't notice I was high.

He is asked a question that upsets him.

No. I know a few people who saw office workers falling out windows, but I just kind of kept my head down and walked away. Why would you ask me that?

He skims, finds the right part and continues reading.

We got a few days off, then we had to start going to Brooklyn Tech because they were still using Stuy as an emergency base. The Tech kids went in the morning, we went later. The tech kids were dicks to us but I liked it, it was closer to home and I got to sleep in. Then we went back a few weeks later.

He is finished reading and addresses the psychiatrist.

That's it, can I have my Aderol now?

No, that was the deal, I write down what happened and you give me Aderol. You know, the stuff helps you study better, it's not like I want real drugs, I'm just trying to get into Brown.

Beat.

I'm not fucked up over it, I know lots of kids are but honestly, it was just something that happened. Lots of people that weren't anywhere near there had their lives screwed up a lot more than me, I don't know why I have to be in counselling. It's like everyone's trying to make me feel shitty for not feeling worse, it's ridiculous. Just give me the Aderol.

He waits frustrated.

Xanax? Are you kidding me? You know, in the three years my parents have been making me come here I've never asked you for anything, and the one time I do you try to prescribe me anti-depressants? I AM FINE, I want to go to Brown and get out of this city for a while, that's it.

He is asked a question.

I just do. I just want to study somewhere else, since when is that a big deal? It's depressing here. Crowded and cold and shit.

You know, it wouldn't kill them to build something there. It's been three years, every day I cross the West Street bridge, and see nothing, it's shitty.

Beat.

Well? Aren't you going to say something? Some fucking psychiatric observation how I'm transgressing my feelings? You know, a lot of good stuff came out of it 9/11. We had heroes, real life heroes. And for a while after, it was like we got over our personal bullshit for a second and were human beings for once. But that's not the whole story. You have all these idiots and pricks that started twisting the whole thing into something else. And if you say anything about how things have changed with the shit they're putting on TV, the random racism against Muslims, wars starting for no reason, they hide behind these American flags that have popped up everywhere and say I'm disrespecting the dead. One day people will look back on all this, you know, the way we look back at World War II, and they'll forget all the stupid shit we did and only remember the romantic patriotic nonsense. But I'll remember.

I did what you asked, can I get my Aderol now?

He holds out his hand and takes the prescription.

Thanks, you're a real credit to your profession. Do I have a choice? See you next week then.

Franklin exits.

*A female news **reporter** sits at a desk.*

Reporter. The world stands silent today as the twin towers, a national symbol of American achievement, were attacked and destroyed. The death toll is uncertain at the moment. Mayor Giuliani has ordered 10,000 body bags. We don't know at this time who or what is responsible, but it is clear that this was a deliberate terrorist attack on U.S. soil, most likely the deadliest in our nation's history.

How was that? Yea? Not too Barbra Walters? Just giving the morose facts, we can worry about the tear jerker material later. Roll it back for me. Come on Dennis, we don't have a lot of time here!

She watches.

Good, good. Wait, hold it! Stop it right there! What is that? Tell me Dennis, you're the director, what am I looking at? Is that a cowlick? This story is going to make my fucking career, do you understand most of the other channels are down? The entire fucking world is going to watch this broadcast and if I tell them the world's changed forever looking like alfalfa you and me are finished? Do you get that? Then where the fuck is hair and makeup? Fuck me...what was that? Did you say something? Something about scratching little itch? Or a little technical glitch? It's hard to understand you when you're way the fuck over there with a Danish in your mouth and I'm going live to tell the world America is under attack so I apologize if my fucking demeanour is anything less than sugary you fucking philistine. You think I'm a selfish bitch? Millions of people can't reach their loved ones because the phones are fucked, you think they want to hear the situation from someone too lazy to apply appropriate hair product? Dennis am I wrong here? Tell me I'm the asshole.

The hairdresser is working on her.

There we go, thanks for waking up sweetheart. Don't pull. Don't pull, just fix it.

What? I'm fine. You think today of all days I'm gonna choke? This is it, the big time. Just keep these amateurs out of my face and we're going to make history. You know you need New York, you know you need unique New York. Okay, ready.

Optional sound: countdown to live.

The world stands silent today...

Hooker *walks into a living room. She sounds like Marissa Tomei.*

Hooker. Oh this is nice! Look at that! You have your little chandelier, is that made of crystal? Plastic? Really? Oh no you can't tell at all, not at all. Should I sit here?

She receives the okay and sits.

This is really nice. I see a lot of dumps, you know? It's nice to go somewhere...nice! You know?

Beat.

So you live here alone? With your wife and kids? Oh okay. It's just that it looks so nice, you know, family houses usually look a lot shittier. Guess you have a maid or something?

Beat.

Is that your wife over there?

She walks over and looks at a photo.

She's pretty! Well she's in her 40s, you expect Cindy Crawford? Oh sure sure, we can talk about anything you want. Oh sure honey, let's get to it then.

She starts to take off her top. She is stopped.

What's wrong? Oh yea? Sure honey, I don't get a lot of that, go for it! Oh you know, take off any of it first, it's all good. Yea! The shirt, go for it! Oooh yea, look at you! Nice hairy chest, ooh baby you know how to work it! Is that Banana Republic? Very impressive! Oh yea, take it off, let's see the goods! Woo! Launch that rocket over here baby!

Beat.

Just give it a sec. What do you mean? Well I can see that, I'm just being supportive. So? Here, let me help.

She is stopped.

Oh sure, sure. No I'm sure you don't need my help, just most guys like my inherent altruism. Sure, take your time, I'm over here whenever.

Beat.

You got any vodka or anything? Oh sure, yea, no it's the same with my kids, you always know what they're up to by how much booze is gone. You don't want to hear about my kids.

Beat.

You wanna touch the girls? (*Indicating her breasts. She is dismissed, she makes a gesture stating that that's fine.*)

Beat.

Want me to sing you a little song? I can be quiet, sure honey.

Beat.

Oh no, no. You're a man, you're a big strong manly man, it happens. You don't want me to try? Oh sure honey, everyone has an off night. Really? No no, I've heard that a lot, it's very common. They say one out of five New Yorkers has some form of Post Traumatic Stress disorder which can often...(*she gestures*) It's very common. That's okay baby. Sure sure, I can go, no problem baby.

She stands and waits.

Sure hon, just need my paycheck and I'm out of here. Well that doesn't matter, you rented me for the hour. A discount? Would you like me to charge you nine dollars and eleven cents? Sweetie, it's been a real nice evening, you're a real nice guy, don't ruin it. Am I going to have to call my friend?

She takes out her phone.

Alright, but you're being silly now honey. (*The phone rings.*)

Hello? Anthrax? Is that you baby? It's me...I'm good. Listen, I've got this real nice guy here who is having a little trouble...yea...yea, another one, his North Tower got knocked down...yea....FEMA won't release their funds....right...oh that's great, thank you baby. Let me see, I'm on second avenue...(*to the John*) what's that? Oh great! Anthrax don't worry about it baby, the nice guy smartened up. Yea, and he's going to throw in some cab fare so I can go back to work, isn't that right? Yea, no he's a sweetheart. Talk to you soon baby.

She sticks her hand out and takes the money.

Well this has been a real nice night. Good luck mister, stop by my corner some time when you're ready to rebuild.

She air kisses and exits.

An office. **Robbie**, *in a white shirt and necktie, is sitting at a desk typing on his computer.*

Robbie. Keep it together Robbie. It's quarter to nine, Harry won't be in until at least 9:30, plenty of time to complete a histogram. Two months of work coming down to blue and red bars. Wait, what about ochre?

He clicks, expresses ecstasy at his choice.

See Robbie? This is why it's all going your way, you are THE MAN at powerpoint! Just factor in the diminishing returns, this will be done with enough time to stop by Au Bon Pain.

CRASH!! His desk shakes

What the hell was that? (*He looks out the window.*) I don't see anything wrong. Well after all of those damned drills if they want me to evacuate they'd better blast the alarm. (*Back to typing.*) I wonder about teal.

The alarm goes off. ROBBIE looks around.

I'll be damned if some incompetent janitor is going to screw up my quarterly report.

He stands and removes the battery from the alarm. It stops.

There are three other people in this office, if it's such a big deal one of them will let me know.

His phone rings.

Hello? Of course I'm in my office, how else would I answer the phone? What? An airplane? You're kidding. No, thank you, I appreciate it. I love you too Jerry.

He hangs up.

What a goddamned fag. (*He continues typing.*) Just keep at it, the Virgin Mary herself isn't going to stop me from getting this on Harry's desk by 9:30. (*Clicks some more. He is shocked.*) I can use a wipe animation with a histogram? Hell yea!

The phone rings.

Goddammit! (*He answers.*) Hello? Yea Jerry I'm still here. I'm gonna go in a few minutes, I'm just finishing something. Well I didn't ask you to wait for me! Goodbye! (*He hangs up.*)

He's really losing it. At this rate I'll have his parking space in no time.

Phone rings.

Jesus Christ! (*He answers the phone.*) Jerry, what the hell do you want now? Margaret? What are you doing calling me, I signed all the papers;

I thought we agreed on joint custody. What? Of course I have a will. Yes Scott's in it. Why? Yea I'm in the World Trade Center, you called me, didn't you? No, I've got a presentation to do. Well thank you I will take my time. Goodbye.

He hangs up.

Just focus Robbie, you're almost there.

He continues working, then looks up shocked.

Jerry, what the hell happened? Well I can see you're bleeding. Yea, airplane, you told me. Fire? Melted metal? Where? What the hell were you doing up there, you said you were leaving! To rescue people? Are you out of your mind? You can't do a push up, you're going to rescue people from a plane wreck? I don't have any band aids Jerry, what do you want from me? Dammit, stop bleeding on my floor! Just go if you're gonna go!

He turns back to his desk.

Honestly, if everyone in this office has Jerry's work ethic I'll make manager by February. (*Phone rings.*) For God's sake!

He answers.

Hello? Harry? Yes of course I'm in my office, I'll have those charts on your desk by nine-thirty, no, nine. You're not coming in? You told me this report had to be on...yes I'm aware the building is on fire, am I the only one around here that cares about a deadline? Fine, enjoy your day off, I'll see you tomorrow.

He hangs up the phone.

Even Harry is softening up, the board of directors is sure to promote me in no time. Things are finally starting to go my way around here!

He returns to work.

*A **mortician** is sitting at a bar. He spots a friend, another mortician, and flags him over.*

Mortician. Jesse! Hey Jesse!

He stands and shakes hands. They have not seen one another in a while.

What are you doing here? Oh yea? Isn't that funny. Feel like keeping me company until they get here? (*Laughs*) You must have had some idea, you know this is my haunt. It's good to see you! Where's your business now? Flushing? Really? You getting the Chinese? Greeks? I guess they're still out there. Ugh, Greek funerals, like I have to tell you. Me? Ah, you know same as ever. Of course same place, same bar, isn't it? Yea well I got this Puerto Rican kid helping me out. No, after you left I got my embalming license. Yea, Stacy still hates you for that, the whole bedroom smells like fluid. What about you, ever get your funeral license? With those hands, nah, someone always needs a good embalmer. Death never goes out of business, am I right?

Hey, let me ask you, you know I get a little philosophical after the third scotch, but do you know when you wanted to get in the funeral business? Did you like have a moment? No? Did I ever tell you my moment? It was...I was six months into my apprenticeship. You know, when the novelty of working with stiffs has worn off and you're thinking, what the hell is wrong with me? Dead people, really? And then one day this kid comes in, sixteen, mangled in a car crash. I mean the kid's face looked like someone put a football in the blender. And they tell me they want an open casket. I'm thinking no way, just not gonna happen, you know? And Simmons, Leslie Simmons, I told you about him, could embalm circles around any Egyptian, he just nods and gets to work. We worked on that stiff for, I don't know, it felt like days, probably was just six or eight hours. When we were done the kid is good as new, I couldn't believe it. So at the funeral the sister, the one that wanted the open casket, she goes up to the kid and, I'll never forget this, she froze and screamed, 'Holy shit, is he in a coma?!' That made it all worth it.

Hmm? Scotch, Glengoyne fifteen. You want one? Oh yea, well, always a beer drinker, but these guys help keep the pounds off you know. So how's business, the Greeks keeping you busy? Oh. Well you know the ethnic areas, its slow slow and then BAM your books are full. I don't know why, all eating the same food or something?

He finishes his scotch and orders another. The other mortician notices his watch.

Oh yea, got that beauty a few months back. Not bad, right? No it's real, though between you and me the stuff on Canal Street is pretty close. Just, you know, I walked by this thing every day for years and one day said why not, you know? So tell me more about you Jesse, you're looking good. Ah come on, a few pounds maybe but you look good. Well yea everyone looks better with one of these (*the watch*).

Beat.

So some season we're having, huh? Mets I mean. In 2000 they're in the World Series and now, you know? You must get to catch the games out in Flushing...well yea, you've got that right, seems like yesterday a ticket cost nine bucks.

Beat.

Jesse, is something going on here? I'm just saying, you know, haven't seen you in a long time, it's good to catch up, but I get the impression you're, I don't know, mad at me or something.

JESSE says something, he listens and becomes upset.

You've got a lot of nerve, you know that? You left me, remember? I had to close the business for three months, three months Jesse! You screwed me! I couldn't afford a new embalmer, hey, hey you hang on right here...if I could afford to pay you more I would have, what's the matter with you? You think I've always had this watch? Huh? Is this a joke? You ruin me, I go out and get an embalming license and reopen the funeral home...yes, summer 2001, and? What do you want me to say, that I didn't get some business after that shit went down? Huh? You've got some nerve Jesse, you really do. I swear, if this wasn't a place I like, if I didn't mind getting kicked out for knocking your block off...so I'm supposed to feel bad about profiting off death? I'm a fucking mortician! It's the business Jesse, I'm sure you would have turned that away, right? Who needs to pay a mortgage, right? You're in the back with the stiffs, you don't have a clue! You don't know what it's like talking to people, being respectful and solemn all the time, if you have a good day you have to bury it! How many businesses do you have to pretend to be miserable when you get a flood of cash?

He finishes his drink.

You know what Jesse, I'm leaving, and I don't ever want to see you in this bar again. I hope you rot out in Queens.

Mortician exits.

*A **police officer** appears on television.*

Police Officer. Hello, my name is Lieutenant Freddy Gonzalez from the First Precinct in Lower Manhattan. On September 11th 2001 the world changed forever for us in New York, for the citizens of our nation and for our allies abroad. Each of us has something that died for us that day, for me it was my colleague and best friend Officer Luis Ramirez.

Officer Ramirez couldn't sit through a scary movie without finding excuses to leave, but that morning he was the first one in the South Tower, fighting against thousands running out of the building. Although everyone's orders were vague, it was obvious our job was to maintain order; it was the fire fighters' job to save people. That didn't stop Luis. He ran back and forth through the smoke and ash guiding people and looking for more trapped inside. No one expected the towers to fall, how could we know? They told us they were designed to withstand the impact from a plane, but the planes in the '70s were a lot smaller. That's what haunts me, that little bit of information that could have saved my friend's life. In the end though, would he have listened? I don't think so. More than anything I wish I could go back to the day before that day, but I can't.

That's why I choose Pepsi. Its crisp refreshing flavour makes every day feel like September 10th. Pepsi, for those who enjoy a pre-nine-eleven mindset.

*A **Tour Guide** gives a tour on a double-decker tour bus.*

Tour Guide. Thanks for your patience, as you can see we've got a bit of traffic around us. Those of you just joining us welcome aboard your City Scenes downtown bus tour, I'm Mike your tour guide. As you can see this is an open top bus and the pictures are better if you stand, but please don't. Those traffic lights are about two feet above your head and they hurt a lot. Speaking of which as you can see I am ignoring my own directions and standing, that's because when you do this all day long your muscles atrophy if you don't stretch them. PLEASE LET ME KNOW IF I'M ABOUT TO SMACK MY HEAD ON A TRAFFIC LIGHT. Do NOT do this. (*He points with his mouth open.*) I don't know what that means. Say 'traffic light', 'duck' is a popular favourite. I'm a lot more entertaining if I'm not face down in a pool of blood. If you have small children that like to run around remember that much like a football they make an excellent projectile if the bus stops short so keep them seated. If you don't speak English then you don't understand any of these safety announcements or what I'm saying right now but that won't stop me from screaming profanities at you like a lunatic if you violate any of them. Any questions? Good.

Here we go pulling out. Now those of you that just got on probably don't realize you were standing at the oldest continually run public building in New York, St. Paul's Chapel. It is where George Washington used to worship, his pew is still roped off. Though still running services on Sundays St. Paul's is more of a museum than anything else, its long history provides us with many plaques inside with a lot more information than I care to learn. It's a miracle that the church is still standing because if you look between the church and the store on your right you can see what a lot of you have been waiting for, the former World Trade Center.

The World Trade Center was in fact seven buildings, not just two, the entire amount of office space lost or damaged that day is more than all of the office space found in the cities of Los Angeles, Boston and Atlanta combined, I kid you not. The only building rebuilt from the attacks is 7 World Trade, the bluish building there with the squarish top, bigger and better than it was before it has more office space than the entire city of Indianapolis. The Twin Towers were one-hundred and ten stories tall. At 1362 feet, or 415 meters they had one acre of office space on every floor. Fifty-thousand people worked there, one hundred thousand were in and out of there every single day. They had their own zip code, their own shooting range. On a clear enough day if you stood at the top you could have seen clear over New Jersey into Pennsylvania. Now if you look on your left you will see the Federal Reserve with more gold than...

I'm sorry? (*Pointing toward the pit.*) The former twin tower site is there. (*Still pointing.*) Right there. You can't see anything because there isn't anything there. Because there were two really tall buildings that were knocked down and now there's nothing, it's the most boring landmark in the world. What? (*He is being asked a question and leans in for further clarification.*) Well it's unfortunate you missed the stop Ma'am, you can just get off at the next one, it's not a far walk. You know, this (*referring to the site*) was pretty bad but honestly more people die every day in car crashes than the September 11th attacks. (*Beat.*) Excuse me? No Sir, I'm not making a mockery of a tragedy, I just think it's been six years and we need some perspective. Well I can see this is hallowed ground for you from the Ground Zero hat, T-shirt and umbrellas you and your children are wearing. Yes, I am from New York. Brooklyn. I was born there. No sir, I don't personally know anyone who died. Well believe it or not it was still a pretty crappy day and I do feel my opinion is valid. Yes your opinion is also valid but no one flew airplanes into Oklahoma City so I think I have the edge on you. It's not a lucky guess, the tattoo on your arm of the Confederate Flag shaped like Oklahoma was kind of a giveaway. I know you had a tragedy there, the next time I get in a car with you wearing a Timothy McVeigh T-shirt asking why you don't have a cowboy hat we'll be on equal footing. I don't care if you report me, there isn't a lot of upward mobility in the tour guide industry. Any other questions?

I don't know when we're going to have anything built. Our governor and mayor have given us a lot of timetables over the years. There's a lot of reasons for the delay, it's obviously a personal issue to a lot of people that all have different interests. Some people want a museum, some a park, some like me want the tallest buildings in the world again, some want shorter buildings, and then you have people like this gentleman calling it hallowed ground that inhibits construction for the rest of us. (*To Ground Zero guy.*) Sir, I don't care if your son is in Iraq, I didn't ask him to go there. Well I was pretty free before he went. (*To a different person.*) No, I don't think more tall buildings are a bad idea, New York sort of invented that and I think it's stupid to change because of a few insane Muslims. Well it's not as if we don't have other tall buildings to hit if they want to strike again. And besides, we're running out of development space in Manhattan and here we have a giant hole to fill, doesn't anyone think this would be a great opportunity to show resilience by competing with Hong Kong, Tokyo, Dubai and Kuala Lumpur and having some modern architecture again?

Ma'am, I already told you I'm sorry you missed your stop...no, I can't let you off the bus. The next stop is very close, it's just taking us a while because of the traffic. No Ma'am, we don't go directly to the Statue of Liberty. Because it's on an island in the Hudson River and we'd all drown if we drove there. (*Addressing someone else and pointing.*) That there's the Hudson River. Those tall buildings are New Jersey. No that's not impressive Miss, don't ever say that. They went up after the attacks because people were scared to be in lower Manhattan and moved to midtown and Jersey. Simply put, everything sucks since 9-11. You can't even go into the Statue of Liberty anymore. No, you can only go up to her feet, there's only one exit so just like everything else it's a terror issue. I don't care what our tickets agent told you, they work off commission, they'll tell you that the Eiffel Tower is on the tour if you'll buy a ticket. (*Back to Ground Zero guy*) Sir, if you call me a communist one more time I'm kicking you off at the next stop. Sure I can, I can do whatever I want. I can tell you about my first grade math teacher if I want. Her name was Ms. Metric and she was hot. She once asked me...(*A traffic light hits him in the back of the head, he is down. He slowly gets back up.*)

Did no one see a giant traffic light coming at my head?! Fuck, I should have stayed at McDonalds! What? It's the goddamned stock exchange you idiot, there's a giant sign right there. No there aren't tours anymore, I just told you since 9/11 if it was cool it's now illegal. Do any of you hicks have aspirin?

*A **Minister** gives a sermon in a church.*

Minister. Brothers and sisters, I welcome you all to another one of God's blessed Sundays. Let us all give thanks to the almighty for all of His blessings in this, His chosen church. Lest we forget it was by the mighty hand of God that our house of worship was spared the ferocious attacks of the heathens. Even as civilization as we know it collapsed around us, a preview of the Book of Revelation with people running in the streets with faces of blood, our blessed house remained untainted. Even now the Greek Orthodox preach the false teachings of the devil from inside a tent of scaffolding at St. Nicholas's church, unmoved by God's neglect of their well being. That is why my brothers and sisters I am so moved to see God-loving Christians before me. Christians who understand it is not a kind eyed Lord sitting on a cloud with a Santa Claus beard with a ring on his head that we have to thank for creation but a vengeful omnipotent giant who will smite us out of existence unless we do exactly as he commands without question or thought. So now, children, let us bow our head in prayer.

Dear Lord. Please don't kill us. We're sorry. We don't know what we did but we're sorry. Show us the way oh Lord, because we don't want the heathen fire and brimstone to destroy us like the Greek Orthodox you despise so much. Amen.

Now brothers and sisters, if history has taught us nothing else it is that the only guaranteed way to please our Lord is to give Him money. He needs it a lot more than you do. Our collections have been a little shabby as of late so I want you all to dig deep into your pockets and feel the spirit of Jesus move your wallets, can I get an Amen from Ben Franklin oh children.

Paula, *a well dressed woman walks up to the security checkpoint at an airport. She is whistling and puts her bag on the conveyor belt. She starts to walk through but is stopped.*

Paula. Oh, the jacket, sorry.

She takes off the jacket and puts it on the conveyor belt. She starts to walk again but is stopped.

My shoes? Oh yea, the shoe bomber. (*Makes explosion noise.*) I'm…just kidding.

She takes off her shoes. Still whistling she walks through the detector but it goes off.

My keys! Sorry.

She takes out her keys and puts them in a bin. She walks through and the detector goes off. She is confused.

The cell phone, right. You know, you always have these things on you so you don't even think about…you don't care. (*To the people waiting behind her.*) Sorry, just one moment.

She takes out her cell and puts it in the bin. She tries walking through but again the alarm goes off.

My ring? It is a bit big, isn't it. (*She takes off the ring.*) Yes, we all have to be somewhere, just hold your horses.

She walks through and it goes off again. She is confused and checks her pockets.

I don't have any more metal on me! Over here? Okay.

She follows directions and walks over to a different area, putting her arms out.

Like this? Maybe I have a piercing I don't know about! (*Losing patience.*) Really now, there's nothing left in my pockets.

Beat.

What? Are you serious? Look, my flight is leaving in twenty minutes, they've already started boarding. No, I understand that it's necessary to have precautions, (*Sigh.*) Fine, but can it be quick?

She picks up her things and goes to a different part of the stage and stops.

Right here? Uh yea, I have a passport. Don't really need one because I'm flying in the country, just to Phoenix to see my sister…Paula Bryer. 2365 Archer Avenue, Flushing. Is this all really necessary?

Beat.

Excuse me? No, I'm not trying to tell you how to do your job, no, I want to get out of here as soon as possible...fine, fine.

She takes her shirt off.

Okay, there, no bombs strapped to me, can I go now?

Beat.

You have to be kidding me. (*She looks around.*) Absolutely not. Okay, have you ever heard of a little law firm called Sullivan and Cromwell? That's where I work so unless you want to be knee deep in litigation I suggest you end this little interrogation...hey, what are you doing? You know what, fine, fine.

She takes off her pants.

You want them off so bad, there you go. Hey, what are you doing?

She is involuntarily spun around into a search position.

Stop that! (*Spins around.*) That does it! I am leaving here now, do you understand? While you're holding me here Akmaad Kameel is walking through with M80s. Why don't you do your job, stop the terrorists and let the real Americans through. White people don't blow up planes. You're damned right I can go!

She exits.

*An Indian **deli owner** is behind the counter.*

Deli owner. Two bottles of Coca-cola, a grilled cheese sandwich and a bag of Doritos, that will be seven eighty-two.

He receives the money.

This is seven thirty-five, you still require forty-seven cents. Yes I am certain, please count yourself.

He holds out his hand.

You have contributed an additional twenty cents, you still require twenty-seven more. Sir, in college I tutored calculus, I am quite certain the sum of your quarter and three dimes is fifty-five cents, twenty-seven short of your goal for this transaction.

He receives the change, and gives three pennies back.

Three cents is your change, thank you, enjoy your sandwich. Next customer please. We do not sell pornography here. Try the Magazine Hut down the block. Next customer please.

What sort of sandwich would you like? The options are listed on the sign above the meat slicer, the ingredients themselves are on display behind the glass. No, we carry no beef of any kind. Because we do not. There is a deli across the street that can address your roasted beef sandwich needs. Yes sir, three kinds of chicken. Which would you prefer?

To a co-worker.

Sanji! Murgi ka bachcha!

Back to the customer.

Anything else for you sir? With the Sprite, that is four seventy-five please. (*He receives money, makes change.*) Twenty-five cents is your change, thank you.

He turns to his television, then back upon being asked a question.

That was Hindi, my mother tongue. (*He turns back.*) Yes, we have ham and pork. Would you like another sandwich? You are thinking of Judaism and Islam which abhor the pig as a filthy animal. I myself am a vegetarian but have no moral conflict in selling meat to those who would eat it elsewhere. No sir, I am Hindu. Islam is a monotheistic religion following the Abrahamic traditions of Judaism and Christianity, Hinduism is the world's oldest spirituality and believes in many deities. Yes sir, I am certain I am not Islamic.

Hands him sandwich.

Here is your chicken sandwich, thank you. Of course I am aware the neighborhood believes I am a Muslim, you should see the graffiti I'm cleaning every two weeks. What is there to explain? The Bronx residents seem uninterested in a lesson on Krishna and the Upanishads. No sir, I was born in India, I have never been to the Middle East.

CRASH, the window is broken. The man at the counter motions to the vandal to run away.

Are you serious? Who broke my window? Get back here you kaala lund! Sanji! Nagara pala gana!

He notices the man at the counter has motioned toward the vandal and is looking after him.

This man is your friend? That is going cost me hundreds to repair! If you do not tell me who he is you are an accomplice as well! Do not walk away! May your chicken be dry and unfulfilling and your Sprite flat and without refreshment! Next customer please! Yes, we have condoms of all assortments, which kind would you like? Magnum sir? Are you quite certain.

*A little league **Soccer Coach** addresses the kids before the big game.*

Coach. Alright kids, pull it in. It's the first game of the season, it's time to play some soccer! Let's show the Blackbirds what we're made of! Richie, get your finger out of your nose son. Now I know a few of the blackbirds are a bit bigger than some of you, but remember you're the Tigers, and Tigers eat birds! Just remember our practices. No one's afraid of the ball anymore, right? We kick the ball to each other or...the net, yea? Just go ahead and nod. There we are. Alright, looks like the ref is ready to go, take your positions and remember to have fun!

He watches, and cringes.

Way to take a hit Devon, walk it off! The ref must have missed that one, but...what was that? You're telling me you didn't see that? I don't care how old he is, that was a spear tackle! Cover your mouth Lawrence, you're getting blood all over your uniform! Time out!

He brings them back.

Okay kids, nice teamwork out there, just focus on your game, pass and shoot. Now look, the idea is to have fun, but if the other team wants to play rough you need to bring it right back at them. Sometimes soccer is about dropping your shoulder a bit when the ref isn't looking. Remember, we're only a minute in, lick those wounds and let's get back in this thing!

They run off.

Atta boy Christian, make him work for the ball! (*Shocked.*) Christian, I told you to wear a cup kiddo! No, you're just fine there on the ground...oh my god!! Get up, they're just going to keep stepping on your face! You don't see any of this, hey ref? Christian, get up now!! Time out!

Brings the kids back in.

Alright, it's time to get serious. All of you stop crying. I said stop crying!! Now you all have your parents looking on, well not you Cameron, your parents are dead, but the rest of you have family that dropped two hundred dollars for you to play some ball, let's do something besides bleed on the field. Get out there and make them proud!

They run off.

Good Lawrence, nice hustle! Now push, push, no, don't run away! I don't care if he kicks you, kick him right back! Richie for the love of God get your finger out of your nose! Come on, move that ball up! Cameron, get in his face! Cameron! Okay Stevie, get in front of that ball! Oh shit,

Stevie? Stevie, can you stand son? Can you wiggle your fingers? Just rest it off. Time out!

Brings them back in.

Listen, this game is barely two minutes in and we're losing with at least, what, eight injured players? You kids need some attitude! Cameron, I'm sorry but this is up to you. You're the only decent player on this team and I need you to step it up, no offence to the rest of you. I know you've got the skills son, I need to see some drive. Now I want you to look at the Blackbirds Cameron. Look at their two best players, what do you see? Yes they are big, what else? Do they look like the rest of us? How are they different? They look a little like terrorists, don't they? Sort of like the people that killed your parents, don't they Cameron? Now I want you to listen to me son. Nothing, and I mean nothing will ever bring your parents back. But you can at least do this one thing for them and stop those lying terrorists from dismembering your teammates. Do you want their souls to see peace or not son? Now get in there and make them hurt.

They run off.

Nice Cameron, that is what I call hustle! This is going to be a great season.

*A **homeless man** steps on to the Q train.*

Homeless man. Excuse me ladies and gentlemen, I hope you are enjoying your commute home on the Q train this evening and apologize for the disturbance. When you get home tonight, be grateful for what you got: a big old house, hot food, a little drinky drink, underwear. I ain't got none of that shit. Ladies and gentlemen, I am homeless. The last place I slept with a roof over my head was over there.

He indicates by an audience member.

I ain't no drug addict. I was, that's why I ain't got no job now, but I'm off the shit. I live off you nice folks. I ain't got no instrument, I don't do no dance, fuck them bullshitters, how you gonna ask for change sounding like Miles Davis with a five piece orchestra in front of Macys? Fuck them homeless with cell phones too, I know you be seeing them around, sleeping next to outlets to charge up, talkin' 'bout 'I ain't got no home, how else do I talk to my peeps?' Fuck that! Folks, I'm the real deal, me and the crippled am the only ones you should be giving money to. Don't be ignoring the man with no legs asking for change, you can have a big mansion and a big tittied hot ass wife but life is still shit if you ain't got legs, how you think it is having no house too? Give to them and me, I'll take food, I'm legit hungry, I'll eat a fucking crayon if the shit's between bread. Please folks, anything at all, one penny makes a difference. Thank you, god bless you all and I'm sorry for disturbing your journey.

He walks around taking up a collection, he receives nothing.

The fuck is this, one penny? Are you shitting me? I wasn't serious, one penny don't do shit! Am I gonna go to the deli and buy one Dorito?

He throws the penny on to the floor.

Fuck you all! You know, you give, what, twenty bucks to some charity and think you're hot shit, but when people are dying around you begging for the change you don't need anyway you ignore me? Suck my cock all you motherfucking...

Someone gives him a quarter.

Is that a quarter?

He is grateful to the contributor.

Fuck the rest of you!

*A **kid** and her stuffed animal are deciding what to play.*

Kid. What do you want to play? We just played with Barbie, I'm bored. We can't go outside, it's all rainy.

Gets an idea.

Let's play 9/11! I'm the terrorist! You were the terrorist last time so now you're the pilot. Here's where the pilot sits, there's the co-pilot, there's the door. Ok, ready? Fly the plane! No, like this!

Demonstrating how to steer the plane.

Keep it steady! Okay, ready! I'm going to kick down the door! Keep flying!

Kicks in door.

BAM! Don't move!

Holds box cutter under the 'pilot's' throat.

We're going to Cuba! I know we're going to New York, I'm just saying that 'cause they'll get mad and attack me like the United flight! Now bring the plane to Cuba! Wait, what happens now? Oh yea! Get out of the seat, I'm flying! Oh I have to tie you up.

Starts tying him up.

Okay, now you tell the people everything is okay.

Makes an announcement on Teddy's behalf..

Shut up you American pig! Ok, tell me I'm heading toward buildings. Die infidels! Ahhh, we're gonna crash!

Explosion sound.

The whole plane is exploded! Agh! We're burning! We're all dead!

Lies down, gets back up.

Okay, now we're in the building. What was that? It was really loud! Okay, now I'm the firefighter carrying you out, you get on my back. Aghh, you're coughing, there's too much smoke! Okay, now there are too many stairs so we're tired. Agh and the fire is too close! No I can't put it out. Because the hose doesn't reach, we're like a million feet up! Run! Aghhh! Okay, we're almost out! We're gonna make it! We can see outside! Oh no the building is falling! Agh! Now we're dead. No, deader. Now we just stay here for a few months. Um, I think that's it.

Beat. What do you want to do now? Iraq War? I don't like that game, it makes no sense.

A black stage. **Franklin** *enters.*

Franklin. Thank you. I want to thank your teacher for inviting me to tell you about September 11th on its fiftieth anniversary. It's important to remember the real story beyond your history books. I had just started as a freshman at Stuyvesant High School, which is a few blocks away from the World Trade Center. September 11th was a Tuesday and I had an early history class, not totally unlike this one. So we were sitting there when we heard and felt the first building get hit. There was a lot of construction so we didn't think much of it. Then the Principal came on the loudspeaker and told us the first tower had been struck by an airplane. We all held hands in the classroom, it was a sombre moment. We turned on the television and saw it live when the second tower was hit. We just sat there in dumbstruck silence. I think we already knew everything was going to be different. The Principal came on the loudspeaker and said we all had to evacuate.

We moved out in a big group, and that's when I first saw everyone else: the workers from the financial district covered in dirt, some totally covered in blood. One man was limping, it looked like his foot was crushed. I didn't want to look up, but I couldn't help it. I saw people falling from the towers, frozen screaming in mid-air. You kids can't imagine it. Somewhere in the confusion a girl from my homeroom, funny how I can't remember her name now, invited us back to her house in the village. We were kids going through a tragedy, we consoled each other, no one knew if their families were alive or dead. We sang 'America the Beautiful'. I eventually made the long trek back to Brooklyn to see my family, we stayed up all night just holding each other.

In some ways the next few weeks were worse. We had to go to a different school for our classes, it was a constant reminder of those poor emergency workers using our Stuyvesant as a base. It took me years of counselling to work through it.

But in some ways the years that followed were even more important. They way we came together as a nation, for a while there was no black, white or brown, just Americans. People were selfless in the way they donated their money and hearts to make the city better. The way we honoured those innocent victims as the heroes they were. And it was nice in a way that they didn't finish the buildings at the World Trade Center site until 2032, because we lost something that day that could never be replaced. September 11th 2001 was a day that defined us as Americans and should be remembered that way.

We had a saying back then that I'll remind you of now: Never Forget. Thank you.

Notes by Mike Poblete

I spent the summer of 2005 on top of a Manhattan double decker tour bus, and was shocked by how visitors to my city treated the World Trade Center site as a tourist attraction. I realized that in a short period of time 9/11 had become a commercialized cliché, with T-shirts, umbrellas and mugs being sold at home; and uncomfortable U.S. foreign policy justified abroad. Somehow in all that, New Yorkers themselves were forgotten. It's hard to express what the Twin Towers meant to us: they were a symbol of safety, strength, and guidance, as they always pointed you downtown. They were the best of what we are, and one day they were taken from us, and to this day we still don't have finished buildings in their place. I didn't write a play about 9/11, I wrote a play that reveals the hurt and frustration New Yorkers feel every day living with a giant gaping wound in our city and in our hearts.

The show was first performed in 2009 with the help of Focus Theatre in Dublin. Living in Ireland I had the distance and clarity necessary to write this material, and it resonated with the Irish people. New York and Ireland have always had a close connection, and I think the Irish had a lot of opinions and sentiments towards 9/11 that they didn't always feel appropriate to express, due to a lack of ownership. This play allowed them to have a conversation they didn't always realize they wanted to have, and I was very touched by its warm reception. This was only possible, of course, because of the enthusiasm and talents of the actors, who though almost entirely non-Americans, gave truthful and vulnerable performances; and of course the direction of Geraldine McAlinden, who took the script to wildly different and amazing places that I could never have conceived of.

In 2010 I workshopped the script in New York. The stakes were much higher, of course, and the feedback, good, bad and otherwise, allowed me to clarify my message. I wrote an additional five monologues and framed the narrative around a cynical high school student, who would one day remember the talking points of 9/11 over his own experiences. The play received good reviews the summer of 2010 at Theater for the New City in Manhattan, and I took the new script back to Focus Theatre in Dublin in 2011, where the original cast and director seemed to agree my edits resulted in a stronger show. I am grateful to Focus Theatre, the Attic Studio where the first monologues were workshopped, and the people of Ireland for helping me tell a very personal and local story.

Francis & Frances

A Nice Slice of Bacon

by

Brian McAvera

Agent: The Sharland Organisation
Tel: 01933 626600
Email: tsoshar@aol.com
tso@btconnect.com

ACT ONE

Proposition 1: There is no life after death.

All of the Propositions are either flown in from the Gods, on a placard, or else projected, either above or to the side of the stage.

FX: *A cold wind is blowing, as if from the Arctic. It's steady and insistent but not especially loud, apart from the odd wind-whipped whine.*

Head 2 *appears on one of the normal mirrors, rear stage centre. The light levels are low and during the following they gradually increase until – for one brief second, which will be that of Bacon's entrance – they will become almost blinding.*

Now we hear a low, insistent, driving, military-style drumbeat, one which will surface and resurface throughout the entire play, like a fabric which the characters can ride over or under.

*In the far distance we can hear the thunderous gallop of horses, as if on hard unspringy turf. This noise, in tandem with the brightening lights, gets closer and closer, louder and louder, almost to the point of physical discomfort until, at maximum decibels and maximum lighting intensity, a body dressed in a belted, full-length (but very elegantly cut) leather coat, as if out of nowhere, seems to be thrown onto the stage, rolling across it at speed, and ending up beneath the projected image of **Head 2**. Immediately cut galloping sounds.*

*The body, it being **Francis Bacon**, straightaway goes onto its hunkers, head bent back, teeth bared, in a simulacrum of **Head 2**.*

*As Francis yowls like a wounded beast, **Head 2** vanishes, and the light levels, at exactly the same moment, return to normal.*

We still hear the low cold wind, and the low insistent military drumbeat.

Slowly Francis's head turns and he becomes aware of the audience, eyes raking them in from top to bottom.

A beat.

Francis. (*Conversationally, as if to a group of old friends*) My life hasn't changed that much, you know.

I still masturbate!

A beat.

Gets onto his feet, dusts himself down. He is very aware of his clothes, and his self-image, taking care to present himself as his own creation. He is lithe, with a very distinctive walk which – though not mincing – is unusually dapper, and composed of rather small steps. He is extremely alert to his surroundings.

He looks around him, as if trying to make up his mind whether he will take this 'audience' into his confidence.

He decides to 'go for it'.

Proposition One: there is no life after death.

He does a double-take as he realizes that this same proposition is written/projected above him.

Ergo: I am still alive.

Takes out a tiny hand mirror and, in a characteristic gesture, runs his hand through his hair, smoothing it back, whilst observing the effect in the mirror.

Ergo: (*Taking in the audience*) *You* are all still alive.

In some cases, that would seem to be a pity!

Never mind.

Now where are we?

Too many bottles of champagne last night...well...yesterday afternoon, evening and night.

(*Gesturing at audience*) You must be one *hell* of a hangover!

A beat.

I should be in the studio now.

Why break the habit of a lifetime?

Maybe I'm dreaming! Yes, that's it.

A beat.

Don't like going to sleep. Don't like dreaming.

I *never* allow myself to remember my dreams, though I did once decide to myself that, if I couldn't be a painter, I would be a film director, trapping images on the big screen.

So, if I *am* dreaming, and seeing that my dream has seen fit *not* to include my easels, my paints, my canvases, and the chaos of my perfectly organized studio clutter, then I may as well dream that I am directing.

That seems sensible, doesn't it?

Don't worry. I'm a benevolent dictator.

Well, maybe not *benevolent*....

(*Ruminatively*) I've always liked Eisenstein, Bergman, Godard, Resnais, Buñuel...

You see, the great thing about movies, is that there are all of these beautiful *men*.

Observes audience attentively.

That's it! You're my extras!

Now that means that you have to do what I tell you.

Conversationally swift: enjoying the ramifications of the idea.

Personally speaking, I prefer to be buggered, on a reasonably regular basis - say once a night – it helps the flow of the work you see. If I don't get it I fret, become irritated, I don't have that element of interruptive relaxation – the arse extended, expanded and comprehensively penistrated into pummelled satisfaction – which is a very necessary prerequisite for the *real* work of fucking on the canvas.

A beat: raking the audience.

Now. I don't like namby-pamby types. A nice Spanish boy would do. A nice Cockney? Large hands, fine fists, forget about the intelligence.

Focusing on some of the women in the audience.

Let's face it dearie, if you want to be shagged, then you don't want his cock to be decorated with twenty volumes on astro-physics and a disquisition on postmodernist intertextuality – now do you?

(*Benignly*) So we'll have some champers.

Calls with an authoritative but languid wave of the arm as if to unseen waiters whom he expects to arrive promptly.

Two bottles of Krug please, properly chilled. And we'll have a little Beluga caviare.

And I'd like to see the wine list...

(*To audience*) We'll have a nice little flirt, a nice little pre-prandial nibbles with drinkies, and then I'll direct the shagging sessions. O.K? You know it's so *tiring* being a famous artist, but I suppose we all want to be liked, and if you are famous then you sell for lots of money, and so you can buy as many people as you like, when you like, where you like.

And then just discard them when you want to work.

None of that messy relationship stuff.

So take it from me, and I'm old enough to know: *don't* fall in love.

It's bound to be with the wrong sort of person, you'll suffer horribly, he'll have piles, your life will be hell, and worst of all, you won't be able to *work*!

Work.

It's really too, *too* annoying, not being in one's studio, one's little womb, one's seedbed for ideas.

Ideas...

Ideas for a movie.

FX: Main theme from the movie Ben Hur, mingled with chariot race soundtrack

This should come in under the previous line, as if stimulating the thought pattern.

Chariot scene in *Ben Hur*, all those nice men in leather skirts and jock-straps.

(*Getting excited*) The entire movie will be a chariot race!

We'll have the English and the Irish, and lots of those *nice* Spanish boys, all entirely nude, dust flying everywhere in the hot afternoon sun, their whips whiplashing – ooh I *like* the sound of that! A little whipping of each other's naked bodies to get arousal, the chariots flying around the arena, the cocks rising in unison, a nice little *frisson* when one of them gets carried away and gets mounted – (*A beat*) 9/11 not by the horse – (*a beat*) 9/11 I'm not that practised a director...yet...

(*Con brio*) Then a fist fight breaks out on one of the chariots, and one of the charioteers – let's make him Irish – goes flying off, desperately holding onto the leather, thong-like, reins as his poor little penis goes bumptity bump, bumpity bump, bumpity bump over the stony, hard-boiled, earth:

GIANT CLOSE-UP!

Pulversized penis, a bloody, splodgy splurge in the most glorious shade of Venetian red, with just a touch of Alizarin crimson...could almost be one of my paintings!...

Music building steadily to a climax just like Bolero.

And *then* he half turns, but one of the other chariots has drawn abreast, *that* charioteer leans forward, and with a downward slash of his whip he cuts off the bloody, splodgy splurge of a penis which goes sailing into the air! And the mouth of the other charioteer – ooh, I do love mouths – you know I have the most beautiful book in my studio, bought it in the thirties, in a flea-market in Paris, on diseases of the mouth, with *gorgeous* hand-coloured plates – I can see it, the image dropping into my mind like a slide, his mouth opening in a screamingly pleasurable rictus of pain; the bloodied gums, sparkling in the sunlight, caught in a rhyme of Venetian red; and the teeth, oh the magnificent purity of the zinc-white teeth, glittering in pearled sunshine, their curved canine points sharpened for the kill; and the tail of the whip, flicking upwards like the tongue of a rodent, ready to razor-kiss the flesh of –

As Bacon is caught in an Attitude, the soundtrack (Ben Hur's stirring theme, plus chariot race maelstrom of sound) abruptly stops.

A beat.

Still in his Attitude, Bacon's head, only, moves cautiously round, first to one side, then to the other.

A beat.

Then, offstage, we hear a single, very loud whiplash.
Bacon visibly relaxes.
(*To audience*) As I was saying –
Simultaneously military drumbeat resurfaces and stage lighting goes as incandescent as possible. Out of the incandescent glow emerges **Frances**, *in high spike heels, fishnet tights, perhaps a short frock jacket, dominatrix-style, and carrying a bullwhip, the whole complete with the 'swish' sounds familiar from SF and FX movies.*

This is an ENTRANCE.

She moves powerfully, purposefully, but sexily, towards him. (*Still in an attitude; head turned towards her*) My, my, my my my! Isn't he a nice young boy!

A beat.

Simultaneously the lighting returns to normal as she lashes at him with the bullwhip. Like a scalded cat he leaps out of the way but she pursues him, whip lashing at him, seeming to get him, him yelping until he ends up, curled into a ball on the stage floor.

Frances. My, my, my my my. Isn't she a sad old hag?

Francis. (*Hopefully. Looking up*) Do I know you?

Frances. Of course you do.

Francis. I do?

Frances. (*Deadpan*) What's inside every gay, fun-loving faggot, fairy, pervert, pansy and poof?

Francis. Heavens! A semantically literate tit, or two.

(*A beat*)

You left out fruit, ponce, shirt-lifter, sodomite, Queen and bum-jumper. Personally speaking I prefer to be ginger beer: queer. You, I presume, are fem, gay, sapphist or dyke.

Frances. Remember when you were a boy? A pretty, pouting, six year old boy with long, fair curls? You adored dressing up and talking about clothes.

Francis gets into a sitting position, one hand stretched out on the floor to support himself.

Francis. Ah! The simple pleasures of childhood. Who told you!

Frances. You did.

Francis. I did?

Frances. Of course you did Francis. I'm you.

A doubletake between the audience and Frances's legs

(*Admiringly*) If only I had your legs. (*Longingly*) And your other bits.

(*Strokes a stocking*) I love Liege silk....

Frances. (*Raises an elegant heel*) You may kiss my spike heel.

Francis. Willingly!

He does so.

Frances. Good girl. Now place your hand on the floor again.

He does so.

Good girl!

She places the spike of her heel square in the middle of the top of his hand.

He breathes in ecstatically.

Francis. I adore spike heels.

(*Hopefully*) You could nail me to the floor.

Still with one spike just touching one of his hands, he lies out flat on the floor

You could crucify me like this!

Frances. Really?

A beat.

And I suppose I could use a giant hypodermic needle, instead of the spear through the side?

Francis. Oh yes please!

Frances. In your dreams, girlie. I'm not part of one of your painted crucifixions.

Elegantly removes her spike heel from his hand: he looks dejected.

(*Smiling. To audience*) Now I'm being a sadist!

To Francis. putting the handle of the whip under his chin and levering him up.

Stand!

He does so: in her heels she is a good three or four inches taller than him, if not more.

Good girl. Now. Take off your coat.

Francis. (*Shyly*) I'm not used to taking my clothes off in front of strangers.

Frances. (*As if to a child*) Francis. For the best part of seventy years you took your clothes off in front of strangers. Every night. Sailors, barmen, militia, builders, rent boys.

Francis. (*Pointing to the audience*) Not en masse!

Frances. Tough!

Suddenly lashes him with the whip.

He yelps with the pain. Then groans with pleasure.

Francis. (*Demurely*) There's no need to be so gentle!

Demurely opens and takes off his leather overcoat, carefully folds it, then just drops it on the floor, revealing a stylishly well-cut suit.

Frances. (*A little too casually*) Your father always liked to be well-turned out...

Francis. (*Out of the blue: A blistering interjection*) He was a silly old cunt, was Daddy. Narrow-minded, brutal, authoritarian, lived only for horses and gambling. Didn't much like women, even when they knew their place – a bloody disciplinarian who –

Frances. (*Sweetly*) Sounds just like you –

He takes a basilisk step towards her.

...in many ways...

He is inches away from her, every muscle in his body straining in anger.

(*Calmly*) You want to hit me. But you won't. Down here, you don't know the rules. Do you?

Abruptly she head-butts him, or smashes him in the face with her elbow, as the military drumbeat resurfaces. He collapses in a heap. She kneels, clasps his head by the hair, shoving it towards the audience and holding onto it, half jailor, half mother.

Anthony Edward Mortimer Bacon. Daddy. Born in South Australia, 1870. Educated at Wellington, then into the Military.

Tell us about Daddy.

Francis.

FX: Mauser rifle fire etc. At first this is dreamlike, as if in an echo chamber.

Gradually it becomes 'real'.

Francis. (*As his father: direct to audience. When he is being his father, his voice changes to a clipped military, and very masculine manner*) Captain Edward Bacon, Sir! Shipped to South Africa, Sir! Boer War Sir!

His neck whiplashes round to her.

Had to attack a pontoon bridge. Heavy fire! Crested the hill 'splendidly', said the General. Bombarded all night by pom-poms and rifle fire. Twenty of us killed. Seventy-six wounded.

His neck whiplashes round to audience.

Action of no military consequence. Sir. Not wounded. Sir. Doing my duty. Sir.

Drumbeat overtow. His neck whiplashes round to her.

Transferred. Transvaal. Cavalry. Boer commanders refused to surrender. Living in the saddle, month after month, sleeping under the open veldt. Hunting down the guerrillas, one by one. Execution. Execution. Execution.

Lighting change

FX: Mendelssohn's *Wedding March* plays cuts in sharply and swiftly and at high volume

She powers him upwards, using the bullwhip under his chin, then cleanly and immediately becomes his wife.

Now they are walking down the aisle, to be man and wife

Frances. (*As wife to be*) How sweet! I'm beautiful. Twenty. An heiress.

A beat.

Innocent.

Francis. (*As his father*): I'm handsome. Indigent. Thirty-four.

A beat.

But I *am* an Honorary Major. And I *do* have permission to wear the uniform: scarlet; dark green facings; bugle badge.

A beat.

We're moving to Ireland dear. Good protestant Ascendancy stock. Near the army barracks at the Curragh, County Kildare. The cavalry need horses. We shall breed them. And race them! Heigh ho! (*As if to priest*) I do.

Frances. (*As if to priest, as wife to be*) I do.

They kiss, very formally.

A military drumbeat interrupts, breaking off the kiss.

FX: Snatch of *Rule Britannia*, at high volume which rises high above the drumbeat, then fades under.

(*As wife*) Lovely country.

A most proper and entirely delightful circuit of The Big House.

Francis (*As his father*) Pity about the natives. They breed like rabbits. (*Sententiously*) There'll be trouble, you mark my words.

A single swift beat on a snare-drum, which echoes.

Frances. (*As herself*) Not only the natives who breed, Francis. Take off your shoes.

He does so. Puts them neatly beside his coat.

Good girl. Take off your jacket.

He looks at her as if to object. She cracks the whip sharply.

Francis. (*Petulantly*) Keep your wig on!

(*To audience*) Quelle horreur!

Takes off jacket and folds it neatly and places over overcoat. As he does so he sniffs and responds with an asthmatic wheeze.

Frances. Have trouble breathing, do we? Pity about the asthma.

Francis. All those animals. Cats. Dogs. Horses. The stink of hair.

Frances. Daddy was determined to make you a proper boy.

> 'Give you a backbone, boy'.
> 'Mount the horse!'

Francis. I fell off!

Frances. 'Mount the horse'!

Francis. I fell off!

Frances. (*To audience*) An alternative educational strategy was introduced.

Francis. I was horsewhipped. By the grooms. At Daddy's request.

Frances. 'Make a man of you yet, boy'!

A beat.

Remember your grandmother's husband?

Francis. I liked my grandmother.

Frances. But not her husband. Hunting shooting n' fishing. Remember the cats?

Francis. He threw them into sacks, waited for the claws to scratch through, then cut off the claws. (*To audience*) Thus armed, he set off to give the hounds a taste for blood.

A beat.

(*Curious. To himself*) It's a different colour.

Frances. What is?

Francis. Cat's blood. Not like human blood: (*To audience*) phosphorescent vermilion.....

A beat.

Whip me.

Frances. No.

Take off your tie.

Francis. No!

Frances. Please yourself. I'll leave you with *them*.

Turns as if to exit.

Francis. Wait! (*Little boy wheedling voice*) I need a shag…

A beat.

(*Grumpily*) Oh very well!

Takes off tie and neatly places it on the pile.

(*Sarcastically*) I suppose you want the trousers off as well!

She cracks the whip at him three times, with real menace. He scrabbles to get them off, then stands holding the trousers in front of him, half genuinely afraid. She waits. Sullenly he folds them and places them on the pile. We can now see clearly that he is wearing women's underwear: fishnet tights, silk panties, and suspenders.

He stares at her defiantly.

I'm putting on my shoes. Whether you like it or not!

Does so.

She smiles, and like a conjuror, gives a little flick of her whip. Undertow of military drumbeat

FX: World War One Air Raid siren: loud.

He dives onto the floor as if a boy, and scrabbles up to an imaginary window.

Frances. (*As Mummy. Coming over to him, kneeling, stroking his hair*) Imagine! At Liberty Hall in Dublin, long columns of Irishmen are swinging past, off to the poppy coffins of Flanders Field.

Look. Here, at home, the soldiers are leaving for Flanders too! Daddy's too old. Desk job in London.

(*Suddenly*) What age are you?

Francis. (*Small voice*) Five. But I'll be brave Mummy. (*Looking out of window*) Why are those men painting xs on the grass in the park?

Frances. (*As Mummy*) It's a phosphorescent paint Francis, so that it glows in the dark. It's to make the bombers think that Hyde Park is full of houses, so that they will bomb the grass, and not us!

Francis. What are those square metal things Mummy, with wires?

Frances. (*As Mummy*) A defence against low-flying aircraft, young man. We need to draw the curtains now. Time for the Blackout.

Francis. (*Peeking out. Pointing Excitedly*) Look Mummy! Huge silver worms!

Frances. (*As Mummy*) Zeppelins Francis.

FX: Anti-aircraft barrage WW1

(*As herself*) Remember Francis?

Francis. (*On his hunkers: no longer the child*) I used to pick up bits of shrapnel...shell casings...in the park...

Frances. Jagged metal fragments, falling thousands of feet, plummeting through the atmosphere...

Francis. (*Fascinated*) Battleship grey, blasted bronze...cleaving through the air like alien surgical knives...Ripening wounds with a soft plosive squelch of chrome red, and the splintering clarity of glimmer white...I'd look out, from underneath the blind: thick, palpable gloom. Suddenly a body would loom out of the darkness, for a brief second frozen like a photograph...then slip back into shadowland.

Frances. (*Almost intimately*) I didn't like going back to Ireland. After the war.

Francis. (*Coldly*) I'm not Irish! Once I left, I never went back!

Frances. (*Disingenuously*) Did I say you were Irish? We were born there. Lower Baggot Street, Dublin. Proper terrace house.

Francis. *You* were born there. I was just domiciled.

Frances. A different Ireland when we came back, girlie. Easter Rebellion.Executions: sixteen. Arrested: Three thousand five hundred. Martyrs. The world of the Protestant Ascendancy:

> Daddy's world; Mummy's world...
> Crumbling like the leafmould of your studio Francis, into dust.

Francis. (*A flash of humour returning*) The Irish getting their own back: Rebellion!

A beat.

Fuck them. I'm not Irish.

Frances. Lower Baggot Street. Where you were born.

Francis. And what was so wonderful about Lower Baggot Street?

When we were eleven, fourteen British undercover agents were executed in their beds. A slaughterhouse of bodies.

When we were eleven, Captain Newbury, trying to escape out of a window in Lower Baggot Street, was shot dead in front of his pregnant wife, and left hanging in the window frame, like a carcass hanging in a butcher's shop.

There was another carcass two months later when she gave birth. When we were eleven, in Lower Baggot Street, another officer, who had lost a leg, chopped off with a certain lack of surgical precision as he fought for freedom in World War One, found that he couldn't move so rapidly; so they put a bullet in his brain, and turned him into a one-legged carcass. Satisfied?

Frances. Do I need to be satisfied?

Military drumbeat undertow.

Our daddy was an Honorary Major. In the Special Reserve. Counter Insurgency tactics were his speciality. Remember Francis? Boer War. Tracking down and executing the insurgents...

A beat.

Now I wonder if Daddy played his part, acted his script, and defined his role...in helping to form the Black and Tans? To fight the good fight against Sinn Fein and the IRA? (*Taunting*) After all, you may as well flaunt what you've got! You may as well use what you were born with! You may as well do what you're good at!

Francis. He was good at nothing.He was a lousy gambler. He was a lousy horse trainer. He was a lousy man.

Frances. But you loved him.

A beat.

Take off the shirt.

Francis. (*A beat. Then coldly*) Why?

Frances. Because I'll whip you if you don't.

Francis. Ooh! What a threat! I *like* being whipped. I've *always* liked being whipped. So there!

Frances. Please take off your shirt.

Francis. Why?

Frances. Because you are me. So you are asking you.

Francis. (*Off handedly. To audience*) Seems perfectly reasonable.

A beat.

Suddenly he gives us a blazing smile.

FX: Stripper music

Playing to her, and off her, he proceeds to undo the button of his shirt, and with the full bump and grind, slowly takes off the shirt, whirls it around and ends up flinging it over her shoulder. Throughout, she remains amused, but unmoved. We now see that in addition to the tights, satin panties etc, he is also wearing a satin undertop. He poses in an Attitude. Music ceases. He crooks his head towards her.

Happy now?

Frances. That's how he found you. Wasn't it? In Mummy's underwear. So he threw you out: permanent exile.

A beat.

You loved him? Well. You hated him. But you were attracted to him. Sexually. He had you whipped. By the stableboys. He watched. Didn't he? Did you ejaculate, Francis? Did the semen spurt, like those hot white splashes across your canvas? What came first Francis? Did you 'come on' to one of the boys? Or did they 'take' you? Mounted like one of daddy's dogs? You've always had to be mounted, Francis? You've always had to be whipped, Francis? You've always had to be beaten, Francis? Why is that Francis?

Francis. You're me. Tell yourself!

Frances. Humour me.

For a brief moment he strikes an attitude, arms akimbo. Then, with absolute dignity, he walks across, takes his overcoat, and, with practised, elegant movements, puts it on – but does not do up the belt. He walks over to her, and in a mirroring motion, goes arms akimbo again, this time with the coat sides, held behind by the arms.

Francis. See. We're two of a kind!

A beat.

You know why. I'm guilty.

Frances. Because you're gay?

Francis. (*Regretfully*) I'm not gay. I wish I were. I'm queer. I was born queer. I am unable to be anything other than 'queer'.

Frances. And Daddy?

Francis. (*Simply*) I was in search of a shag. I just didn't know it at the time...

He belts up the leather overcoat.

We need a drink! (*Yells*) Service! Champagne! Where's the bloody Krug? I ordered two bottles. And Beluga caviar. *And* the wine list. (*To audience*) I'll give the *maitre d* a right bollocking when he comes.

Frances. Your first proposition?

Francis. What?

Frances. Your first proposition: there is no life after death.

Francis. So?

Frances. You're dead. Yes?

Francis. How do I know?

Frances. We remember perfectly well how we died. Don't we?

Francis. Fine! I'm dead.

Frances. In which case, your first proposition is wrong!

She cracks the bullwhip and starts to exit in a haze of light.

Francis. Hey! You can't do that! I'm the director here. This is my movie!

She stops and half turns: amused.

Sound!

FX: *Military drumbeat.*

Lights!

The lights immediately incandesce to their highest point, then swiftly return to normal as she strides back to him.

Action!

Frances. (*To audience*) Proposition Number Two:

Francis looks up, just in time to see the placard/projection of this Proposition

Pleasure is Pain**!**

Immediately **FX:** Pulsating Tango Music

She launches straight into a tango with him, except that she is dancing the male part. It is fast, driving and erotic: he is spun round, dominated and, on the off beats, he is smartly slapped on the face and, at the climax, bitten on the lip.

Francis. (*Yelping*) You've bitten me!

Frances. (*Deadpan*) It's a sign of love.

Cats do it. Dogs do it. Baboons do it. Even cantankerous old poofs do it!

Francis. (*Trying to work it out*) If you're me, claiming that you've bitten *me* out of love, then you're suggesting that I love myself so much that, knowing that pain is pleasurable, I bite myself to pleasure myself?

A beat.

(*To audience*) Sounds reasonable! (*To her*) O.K. Psychoanalysis over. You can fuck off now. (*Screams*) Service!!!!

(*With all the insolence he can muster*) Garçon! (*To audience*) I've never tipped less than twenty percent in my *entire* life! Waiters worship me. Garçon! (*Icily*) If they don't bring me two perfectly chilled bottles of Krug – (*Being reasonable*) I'll accept Tattinger or Chateau Petrus – (*Yells*) And I've changed my mind about the caviar. Bring me oysters! Two dozen. Properly presented on a bed of ice! With linen napkins! (*To audience*) You just can't get the service these days, it would seem. (*To her*) Where are we? Doesn't look like Wheeler's Restaurant. Doesn't much look like Old Compton Street for that matter. (*Offhand*) Wherever it is, just tell them to run up a tab.

Frances. Wise up Francis. (*Slyly*) I expected more of you. You're not even asking basic questions. You're making assumptions.

Francis. (*Petulantly*) What assumptions?

Frances. (*Taking centre stage*) You're assuming that *here*, you still have the gift. You're assuming that here, you are the centre of attention.

Francis. Well sweetie, you sure as hell don't!

(*Taking the piss*) Come up and see me some time...I'm off! (*To audience*) There's got to be a decent seafood restaurant around here...Somewhere.

He takes about three steps in the direction of the audience central aisle, only to find that his arms, indeed his whole body, is being restricted by some unseen force. Effectively, in extreme slow motion, he comes to a halt, the whole body straining with the effort of attempted movement.

Frances. (*Enjoying it*) You're off, are you?

She watches him, engagingly. He strains: unsuccessfully, grunting and whining with the effort.

Francis. (*Abruptly, like a sulky child, he stops*) I'm not playing this game anymore. So there!

Frances. My my. You're learning! It *is* a game Francis.

Suddenly produces a pistol and shoots him in the head. The noise is deafening. He seemingly falls down dead.

(*To audience*) So endeth Proposition Two.

Puts one elegant spike heel onto the recumbent body.

See ya!

Military drumroll.

Then the magnified sound of a ball in a roulette wheel in a casino, skipping along the grooves and coming to a halt.

Francis. Wait! (*Being amazed at the words which erupt from him*) Proposition Number Three:

Checks to see if the placard has appeared.

Chance is the Best Artist!

A pack of cards appears in his hand.

Care to play?

Frances. (*Sweetly*) I always play.

A beat.

You prefer to obfuscate.

Francis. That's what *gamblers* do Frances. You take their attention and you divert it away from the real action.

Frances. The real action...

Just so.

(*As a brutal statement of fact*) There was nothing left to chance in your work, sweetikins.

Francis. (*Haughtily*) Real painting Frances, real, actual, perspiring paint is a continual and mysterious struggle with chance.

Frances. (*She does a doubletake off the audience*) Really? The same struggle with chance that produced the working drawings which you claimed you never did? The same struggle with chance that used a T square and lettraset?

Francis. (*Conspiratorially*) My dear boy, the idea and the technique must become inseparable. The brushstroke has to create the form; not fill it in!

FX: In magnified sound, the ball skites along the roulette wheel and dribbles to a stop.

Frances. I'll tell you what you do Francis –

Francis. (*To audience*) How thoughtful....

Frances. You tame Chance.

Francis. (*A beat*) I do adore roulette...(*Suddenly declaims*) I am a machine which took accident for its bride!

Frances. (*Sardonically*) How clever! How witty! (*To audience*) How utterly true!

Francis. (*Genteelly*) I prefer to tell lies. (*To audience*) How else can one keep the social fabric together? (*To her, deadpan*) You really are so intelligent.

Frances. (*A beat*) True. I retain all those qualities which, in you, are conspicuous by their absence.

Francis. (*To her. Eagerly. Like a child*) Once, when I was attempting to make a bird alight in a cornfield, the lines that I had drawn suddenly started to suggest something totally different. (*To audience*) I had no intention of creating the painting that I actually ended up *making*. One suggestion, one accident, created another, and then another: shape-shifting. (*To her*) What was illustration cannot be left as illustration. A sock, a sweater, an edge of ribbed corduroy. (*To audience*) I've painted a Head, but it just illustrates a head, so, ribbed corduroy in hand, with a flick of the wrist I unwrite the image, blurring it into vision, connecting viscerally into the nervous system.

(*To her*) I foresee what I want to paint but accident allows me to unmake the image, to unsex myself, to breed an interior vision into the darkness of the light.

Frances. (*A slow handclap as she doubletakes off the audience*) How wonderful, old girl. (*To audience*) That was almost a soliloquy!

Francis. Shag off bumboy –

Frances. (*Preening*) I've a better bum than you. *Analyses him dispassionately*. Raddled. (*To audience*) Poached in Chateau Petrus. Piles. (*To him*) Spare ribs...

Francis. (*Placatingly*) Dear boy. Man is an accident, adrift in a game without a purpose.

A dangerous pause as she stares at him, then approaches him as if she might be intent on doing real damage.

Frances. You do have a propensity for pompous one-liners, Francis.

A beat.

Play your part properly.

Francis. What 'part'? There *is* no end-game.

Frances. Of course there is Queenie.

(*To audience*) We're here to bring home the bacon!

(*To him*) And you are the cured ham!!

Francis. We – are – animals. We are born, we die, and that's it. (*To audience*) Nada. Zip. Bugger all. (*To her*) There's nothing else. We are just potential carcasses.

Frances. Ah!

Francis? Ah? Ah? That's a very irritating habit you've got bumboy. So – ah what?

Frances. You can admire my legs.

Francis. Ah what?

Frances. (*Cupping her breasts*) And you won't find bazookas like these every day of the week! –

Francis. (*Threatening to go for her*) Ah-bloody-ah-ha what?

Frances. (*Sweetly*) And I've such a slender waist. Unlike yours.

As he lurches forward to grab her neck and throttle her, she brings up the handle of the whip sharply, under his chin, forcing it upwards.

FX: Magnified sound of ball in roulette wheel skiting along to a stop.

Not *potential* carcasses, Francis.

A beat.

Actual carcasses, Francis. Actual. Carcases. You always said that life was a game without a purpose, and not of your own choosing. Well, death isn't of your own choosing, either, Francis. (*To audience*) But it does have a purpose. (*To him*) Now, be a good little protagonist. You always did like throwing yourself in the gutter.

Francis. I always think that something marvellous is about to happen. So the game of painting becomes the game of how to entrap the transient, how to pin it on the canvas.

Frances. But something marvellous is happening, Francis. You are in the gutter of your own making, and you *have* entrapped the transient: yourself! And you are pinning it on this nth dimensional canvas...aren't you?

Francis. (*Preening just a little*) I am?

Frances. (*Leans over and kisses him full on the mouth*) You do love yourself!

Francis. (*A beat. Smelling a rat*) Shouldn't that be the other way around?

Snaps into one of his role-plays.

I don't know what I'm doing. I've never known what I was doing. Accident just takes over. I create chaos in the studio. I play with painting as I would play with roulette. (*A slow ironic handclap from Frances*).

Frances. You really are an old ham, Francis. From ingénue to bit-part player! What a journey!

Francis. A little less of the bit-part player, thank you very much. I was *the* player. (*To audience*) My contemporaries were insignificant.

Frances. 'Losing is better than winning'. I believe you said that. (*Sweetly*) So you played at painting – you didn't even really start until you were thirty – and you played a losing game...

FX: In magnified sound the ball spins along the roulette wheel before coming to a guttering stop.

Francis. (*A rapid virtuoso shuffling of his deck of cards*) Listen dearie, if an image *works*, it's because you can't explain it. You can't use logic. You can't put it into words.

Frances. You can't have a story, you mean!

Francis. Get your technical terms right, dearie: no narrative.

Frances. My my. (*To audience*) What hubris. (*To him*) That technical enough for you? You're so vain, you pumped-up little pervert, that you think you can dispense with the key element in Art, used for centuries –

Francis. (*Petulantly*) Picasso dispensed with a key element dearie. One point perspective. Shoved cubism up your none-too-lubricious little arse!

Frances. Ah!

Francis. What do you mean 'Ah!'.

Frances. Picasso...

Francis. So What?

Frances. Jealous, are we? Insecure in the wake of a genius?

Francis. Ballocks.

Frances. Not interested in yours.

Francis. Can't I get it through your thick arse – content, in a painting, should be minimal.

Frances. Is that so?

Francis. Yes.

Frances. How come your images are layered?

Francis. (*Rather too quickly*) Not the same thing.

Frances. (*Quietly, but with absolute authority*) Yes it is.

Francis. (*Seeking to sidetrack. Grandly*) I create enigmas!

Frances. An enigma is a narrative. It's just not in a straight line. Why else do you use tryptchs? (*To audience*) It's a story with the obvious bits chopped out!

Francis. Fuck off!

Frances. Imagine three of me – your very own, very personal, your very elegantly violent Eumenides – your personal avenging demons –

Whips him.

Francis. (*Whinnying with pleasure*) More! More!

Frances. (*Looking at audience*) Masochist!

Francis. (*Looking at audience*) Sadist!

A beat.

We suit each other....

Frances. (*Whips him*) Liar! (*Whips him again*)

Francis. (*Ecstatically*) Yes!

Frances. Thief!

Whips him.

Francis. (*Ecstatically*) Yes!

Frances. Charlatan!

Francis. (*Normal voice*) Now just a moment –

Frances. (*Whips him*) Hoist with your own petard. Boy!

Clicks fingers: a trumpet sounds.

Proposition Number Four:

He scoots over to check if the Placard has descended from The Gods.

While Europe Burns, Opportunities Beckon!

Turning to him.

When you were younger, when as a painter you had fire in your belly...

Francis. I *always* had fire in my belly...

Frances. Pomp, flummery and melodrama. That's called perspiration, not inspiration.

Opens his coat a fraction with the butt-end of her whip.

(*To audience*) An ego the size of the Imperial War Museum!

(*To him: Uses whip as a microphone*)

When you were *younger*, what did you want to achieve?

Francis. (*Dismissively*) I wanted to short-circuit the self-destructive thrust of an entire continent into a single image!

Frances. (*To audience*) Dear God!

(*To him. Sweetly*) You were a child of your times!

Francis. Psycho-babble, dearie.

Frances. Is that so? (*To audience*) Nineteen forty-three. (*To him*) Remember Francis. You'd managed to avoid the draft Francis. Hired a nice little doggie from Harrods, the day before your medical inspection - and you with your asthma, and an allergy to dogs. (*To audience*) Holed up in seclusion in the Bedfordshire countryside, courtesy Eric Hall. You were a good leech, Francis.

Francis. (*Not getting angry. With pride*) I was a prettyboy, Frances. I was accommodating. I was young...(*To audience*) ...ish. I took care of myself. It's only human nature that old men should pay for what they want.

Frances. Just like you – when you were old?

Francis. (*Equably*) Just like me. I always paid my way.

Frances. A child of your times...!

Francis. (*Languidly*) Whatever...

Frances. (*As a statement of fact*) *When*ever. (*To audience*) Nineteen forty-three, (*To him*), remember?

Francis. Remember, remember, the fifth of November –

Frances. You've decided to blow up parliament?

Francis. (Grins: a brief softening. Does a music-hall *routine*) Guy Fawkes, Guy! Hit him in the eye! Hang him on a lamp-post. And leave him there to die.

Frances. (*Taunting. Doing a music-hall routine*) Since when were you a working-class little boy!! (*Speaking posh*)

> Kaiser Bill went up the hill
> To see the British army.
> General French jumped out of a trench
> And made the cows go barmy!

Francis. Touché mon brave.

(*To audience*) Quelle horreur!!

Frances. And indeed it was Francis. (*To audience*) Nineteen forty three. (*To him*) Swoosh! Swiish! Swoosh! Atomic bombs falling, falling,

falling...On those teenie-weenie, naughty Japanese. (*To audience*) Nagasaki...Hiroshima. (*To him*) One hundred and fifty thousand dead. Another three-hundred thousand radiated, mutilated, flesh eroding like iron in a sluice...Rotting slowly as their children birth-mutated, deformed, stumps for arms or legs, small fleshy carcasses...An opportunity, Francis? (*To audience*) An opportunity?

Francis. (*Loftily*) Politics is boring. (*To audience*) I'm not interested in subject matter.

Frances. World War Three. In the offing, Francis. Atomic weapons exploding like firecrackers. Radiation! (*To audience*) Man reverts to a bestial, genetic mutation! (*To him*) Wasn't that what you painted, Francis?

Francis. Poppycock. (*To audience*) A cock n' bull story for the credulous.

Frances. Man metamorphoses into an alien creature!

Francis. Who's being melodramatic now?

Frances. Really? (*To audience*) *The Quatermass Experiment*. (*To him*) Nineteen fifty-three, in case it slipped your mind. *The Day of the Triffids. The Invasion of the Body Snatchers*...

Francis. (*Sweetly*) Frances. I do realize that you are both physically and intellectually challenged. (*To audience*) Why? (*To her*) Because the worst *already* happened long ago, Frances. Man is mindless, witless, a baggage of skin and bones, infected with violence, which suppurates malignity like a boil oozing puss...

Frances. (*To audience*) Francis as phrasemaker!

Francis. (*Snapping into a position only inches from her mouth*) I have a proposition for *you* Frances. If, as I believe, there is no meaning to life, no reason for us to live, then it follows, as champagne follows Chablis and oysters, that the act of painting, the continuous struggle to achieve a single image which will summarize the self-destructive push of an entire continent, is in and of itself, the only meaningful act in a world devoid of meaning.

Snaps away from her. He bows, pleased with himself.

Frances. (*A beat*) Isn't that just a touch pretentious? Portentous? (*To audience*) Contradictory?

Francis. (*Quick as a flash: snootily*) An artist is the intersection of his contradictions –

Frances. (*Gleefully*) Oh we are so clichéd, Francis.

(*To him*) You'd think you were talking to Melvyn Bragg, girlie.

(*To audience*) Again!

Francis. (*A beat: then, as a small tour de force*) Of course, if you are me, then any attempt at intellectual foreplay is clearly a reflection of me, projected onto you, in an attempt to unlock the inherent complex dualism that is clearly at the heart of my nature, rendering you a mere shadow of the real substance, which is me. Philosophically speaking, I'm a fatalist, so do as you will. (*To audience*) I'll do what *I* want to do. (*To her*) Endgame.

Frances. Not even checkmate, bozo.

FX: In magnified sound, the ball in the roulette wheel hops and skips before skittering to a stop.

Francis. Bozo? How appropriate Frances. (*To audience*) Etymologically, it's gangster slang, meaning guy, chap, man, a youth and (*coyly*), in Spanish, it's the soft down growing on the even softer cheeks of a youth...(*To her*) I accept the compliment!

Frances. To heel, Francis. You turned down the role of War Artist.

Francis. (*To audience*) All those smelly uniforms. (*To her*) Hoi Polloi!

Frances. You had no wish to perform a *useful* role in society.

Francis. My dear boy, my proper place was in the French pub.

(*To audience*) Then a gargle in the Gargoyle with Minton and Freud.

Frances. You keep turning a phrase, Francis. (*To audience*) That's what happened in the painting too...

Francis. (*Bridling*) You think you're pretty, don't you? Well you're not. (*To audience*) A face like a constipated donkey's arse-

Frances. It takes one to know one...

Francis. (*Almost snarling*) Since when did you develop a critical acumen?

Frances. At the same time you did, Queenie pox. (*To audience*) We were both late developers. (*To him: Off hand*) Do you believe in redemption?

Francis. If you're me, you already know the answer, (*To audience*), so talk to yourself!

Frances. Francis!! Here I am, thinking that you're a nice Protestant, Anglo-Irish girlie whose manners are better than her morals.

Francis. (*A long beat: he almost bows. Scuttles over. Disarmingly*) I apologize. (*To audience*) An old poof like me should at least retain the outward show of a gentle lady.

Frances. Thank you Francis. You lie with such blinding aplomb that it would be churlish not to accept your apology. Do you believe in redemption?

Francis. Of course not! (*To audience*) We were born evil. (*To her*) Morality is a luxury that we can only obtain with age – (*to audience*) and financial security – (*to her*) if at all.

Frances. So we are without hope of redemption?

Francis. Quick on the uptake, aren't you? When I was a child...

Frances. When you were a child in London – (*To audience*) World War one –

Francis. (*A beat*) That's another very annoying habit that you have.

A beat.

Yes.

When I was a child...I remember the sound of the barrages...London...covered windows...the streets wreathed in the looming thickness of shadows...I'd be short of breath...I didn't know it was asthma...I didn't know my sinuses were infected...nobody did...

Her voice, as she comes up behind him, echoes behind his.

I'd wait in the dark, knowing they were going to come, knowing that they were looking for me, waiting, listening for the moment when I would hear the quiet ominous drone of the engines, waiting for the darkness to become palpable, for the furies to coagulate out of the shadows and batten onto me, waiting for the whuup, whuup, whuup, seeing the lines of shellbursts approaching, illuminating the cage-like structure of the steel grids, erected to stave off impending doom, hearing the plosive, plump bowel movement of houses exploding outwards, their body parts flanging outwards in search of soft and successful landing.

Frances. And so you welcomed World War Two like a long-lost friend...

Francis. I'd had an operation on the roof of my mouth. (*To audience*) Large dose of M and B to keep the sinuses in check. (*To her*) No antibiotics then. No drugs for asthma. (*To audience*) Did you know that Proust suffered from asthma?

FX: The ball rolls smoothly along the roulette wheel and comes to a stop.

Frances. Stop prevaricating. The Blitz?

Francis. (*A long beat*) You know perfectly well. The yellow flash of gunfire. Flames of the finest coppery red. The greeny-white underwater glow of incendiaries. And the criss-cross hatchings of searchlights, lancing the sky like scalpels slicing through flesh...(*To audience*) I needed a drink in the Gargoyle. Several drinks in the Gargoyle. Enough drinks in the Gargoyle to dull the razorblade of memory. (*A precognition. To her*) The reek of human blood smiles out at him', eh?

Frances. (*To audience*) Nothing like a cheerful chappie. (*To him*) Chin to the wheel, eh?

Francis. It's wheel to the grindstone. Chin up. Or take it on the chin and come out fighting. (*To audience*) You might at least get your slang right!

Frances. So now you're an expert on the English language Francis? (*To audience*) Is there anything that this prodigy before me does not know?

Let's see: (*To him*) Concentration Camps.

Francis. Never been in one.

Frances. Don't be flippant. Buchenwald, Belsen, Auschwitz –

Francis. So what?

Frances. You collected photos of them.

Francis. (*Discovering. To audience*) Actually, it was then that the very idea of Christ Crucified became real (*To her*) to me...

Frances. Degradation, cruelty, vulnerability, loneliness, mutilation, (*To audience*) torture. You *liked* the horrific. You *liked* to visit the carcases in butcher's shops. You *liked* medical bookshops; the Black Museum at Scotland Yard.

Francis. (*To audience*) I – we – were all like sheets of blotting paper. (*To her*) We soaked up the chaos, the brutality. It was the world we lived in and it was all around us...

Frances. (*To audience*) Convenient. (*To him*) And what else did you 'soak up' Francis? (*To audience*) Let's see. (*Like a child joining the dots to make a picture. To him*) Your first major lover, De Maistre, who set you up financially, introduced you to Douglas Cooper, who bought your furniture, and made the introduction that got you your first major exhibition at Agnews, and who knew our nice Alderman Eric Hall who introduced you to Kenneth Clark and John Rothenstein –

(*To audience. Sweetly*) Now weren't they the key figures at the National Gallery and the Tate – (*To him*) not to mention nice Graham Sutherland – (*To audience*) all of whom got you your first commissions. (*To him*) My my, but you were a busy little queer bee, weren't you?

Francis. (*Offhandedly*) They could recognize talent –

Frances. What's a shag worth Francis, as you sleep your way to the top?

Francis. (*To audience*) I think you'll find that even Queen bees do it Frances.

(*To him*) Did *you* enjoy it?

Frances. I'm not a bum person, myself, Queenie hag.

Francis. That's not what I asked you. (*To audience*) I do believe that even the female occasionally enjoys anal sex.

Frances. That's a rumour spread by married men who are gay.

Francis. Ballocks!

Frances. (*To audience*) Disgusting objects. (*To him*) If you weren't dead already, I'd have yours cut off!

Francis. (*To audience*) Anyone would think that you don't like me, Frances.

Frances. (*To audience*)Why should I like a treacherous, manipulative piss-artist (*to him*) like you, Francis? Once you'd squeezed any usefulness out of decent people who wanted to help you, you tossed them into your very own gutter.

Francis. Ah! (*To audience*) A drama queen in the making! (*To her*) Ahh! I see. (*To audience*) I wine and dine everyone around me, I give away my books, my paintings –I'm so generous that it appals your parsimonious nature!

Frances. You wined and dined because you liked to hold court, to be the centre of attention, and because you hated being on your own unless you were painting. (*To audience*) The only books you gave away were novels which people gave to you, and which you didn't want to read. (*To him*) You took advantage of every piece of human flotsam and jetsam that came your way. You're not a very nice girl, Francis.

Francis. (*Urbanely*) I'll have you know, my little Christmas fairy, that I am famed for my fastidious manners, my generosity of spirit, (*To audience*) my charm –

Frances. Oh, you had *that* in lorryloads! Charm! (*To audience*) It oozed off you like brylcream under a hot sun! (*To audience*) The silk glove over the hatchet!

Francis. (*Drawn by the word*) Hatchet? (*To audience*) Oh yes please. (*Hopefully: To her*) Could you draw blood?

Frances. (*Unexpectedly*) We remember, don't we, Francis. (*To audience*) We wore such adorable little frocks, (*to him*) and we were so expert with lipstick and rouge.

Francis. Where's this 'we' coming from?

Frances. (*Ignoring him*) Distant gunfire at night. The British Cavalry galloping up the driveway of father's estate at the Curragh. Manoeuvres! (*To audience*) Horsemen on manoeuvres, drilling in anticipation of the conflict in Europe. (*To him*) Drilling in anticipation of an intervention into Ulster as those loyal laddies prepared for civil war. (*To audience*) Black and Tans. Political assassinations. We should go to Ireland Francis –

Francis. (*Sweetly*) How can we go to Ireland if we're dead?

Frances. We can go anywhere if we're dead, Francis. (*To audience*) For the moment. (*To him*) Would you like to go to Ireland?

Suddenly gasping for breath as if an asthma attack is about to start.

Francis. My asthma! I'm allergic to Ireland! (*To audience*) I wouldn't be seen dead in the place!

Frances. Your mother, when she was pregnant with you, was afraid that a genetic monstrosity would be born.

Francis. What's that got to do with anything? (*A beat*) You were born too!

Frances. You see Francis, things are improving. You acknowledge me as yourself. Mother was only afraid of the male side. (*To audience*) Bad stock. (*To him*) She would have liked a girl.

Francis. (*Acidly*) I did my best!

Frances. Not good enough, girlie. All those memories of Ireland, of the First World War, festering away inside you, (*to audience*) sandpapering your sweet little girlie nature –

Francis. At last. (*To audience*) An accurate description: 'Sweet'. I could be dainty. And my underwear costs a fortune!

Frances. (*To audience*) World War Two. (*To him*) All those childhood memories are being scored, scratched, scraped, sliced, overlaid by the images of the concentration camps – just like your working drawings Francis. At what point did you decide to make *use* of them? (*To audience*) To *use* them, just as if they were nudes, or still-life images, or landscapes. Simply *stuff*. Do tell!

FX: Ball skips uncertainly along roulette wheel before coming to a stop.

Francis. (*Disarmingly*) Freud stated that the female of the species is inherently more unstable than the male.

Frances. (*A doubletake*) You've just made that up!

Francis. (*To audience*) Ah! (*To her*) So you acknowledge that it's true!

Frances. I acknowledge that you are trying to sidetrack the question...

Francis. What question?

Frances. At what point did you decide to make use of other people's suffering?

Francis. (*To audience*) Other people's? (*To her*) Oh, that's rich coming from you! (*To audience*) I was the one who was whipped by the stableboys. (*To her*) I was the one who was born queer as a coot. I was the one who was committing a crime, just because I was following the sexuality given to me when I was born. (*To audience*) Criminalized. (*To her*) I was the one who died a little every day as I gasped for breath. Something else I was born with, queenie. So don't tell me there's a Good Lord out there. (*To audience*) If there's anyone out there he's a bloody sadist.

Frances. Bravo! What a self-pitying whinger you are, Francis. (*To audience*) You liked suffering. (*To him*) You liked using other people's suffering. You were just like that sweet little serial killer, Neville Heath. (*To audience*) What was it he said? (*To him*) 'I got excited, and it went too far'. You got excited, didn't you Francis. Gave you an erection, didn't it Francis? (*To audience*) You could spray your inert seed over the canvas, couldn't you Francis!

Francis. So what if I did? (*To audience*) At least I wasn't some poor little masturbator, jerking off in a corner, with nothing to offer but a sense of inadequacy. I used my weaknesses. (*To audience*) I *made* myself. (*To her*) Everything – everything – was grist for the work. (*Bellows*) Everything. I tore at anything that came my way, ripped it, pulversized it, turned it into a visual compost. And then I gorged on it, surrounded myself with it, excited myself with it, masturbated over it – but I *used* it, Little Bo Peep, I used it, I made something from it, (*To audience*) I turned base metal into golden Art.

Frances. Base metal? (*To audience*) Interesting analogy. The Algerian rebellion in 1957. (*To him*) You enjoyed that. All those photographs of throat slittings, mutilations, decapitations. You enjoyed them so much that your sludgy little fingerprints crawl up and down the photographs like slime from a snail. (*To audience*) I suppose that was an aesthetic response, eh girlie?

Francis. (*A beat: then a considered reply*) It reminded me of Ireland.

Frances. Ha! (*To audience*) Clever...Post colonial Africa as colonial Ireland writ large! (*To him*) Of course there's a problem Francis.

Francis. What problem?

Frances. You and daddy were Anglo-Irish, Francis. You were colonial. You were part of the problem. (*To audience*) Which is why you left Francis. (*To him*) You liked the Anglo, but you didn't like the Irish.

Daddy at least employed Catholics as servants, even if that was a tactical decision by mother. But you only employed your nanny, and she was Protestant to the core. (*To audience*) Apart from the shop-lifting! (*To him*) So let's ignore Ireland, shall we?

Francis. (*A long, long beat. Then finally*) I agree with Mister Yeats. Sailing to Byzantium. Art endures. It has no other duty, but to itself.

Frances. How very, very convenient! But then, of course, Mister Yeats was Anglo-Irish, just like yourself! (*Claps her hands gleefully*) You lost that round Francis! For Propositions five to ten, including prurient details of our sex lives, a philosophical disquisition on assault and battery, and the healing power of booze, you'll have to wait.

A beat.

I know: pure hell!

ACT TWO

FX: In heightened sound, a ball skitters along a roulette wheel before coming to a stop.

Frances. (*To audience*) Heigh ho! (*To him*) Proposition Number Five: (*To audience*, using whip as microphone) Is Bacon the painter of the modern world?

The following done as if a TV interview. She steps out and looks at the placard descending from the Gods. He looks at it, then turns away.

Francis. (*Quietly*) I tried to paint the history of my times.

Frances. Tried? Tried? (*To audience*) How unexpectedly restrained of you!

Francis. I make no claims for history, politics, sociology –

Frances. (*To audience*) How thoughtful of you!

Francis. (*Throws dice*) I'm not an Expressionist.

(*To audience*) I have nothing to express.

Frances. Your paintings say nothing…mean nothing?

Francis. Correct.

Frances. (*To audience*) Clever.

Francis. What do you mean 'clever'?

Frances. You tell critics, and the general public, that you have nothing to say. Naturally, they disbelieve you.

(*To audience*) So they *invent* something to say.

Francis. (*Bridling*) What do you mean 'invent'?

Frances. It's the Emperor's New Clothes. (*To audience*) There never *was* anything. (*To him*) *You* claim there never was anything. Everyone invents to prove you wrong. (*To audience*) Such a clever strategy. (*To him*) You really *are* of no value.

Francis. Now just a minute dearie…

Frances. I'm not your dearie Francis. (*To audience*) I'm *my* dearie.

A beat.

Are you the painter of the modern world? (*To audience*) Or are you the Norman Hartnell of the Horror Movement!

Francis. (*Camply*) Oh how cutting! Why don't you tell me Frances.

Frances. (*To audience*) You'll do it so well! Let's see. 'Modern'. Is there anything 'modern' in your paintings? (*To audience*) Venetian blinds?

(*To him*) Bauhaus furniture! (*To audience*) Crime Scene photographs. (*To him*) Nazi armbands. Hypodermics. (*To audience*) Rip-offs from film directors like Eisenstein, or Buñuel. (*To him*) Getting Deakin to take photographs of those whose portraits you were going to paint...(*To audience*) Shall I go on?

Francis. My my. You have the grace and the linguistic capacity of a Harrods catalogue. (*To audience*) Itemization is as useful as an academic's arse. It tells you, quite precisely, nothing, so you invent to fill the spaces in between. (*To her*) Modern? (*To audience*) I'm not interested – I never *was* interested – in painting for the contemporary. (*To her*) I want to endure. To hammer out an image which will contain the world I know and speak to the world that I don't know.

Frances. You're sneakier than that, Francis.

Francis. Sneakier? (*To audience*) That's not a Baconian word!

Frances. Sneakier. You knew that you couldn't do it! (*To audience*) So you devised a stratagem. (*To him*) You put museum-sized frames, which you insisted be painted in gold, on your paintings (*to audience*) so that the audience thought that these works *had* to be of museum quality. (*To him*) Then you glassed them in.

Francis. (*To audience*) It's called: (*To her*) protecting the paintwork from hoi polloi.

Frances. No Francis. It's called: (*To audience*) having the audience reflected in the glass, so that they become a part of the painting, and as the audience continually changes, so the painting seems to stay modern. (*To him*) Clever.

Francis. (*To audience*) Anyone would think that I planned out all of this...stuff!

Frances. You did. You're a devious little bugger. (*To audience*) That's why you didn't want explications of your work.

Francis. (*Disarmingly*) I was trusting the good sense of the average punter who looks at my work. (*To audience*) Why should people be told what to think? (*To her*) Why not let them make up their own minds?

Frances. (*Sweetly*) I thought you said that man was an animal, a beast, no ratiocination!

Francis. (*To audience*) I'm delighted to see that you can stoop so low.

Frances. I don't have to stoop at all. (*To audience*) You were simply a product of your time, Francis –

Francis. Most people are. The great artists are the ones who can ride above it. (*To audience*) Like me.

Frances. *All* people are a product of their time Francis, even you. And you weren't particularly original –

Francis. (*Piqued*) No? (*To audience*) Who else was portraying the human condition as isolated figures enclosed in a windowless space?

Frances. (*To audience*) So it's the human condition now, is it, and not just the painter of modern times. (*To him*) Careful girlie. All you did was to transpose from another medium, Francis. (*To audience*) Who else? (*To him*) I'll tell you who. Arthur Koestler did, in *Darkness at Noon*. (*To audience*) Sartre did, in *Huit clos*. (*To him*) Camus did in *L'étranger*. (*To audience*) And that's before we look at Kafka – *Metamorphosis* might come to mind. (*To him. Bows*) I rest my case.

Francis. (*Almost offhandedly tossing these arguments aside*) So what? (*To audience*) Painting is superior to literature. (*To her*) If you get it right – and I often did – it's visceral. (*To audience*) It's like injecting into a vein, the adrenalin rush when you orgasm. It communicates directly – without the bother of having to read the whole way through a fucking novel!

Frances. Charity your strong suit? *A beat.* You said 'did'.

Francis. So?

Frances. Painting. You often 'did' get it right. (*To audience*) So you accept that you're dead!

Does a little dance.

Yo!

Francis. (*Waits patiently. Smiles*) No. This is – (*To audience*) what do the Irish call it – a wind-up!

Frances. A little etymological exactitude please, Francis. (*To audience*) Do you mean (*To him*) to wind up the proceedings? (*To audience*) Or, to take the piss!

Francis. (*Riposting*) You know the answer, so talk to yourself. (*To audience*) You'll find it soothing.

Frances. But they don't. (*To audience*) So: Proposition Number Six!

(*Slyly*) Which is?

She points to the descending placard/projection.

Francis. (*Sourly: finding the words coming out of his mouth*) The Studio Equals Sex.

A beat.

(*To audience*) Sex: I'm alive!

Frances. No you're not. (*To audience*) I'm with you.

Francis. (*Dismissively*) You're me. So me, plus me, is simply loneliness squared.

Frances. (*Gesturing. Quietly*) You've an audience.

Francis. (*To audience*) They only exist in my imagination or, possibly, we only exist when they are here.

Frances. Maybe they are all a part of us?

Francis. (*Interested*) Ooh!

(*A beat, then decisively*) No. Don't be ridiculous.

Approaching audience: indicating one of them.

I could never be seen dead wearing a suit like that!

(*Points to another*) And I do *not* have carnal thoughts about women!

Looking around him.

However – men...I do like a nice muscular body in a three-piece suit...I've this plastercast by Michelangelo in the studio. A male nude.

His eyes rove the audience.

If you want feminine meat, then you can go to Ingres! I don't do classical nudes myself.

Swinging round to her. Not *modern* enough!

Frances. (*Starting to giggle*) Someone once said that you were the most over-rated artist since Bougereau.

(*Sweetly. To audience*) He's forgotten now, Bougereau, isn't he, less than a hundred years after his death. (*To him*) Might be you, Francis...some day...

Francis. Don't be ridiculous! (*To audience*) I still flirt as if I were only fifty! (*To her*) I may be getting on a bit, but I still like looking at men. (*To audience*) Passion keeps you young. (*To her*) When I paint, I am, absolutely, indisputably, irredeemably, ageless! (*To audience*) Hands up. Is there an artist in the house? Ah! (*Witheringly*) No, I don't need to see your work. I've seen your tie.

Frances. Don't be unkind Francis.

Francis. Why not? I am to myself. (*To audience*) One of the world's best painters, and one of the world's leading alcoholics!

Frances. Jekyll and Hyde.

Francis. Tweedledum and Tweedledee?

Frances. Castor and Pollux.

Francis. (*Pointing to himself*) Beauty (*pointing to audience*) and the Beasts!

Frances. Dick and Dora?

Francis. Mother and Father?

Frances. Clever: you must have read Freud.

Francis. He must have imagined me!

Frances. Perhaps a child psychologist would be more useful. When Daddy died, you were elated. (*To audience*) Set free.

Francis. Oh dear. Here we go again. Look. I don't see why you should have all of the fun. It's my turn. Let's see. (*To audience*) A sweet little girl in the embryo, struggling to be free, but imprisoned in a man's body. (*To her*) How awful! All that testosterone!

A revelation seems to strike him.

(*To audience*) Dearie me. So that's why I felt attracted to dear Daddie. (*To her*)You wanted to cuddle him, kiss him, jump into bed with him. (*To audience*) Ah! That's why I dressed up in mummy's lingerie! I clearly imagined myself as Mummy, about to be fucked by Daddy!

Strikes a pose.

Oh, it's so blindingly clear now. How could I *not* have seen it all before!! *Oozing sincerity.* Dear Frances, this has been such an education for me. Thank you so very, very much.

Checking his hair in the hand-mirror and preening.

So, now that you have successfully psychoanalysed this poor malcontent, You can fuck off! I'll get down to painting. Now...

Frances. (*Imperiously*) Sit.

Francis. F-

He was about to say 'Fuck off' but finds himself sitting down, as if being forced to do so.

Frances. (*To audience*) I *like* this game. *Pointing to him.* That's you in the morning, Francis, purple in the face –

Francis. I look a damn sight better than you would after champagne and Chablis for twelve hours!

Frances. Don't forget the uppers...

Francis. (*Sing-song*) And I won't forget the downers!

Frances. And now you *do* need more uppers, otherwise you won't even be able to get out of bed. (*To audience*) But you do talk a lot. (*To him*) You babble.

Francis. I do not babble! I'm remembering the paintings that I did in my dreams.

Frances. Ah!

Francis. Here we go again.

(*To audience*) Who will rid me of this...upstart!

Frances. (*To audience*) Life is but a waking dream. (*To him*) Calderon.

Francis. Was he a nice Spanish boy?

Frances. Ah!

Francis. Arrrh! That's a very irritating habit you've got, you female faggot!

Frances. (*Imperturbably, to audience.*) You know, that's the second time you've mentioned a nice Spanish boy. (*To him*) Did you love him, raddled and all as you were when you met him first, at the age of eighty-one? (*To audience*) Fifty years younger than you, was he?

Francis. (*Riposting*) Forty.

Frances. No wonder he dumped you. (*To audience*) No fool like an old fool, eh?

Francis. (*Sullenly*) I loved him.

Frances. You were infatuated by him, just like those old coots who marry nubile young models. (*To audience*) Like me!

A beat.

We survive! (*To him*) You didn't. (*Giggles*) There you were, the genial atheist, in a Spanish hospital, surrounded by nuns! (*To audience*) Quelle horreur! (*Bluntly, to him*) In the morning. Bedroom off the studio. (*To audience*) Our mother was excessively tidy.

Francis. What's that got to do with anything?

Frances. (*To audience*) Oh, the joys of juxtaposition! Fastidious Francis, whether in three piece suit, or fashionable jeans, shirt carefully pressed, cuffs ironed, and that watch, that expensive, flashy watch that you oh so obviously fiddled with – just enough to tell the punters that you were rich and could pay for it handsomely – and then, the studio swamp!

Francis. (*To audience*) Mister Freud again? (*To him*) You're becoming obvious Frances.

Frances. But you *are* obvious, Francis. That was your spectacular conjuring trick. (*To audience*) How to be obvious but con people into thinking that it wasn't.

Francis. (*Snarling*) I'm never obvious!

Frances. Oh? Oh? Two naked men, one on top of the other, in the grass. (*To audience*) An exploration of the human condition eh? We know what your little coterie called it in private, don't we Francis. (*To audience*) The Two Buggers! Just what is *not* obvious about two naked men, whether one of them is being buggered or masturbated, complete with big white taches of seminal fluid, eh Francis? (*To audience*) Who gives a toss who ejaculates whom! It's your great subject Francis. Not love. Not affection. Not relationships. Not decency. Just fucking. Loveless. Aimless, passing-the-time fucking. (*To audience*) The wanker's paradise! You didn't paint the human condition, Francis. You painted your masturbatory dreams!

He is glaring at her, from a distance of two or three metres, almost unable to control himself. We can however observe his ruthless willpower as he forcibly begins to do so himself. Slowly, ever so slowly, he almost minces towards her, like a parody of queerness. Then he seems to straighten up as if he were becoming six foot tall. His arm sweeps back as if he were going to hit her across the face. Then he observes his hand. Suddenly he seems to relax

Francis. (*Smilingly, to audience*) Wouldn't want to bruise a painter's hand, now would we? (*Sweetly to her*) I don't apologize for anything that I have done, Frances. I was born this way. Queer. I didn't write a letter to my dear, unlamented parents, asking to be delivered as a mewling, puking queer. (*To audience*) I didn't offer up a prayer to that great, so-called God-in-the-sky that so many of you morons seem to believe in. (*To her*) I didn't ask Him, Her, It, or whatever, if I could be placed on Queer earth. (*To audience*) I didn't grow up *wanting* to be queer. (*To her*) I wanted to be *normal*, just like everyone else, (*To audience*) throwing cats to the hunting dogs, shooting Sinn Feiners in the dark, walking in the shadow of Father as he ignored my mother, spent her money, trained his horses; walking in the shadow of mother as she ignored my father, kept out of his way, went off to parties and left me *alone*. Do you remember, dear Frances, when we were four. The pair of them were individually out. (*To audience*) We had a baby-sitter, who had better things to do than babysit a squalling brat, (*to her*) so she took us to the top of the stairs, to the cupboard on the landing, and she locked us into it, and as we screamed into the blackness, into the blackout of the blitz that was all too soon to come, downstairs, below stairs, in the curved open spaces of the Reception room, she screamed as her boyfriend mounted her, her flanks juddering against the table, her breath, soughing in great gobbity gulders, until, pain and passion coagulating into orgasm, (*to audience*) he shot his bolt and she shagged on his shaft until...until...there was only a horse's whimper of passion left...and she subsided into silence.

Don't tell me, Frances, about what I do or do not paint. I am a forked animal and that is what I paint. (*To audience*) I am a forked animal which is both male, (*to her*) *and* female, the two sliding and slithering and sloughing within me, so I have the whole world inside me Frances, all of creation, all of that inchoate, uncouth, *blubber*, that animal fat, that carcass of flesh that gangrenes into what you loftily call Humanity. I AM. (*To audience*) I work with what I have been given: that's my curse. (*To her*) And my...animality...sexuality...sensuality...my 'condition' is what I put onto the canvas, and to be able to put *anything* on the canvas, I have to be stimulated; (*To audience*) and to be stimulated into ideas, into exploration, into sublimation, I have to be sexually stimulated so that ME, all of me, everything that I am, is pressing down on the idea, squeezing at it like squeezing a pimple, so that the succulent puss can stain the idea, and so breed others.

The studio is my cage Frances, my friendly prison, my interrogation centre, my torture chamber, my cabinet of dark curiosities which contains the images of lovers, dead and alive, for the dead are even more alive in the imagination Frances; which contains all those nice pinups of bodybuilding men, sportsmen, boxers, bull-fighters, cricketers, physical physique instructors, which contains the flayed photographs of corpses, the diseases of the body, the beauteous wounds, the nude boys of Michelangelo, which contains my bathrobe, my stained towel – bullfighting is like boxing: a marvellous aperitif to sex, don't you know? – which contains the world in my head.

(*To audience*) Anyway, whoever heard of anyone buying a picture of mine because he liked it!

Frances. Got that off your chest, have we? (*To audience*) I'll bet Picasso would have said the same!

Francis. We both liked the studio and we both liked dust!

Frances. Is that supposed to be profound, or just gnomic?

Francis. Both. (*To audience*) My round, I think!

Frances. Not so fast, Queenie. You're just a self-aggrandizing, self-dramatizing, theatrical invention. (*To audience*) Of mine! (*To audience*) What a performer, eh? Manipulative. (*To him*) Good at accents. You like the odd Cockney touch in between the Sloane Ranger bits! (*To audience*) Wow!

Francis. Ah! Ahhhh! (*To audience*) Now I get it. (*To her*) You're afraid! I'm the stronger one. (*To audience*) I'm the one who invented a style, a personality, a world that is seen through my eyes. (*To her*) You are afraid that I am going to vanquish you – which I am! (*To audience*) Which is why –

Frances. (Gleefully) We have: Proposition Number Seven.

(*To audience*) Photography is your Prop!

(*To him*) Yabooosucks, and up your nose!

Francis. (*To audience*)You see what I have to put up with! *Points to the placard/projection above his head.* Inelegant. Unintelligent. Ignorant of photographic history. *(Grandly)* Photography, my dear young boy, records appearances. Painting needs to go under the world of appearances, or beyond that world. (*To audience*) Painting searches for inner, and not outer truth. (*To her: bows*) To quote a phrase of yours, I rest my case!

Frances. Deakin. John. Photographer.

Francis. (*To audience*) Horrible little man. (*To her*) Of no consequence.

Frances. Really? (*To audience*) You said that he was the best portrait photographer since Nadar and Julia Margaret Cameron.

Francis. (*Innocently to audience*) Did I? Dearie me. (*To her*) Must be getting old. (*To audience*) Memory doesn't function as well as it should.

Frances. (*Squaring up to him.*) We'll come back to Mister Deakin.

Francis. (*To audience*) I could almost construe that as a threat.

Frances. (*Smiling*) Maybe it is....

(*To audience*) Muybridge, Eadweard Etienne Muybridge (*To him*) Those massive volumes (*To audience*) *The Human Figure in Motion* (*To him*) *Animals in Motion.* (*To audience*) Expensive volumes. (*To him*) Didn't stop you buying four separate copies. (*To audience*) Tearing out the pages. Mounting on cardboard. Pinning them up on the studio wall. (*To him*) Drawing over them in Indian ink. Scraping away at them with steel wool, or a razor blade. (*To audience*) Painting over them.

Francis. (*Throwing himself onto the ground beside her, and stroking her legs*) Listen 'Legs'. Muybridge did something new. He showed us animals, and people, *in motion.* (*To audience*) Not the way painters had portrayed them. (*To her*) But as they actually were. (*To audience*) Why should I do that when Muybridge had done it before me? (*To her*) You need intelligence to be a *major* painter, Frances. (*To audience*) So I used *my* intelligence. I *used* photography, not as a prop, but as a trigger. (*To her*) You have to breed images in the mind Frances, breed them until they swarm, breed them until, like a ravening of wasps, they see a swirl of movement and attack, plunging their stings subcutaneously into the flesh, dying in their thousands so that they form a compost from which will spring a sturdy shoot, an image ripped out of the mind's womb.

Frances. (*Claps*) Bravo, mon pederast! That's your third soliloquy! (*To audience*) I must get getting good at 'triggering' too! (*Thoughtfully*) Of course, it wasn't just nice Mister Muybridge. (*To audience*) Handy, wasn't it though, that all of his subjects were nude! (*To him*) Those naked wrestlers, one atop the other.

Your studio floor, leafmoulded with photos of animals, Nazi generals, dictators, photos ripped from magazines, newspapers, stills from movies, big-game hunting photos, bullfight 'kills', clinical operations on diseases of the body, gun-shot wounds, knife wounds, throat-slittings – and of course, photos of your good little five-foot-six self. (*To audience*) Some taken by Mister Deakin. (*To him*) Some taken in photographic booths: little strips of passport photographs; this is my good side; this is my bad side; that is me frontal on...(*Melodramatically, to audience*) Oh, I'm so ugly I just *have* to have my photo taken again and again and again and again.

Francis. (*A beat. Then airily. To audience*) Of no great importance. (*To her*) Most of them I just threw on the studio floor. So what?

Frances. Ah ha!

Francis. (*Pretending to be bored with this game, but very much on the alert*) (*To audience*) 'Ah ha'. (*To her*) Your linguistic skills seem somewhat...repetitive.

Frances. Deakin.

Francis. (*Fondly*) The Mona Lisa of Paddington. (*To audience*) Self-styled.

Frances abruptly becomes him. This is not an impersonation. She role plays him, playing true to the emotion and lightly characterizing him as a man, but without any help from costume. A clipped, slightly seedy English accent. A controlled, observant, self-loathing presence.

Frances as Deakin. Was I always a photographer?

Francis. I don't know.

Frances as Deakin. You're lying. You were my closest friend.

Francis. You had no friends.

Frances as Deakin. When I died, you were named as my executor.

Francis. (*Sourly*) Your little joke.

Frances as Deakin. Was I always a photographer?

Francis. (*Seemingly bored*) You told me that you were at a party, in Paris in 1939, dead drunk. When you woke up you found a camera, so you stole it. O.K?

Frances as Deakin. What did I do before I became a photographer?

Francis. How do I know?

Frances as Deakin. You *do* know.

Francis. Please yourself.

Frances as Deakin. I was a painter. Did you ever see my work?

Francis. No.

Frances as Deakin. You're lying.

Francis. *Please* yourself.

A beat.

You obviously stopped painting.

Frances as Deakin. Self-loathing. I thought I was no good.

Francis. (*Equably*) Maybe you were right?

Frances as Deakin. I didn't think my photographs were any good either, did I? I even stopped being a photographer. But I kept on working in my room, didn't I? Collages. Little quirky paintings. Papier-mache and chickenwire sculptures. Monstrous dolls' heads. You were my friend. I suppose you forgot to encourage me, either as a painter or as a photographer?

Francis. (*Sharply*) It's not my job *pour encourager les autres*. I gave you work. I commissioned you to do portraits. (*To audience*) I bought the bugger drinks on a non-stop basis. I was your patron! Even when no one else was!

Frances as Deakin. (*Sweetly*) Because I was useful. I was your alter-ego. I was the stool on which you stood to achieve elevation. Were you ever in my room? One room, top flat, Berwick Street.

Francis. No.

Frances as Deakin. Liar. Prints, negatives, nice and neatly ordered like any other photographer's archive, eh?

Francis. Possibly.

Frances as Deakin. (*Starts to laugh.*) You are a hoot, Francis. I was a *dangerous* photographer, which is why I kept being fired. Unsparing. Unsentimental. Unlike you: untheatrical. Long before the Germans, I was showing every pore, every pockmark, every blemish. Every incised line. Every quiff of absent hair. Every bloodshot eye. The brutal gaze.

Francis. I quite agree. That's why I commissioned you.

Frances as Deakin. My room. Strewn with prints and negatives. Spattered with bleach, spittle, booze, the gutterings of take-aways.

Trodden on, cut up, mislabelled, torn, creased, dog-eared, jammed into cabinets, stuffed under the bed, scratched. Sound familiar?

Francis. (*Innocently*) You mean you were untidy?

Frances as Deakin. I was *like* you. But I was born with neither the charm nor the money, so I went to the wall. I *was* like you. Which was why you kept me around. I was a reminder of what you might become. And I knew it. Which is why I loathed myself. Because I couldn't stop myself. Because I knew I had as much talent in my little finger as you had, but I couldn't express it in paint, but I could express it in photography, but photography wasn't regarded as Art, *then*, was it, so I gave it no value.

Francis. My my. But you're a great one for lost causes and lame ducks. You need to make your own luck. You didn't. Skin infection first. Then cancer. They gave you the wrong treatment. (*To audience*) Mind you, once at the bar, he swallowed a glass of Parazone bleach by mistake! (*To him*) Quite funny, really. You were not a lucky girl. *I* gave you the money to recuperate, after the operation. (*To audience*) So what does he do? You go down to Brighton, book yourself into a decent hotel, and instead of taking it easy and taking the sea air, you go out on a bender, get pneumonia, and I have to go down to identify the body.

Frances as Deakin. I committed suicide.

Francis. Don't be delirious, duckie.

Frances as Deakin. Delirious? I've lung cancer. I've just had a major operation. My liver's shot to hell. You've given me money to recuperate. And within a day, I leave the safety of the hotel, and I go out, in winter, on the town, and I drink and drink until I can no longer stand up, no longer know where I am, so I fall down into a gutter, at night. What else do you think I was doing, if not committing suicide?

Francis. (*A beat*) It's not my concern.

Turns to her. (*To audience*) In the morgue, there she was, with her trap shut for the first time in her life. At least I buried you.

Frances as Deakin. With how many others?

Francis. (*Swiftly*) I am not responsible for others. I am only responsible for myself.

Frances as Deakin. I had a good eye though, didn't I?

Francis. (*A momentary relaxation*) That you did.

Frances as Deakin. Encouraged you to look at Soutine didn't I? When no-one else rated him?

Francis. Soutine? Minor painter.

Frances as Deakin. Is that why you had more than seventy of his drawings in your studio?

Francis. An artist needs a model, even if it is only a photograph.

Frances snaps out of being Deakin.

Frances. Gotcha!

Tootles as if on a trumpet.

Proposition Number Eight.

An Artist needs a Model!

Francis. Really!!

Looks up at placard/projection.

How intelligent of you to arrive at *that* conclusion!

Frances. It's both a conclusion and a proposition. (*To audience*) What is he? (*Answering herself*) He enjoys inflicting pain as well as receiving it. (*To Francis*) You're a sadist.

Francis. (*To audience: triumphantly*) Now you know *not* to trust her. Doesn't the world and his gigolo know that I'm a masochist!

Frances. (*Slyly*) Didn't stop you finding sadism in Christian iconography, did it? The Crucifixion! (*To audience*) All those nails...the crown of thorns, the spear through the side, not to mention dragging half a tree for a few miles! (*To him*) Oh, and then there's cosy little Saint Sebastian. (*To audience*) A luscious, muscular male nude – rough trade really – but with all those arrows perforating his flesh like knitting needles penetrating an angora sweater. (*To him*) Nice!!

Francis. (*Patiently*) 'Finding' sadism is not the same thing as being a sadist, Frances.

Frances. (*As if to a child*) It's a form of self-medication, Francis. (*To audience*) Some people use alcohol or gambling – (*To him*) Now that I come to think of it, both of those appertain to you! (*To audience*) Some people would experiment with drugs...(*To him*) That would appertain to you too, Francis...all those uppers...You search for the one that heightens your arousal, that relieves your pain,that ameliorates your sense of worthlessness...It's an illusion of relief, isn't it Francis? (*To audience*) You don't want to feel depressed, empty, isolated...So what do you do? (*To him*) You take young George Dyer. You batten on to the insufficient, the incomplete, the intellectually challenged. You give him enough money to stay permanently pissed. You make use of it when you feel like it, then you dismiss him like a servant when you're not in the mood, so when his self-esteem implodes, and the dozens of pills take their lemming-like leaps down his throat, and his sagging body slides onto the lavatory seat, head lolling, spittle squeezing like toothpaste through the graveyard slabs of his teeth, what else does one call it but sadism?

(*Taunting him*) Remember what you did to Eric Hall? (*To audience*) The man in the suit except that all there is, in the suit, is flesh – no head, no eyes, no heart. (*Brutally. To him*) Who's the Frankenstein Francis? The body on the lavatory seat? The empty suit? Or is it just a smiling Francis, ever ready, like the battery, to display its charming energy…(*Quietly*) What are you Francis?

Francis. (*Smoothly*) What are *we*, dearie? That's the question. The human animal…(*To audience*) Flesh? Blood? (*To her*) No. Have you ever been to a slaughterhouse, dearie? They can sense it, the animals. There's a look in their eyes. A ripple in their muscles. They know that extinction is at hand. That's why we're here, isn't it dearie? We're the animals. (*Points to audience*) They're the executioners.

Frances. (*Role-playing*) You're the animal, Francis. I'm a lady!

Francis. You're disembowelled intestines, offcuts of offal, sheets of skin wrapped around a skeletal frame. You're a nice slice of Bacon!!

Begins to laugh.

She waits patiently under his laughter subsides under her enquiring gaze.

Frances. (*A beat*) You became *old* Francis.

Francis. (*Refusing to acknowledge*) I was only a *boy* in Paris, eighteen, nineteen…(*To audience*) I was fascinated with this pickup: he looked so…young. 'Listen Franceees', he would say to me 'Je me fais jeune'

Frances. (*To audience*) 'I can make myself young'. (*Shafting*) But you can't anymore.

Francis. (*Sententiously*) You can only stay young if you are in love…

Frances. (*Lancing in*) Love? Peter Lacey?

Francis. (*Without missing a beat*) An irresistible, animal attraction…

She becomes him, a role-play of a RAF fighter pilot, retired, in his mid fifties, upper middle class, who is equally as self-loathing as Deakin. Middle-class accent, strangulated vowels.

Frances as Lacey. I tied you up.

Francis. Yes.

Frances as Lacey. Then I whipped you – with a bullwhip.

Francis. (*Longingly*) Yes!

Frances as Lacey. Until you bled haemoglobin red!

Francis. Yes!

Frances as Lacey. Then I kissed you, lovingly...

Francis. Yes!

Frances as Lacey. Then I bit you, and bit you –

Francis. Yes!!

Frances as Lacey. Then I bent you over the table, tied arms outstretched –

Francis. Yes!

Frances as Lacey. Then I pulled someone in, off the street – docker, sailor, some musclebound bimbo with a brain the size of a peppercorn, and a penis the size of a gentleman's steel umbrella...

Francis. Yeeesss.

Frances as Lacey. And then I motioned the muscleman to yank down your trousers, and I watched as you were fucked up the arse...

Francis. Yes!

Frances as Lacey. And then – only then – did I take you myself...

Francis. (*Very, very gently, almost whimpering at the very idea of it*) Yes...

Frances as Lacey. And then, when I had ejaculated into a semblance of serenity, I'd pull out, cut the cords on your wrists...kiss you ecstatically...?

Francis. Yes!!

Frances as Lacey. And then I'd lovingly, oh so lovingly, lick the blood on your flayed back, and kiss your bruised wrists, before kneeing you in the groin, tossing you onto the floor, and kicking you, as you rolled into a ball, kicking you in the hope of splintering a rib or shattering a kneecap...

Francis. Yes! Yes! Yes!

Frances as Lacey. (*A beat*) I was a trifle unreasonable, don't you think?

Francis. It was four years of continual horror...(*Awed, despite himself*) And I loved it...

Frances becomes herself again.

Frances. (*Diffidently*) Maybe, in your own way, you did unto others what they had done to you. But in a different register...

Francis. Couldn't we have Mister Jung for a change, instead of Mister Freud?

Frances. All perfectly normal. Daddy has you whipped. You feel sexually attracted towards him. So you gravitate to father figures, Roy De Maistre, Eric Hall, nice men, cultivated, learned, intelligent, artistic, cultivated, all the things that Daddy wasn't. Then the love of your live arrives in the form of Peter Lacey, and he's an unremitting sadist who does what daddy did – brutalizes you. But you won in the end.

She becomes Lacey again.

Frances as Lacey. Was I a good model?

Francis. What do you mean, 'won'?

Frances as Lacey. Well, you left me, didn't you, and lo and behold, doesn't the nasty man drink himself to death and carefully die on the eve of your first major triumph, your retrospective at the Tate Gallery! You see: there *is* a God after all!!

Francis. (*Screaming*) You – bitch!

Frances as Lacey. (*Sweetly*) Shouldn't that be 'bastard'? I thought old poofs like you always inverted?

Francis. (*A long beat*) I *loved* you.

Frances as Lacey. Love? Don't be unintelligent Francis. It doesn't suit you. You were besotted. All the things you liked Francis. Danger, pain, damaged respectability. A fighter pilot in the war. Goodness! Playing piano in a bar in Tangier. Romantic dross. You knew what I was.

Francis. (*Violently*) You were what I wanted! You were all the things that made me feel life more vividly, intensely, passionately. You were a forked animal who fucked me because that was what you were good at, who beat me because that was the only way you could express yourself and that excited me, and yes, you were a voyeur who watched other men effect rear entry, but isn't that what I am? Watching the others in the splintered glass of the Gargoyle Club, watching those around me at Wheeler's, in the French pub, looking at photograph after photograph...of other men. You were all the different bits of me – you just didn't have them in the right order! And you hadn't the self-discipline to take yourself in hand.

So yes, you were a 'good' model because all I needed was a photograph and my cock would itch in my pants and I'd want to start painting, to register the intensity on the canvas. Satisfied?

She snaps out of being Lacey.

Frances. George Dyer.

Francis. Lawdy lawdy lawdy! (*To audience*) The boy doth repeat himself!

Frances. Not repetition Francis. Excavation…What a waste of a life. Dying at thirty-seven.

Francis. You are like Hieronymous Bosch, but without the humour!

Frances. (*Gleefully*) That's what people said of you, Francis…

(*Declaiming to audience*) A painting is never finished, only abandoned.

Francis. (*Before he can help himself*) Valery said that!

Frances. Indeed he did. 'I always used everybody to get what I wanted'. (*To audience*) You said that.

Francis. I was younger then, we all…

Frances. Diseases of the mouth, mutilated corpses, and young men in underpants –

Francis. *I* am the greatest English painter since Turner.

A beat. (*To audience*) Admittedly, there's not much competition.

Frances. George Dyer. (*To audience*) Choral barbiturates. Booze on tap.

(*Becomes Dyer. Working class Cockney accent*) I only wanted your attention Francis. I wanted affection.

Francis. You wanted to be the centre of attention and (*To audience*) I couldn't give him that!

Frances as Dyer. How many suicide attempts? Two? Three? (*To audience*) New York. Nearly got it right. And then my pièce de résistance. Just like Peter Lacey. (*To him*) Didn't pay any attention to warning signals, did you?

Francis. (*To audience*) I was the *only* living painter to be honoured with a retrospective at the Grand Palais in Paris, other than Picasso. (*To her*) You *know* what that entails, curators, writers, publicists, museum officials. Pompidou, the President himself, was going to open it –

Frances as Dyer. Ah!

Francis. Enjoyment is a form of sadism!

Frances as Dyer. (*To audience*) The man who refused all honours in England, is overawed by a French President! Ah! What did it feel like, Francis, when just before the opening, they took you aside and told you that George, *young* nubile, drunk George, had swallowed a bottle of barbiturates while sitting on the toilet, vomited – quite copiously – and considerately passed away!

Francis. (*A long beat. With an effort*) I was shattered.

Frances as Dyer. (*To audience*) Funny way of showing it. (*To him*) But I do like the clichés Francis. I'm making a collection of yours. There you were, in the photographs, laughing, smiling, grinning, giggling, lapping it up while poor George was on the mortuary slab, being sliced open to determine the inexact cause of death. (*To audience*) A broken heart. (*To him*) What did you take Francis? Mother's little helper? A purple heart? Or was it simply *easy* to shrug me aside, and be to thine own self true?

Francis. (*With dignity*) I am not your specimen, your psychoanalytic patient, your set of Russian dolls. When I want to talk to myself, I'll do it out of the limelight.

Frances. Tough.

Proposition Number Nine: Teeth and Tongues: It Takes Two to Tango!

Francis. (*Looking upwards*) And just how many propositions do I have to endure?

Frances. Relax Francis. As in a Greek tragedy, this is the penultimate scene!

There is a long beat as Francis absorbs the implications of this.

Teeth and tongues: The Mouth!

Frances. Your bellowing popes!

Francis. The scream of dumb, impotent rage.

Frances. A scream of pain, or anger? Or release?

Francis. It's the gateway to the body – the front door.

Frances. What about the back door, Francis?

Francis. Slits, openings, wounds in the flesh.

Frances. And you like wounds, Francis. Syphilitic sores –

Francis. My God, I'm lucky I don't have those!

Frances. War wounds. Tumours. Entrails...

Francis. (*Frances is now behind him, her voice echoing his*) The beauty of those flayed bodies, the flesh stripped back to the revelation of muscles, and sinew, the soft dissection to uncover veins and nerves...The interior of man made manifest...

Frances. So what did you want to be, Francis?

Francis. To be? As flies are we to the Gods. I wanted to be at a dentist's distance from lips, nose and mouth. To excavate the lineaments of touch. To scent the fetid breath of each and every lover.

To swallow the bruised blood of split lips. To enter eternity in the orgasm of the moment.

Frances. The mouth, orgasm, and Freud. (*To audience*) That about wraps it up –

Francis. (*Urgently*) Wait!

Frances. What for?

Francis. (*Disbelievingly*) What for? What for? (*To audience*) I have so much more to say-

Frances. No time!

Francis. Wh...

Frances. The Tenth Proposition, my very own commandment!

Drum roll. Military fanfare.

Beware Greeks Bearing Gifts!! *Francis glances up, horrified.* (*Getting carried away*) Let's Rock n'Roll!

Francis. Excuse me. 'Let's Rock n'Roll'? (*To audience*) I wouldn't be seen dead listening to Rock n'Roll! A nice classical string quartet by Mozart or Brahms –

Frances. Schizophrenia. Dualism? (*To audience*) Who cares? (*To him*) My my my girlie. I think you need to have some exercise!

FX: Military drumroll.

Either a yardbrush is flung on from the side of the stage (preferably high into the air) and caught expertly by Frances; or else it is lowered from the Gods. As this happens Francis's head only turns, with great effort, to observe.

Frances takes the yardbrush (a good five to six foot long in the handle) and sashays over to him.

Frances. Bend!

Francis finds that some force is pushing him so that his back is bent forward at perhaps a thirty degree angle, and his hands have grasped the tails of his leather overcoat and lifted them outwards, so that, to the viewpoint of Frances, his buttocks are revealed.

Now I know, Francis, that you like to be buggered, so it is only reasonable, bearing in mind that abstinence has been your unwilling companion for the past few years, that you be buggered in some style.

(*To the audience: like a conjuror's assistant*) As you will now observe, ladies and gentlemen of the congregation, the handle of the brush is placed at a forty-five degree angle to the floor, and gently inserted into the declivity of the buttocks.

She does so, then sashays around to face him sideways on.

Now Francis, we realize that you are instinct with carnality, animality, and an enormous sexual compulsion, *but* down here, the pleasures of the flesh emerge in a rather different form.

You'll have to make do with a yardbrush up your bum.

You will, I am sure, find it an engaging experience, and one which will feed into an imaginary, painting frenzy.

Alternating between audience and Francis.

We observe the expressions on his face which range from extreme lust to extreme fear.

Now, upon my command, the handle of the yardbrush will proceed to insert itself into the rectal cavity. Just as with a vibrator, beloved by lonely housewives everywhere, this handle can rotate to the left or the right, vibrate to any frequency, thus tuning in to the pleasure-pain principle, and, when commanded to extrapolate the sensations of multiple, blinding, deadly orgasm, it will drill its way through the human anatomy, comprehensively exploring the intestinal pathways, before punching through the thorax, explosively decompressing through the windpipe, and exploding outwards, through the teeth, to provide a glorious focal point: the human animal, pinned, skewered, butchered – a lump of meat decomposing in a shower of fushia-red tears.

A beat.

Francis. Ah...!

A beat.

Could I have a cup of tea first?

A beat.

Perhaps not.

(*To audience*) The service simply isn't up to it...

A beat.

(*To her*) It's really very kind of you to be so concerned as to my carnal satisfaction. I hope I can replay your generosity sometime...in kind.

A beat.

(*With charm*) You know...Frances...it is Frances with an 'e', isn't it? ...You seem to know your way around this rather peculiar...special... particularity...I'd be most awfully obliged if you could acquire for me an easel, canvas – at least three metres by three – and some paints. I feel like WORK!

Would you be so kind?

Frances. (*Wide-eyed*) Of course Francis.

A beat.

They're in front of you.

Francis. (*Suspicious*) Where?

Frances. Concentrate Francis. Focus. In front of you.

Francis. Why so they are. How marvellous!

Frances. (*Happily*) I'll inspire you!

Glances at yardbrush.

(*To audience*) Insertion will (*clicks fingers*) commence!

He screams, half in agony, half in pleasure.

During the following, his moans, groans, gutterings and soughings will slowly increase until, painting finished, he climaxes.

Francis. God! Images, like slides, tumbling into my head. I'll gorge on a painting of mine.

'Study for the Nurse in Battleship Potemkin.'

(*Bitchily*) Critics used to say I cannibalized myself. Shows how much they know! Aaaawh! Odessa Steps sequence. Still of the nurse: her head. The bullet exploding through the right lens of her glasses, and into her eye. Her beautiful mouth, soundlessly screaming. The velvet blood, as sweet as a ripe pimento, kissing her cheek, and nuzzling the nape of her neck.

Oooaaannh!

Frances. (*To audience*) Insertion at intestinal level. (*To him*) Poussin. The scream in 'The Massacre of the Innocents'?

Francis. No! Aannnnh! Coloured plate: diseases of the mouth in gorgeous eruption! Imagine her body. Strip her nude. Deform her into life. Cage her with tubular steel. Aaaannnnnnhg! Muybridge. Photo of Woman sitting down in Chair and drinking tea.

Frances. (*To audience*) Insertion: erupting through the thorax. Francis?

Francis. Newspaper photo of a crowd, scattering in panic across Saint Petersburg Square. Carcass in a butcher's shop, the veined flesh as beautiful as a Rembrandt. Awnerannngh! Berlin! The Thirties! The white halves of a hog, hanging on iron posts.

Frances. (*To audience*) Insertion: erupting through windpipe. Won't be long now!

Francis. Clinical photos: extreme cases of hysteria (*Groans voluptuously*) Looks just like sexual ecstasy! (*Screams*) The eye slashed in 'Un chien Andalou'!

Frances. (*To audience*) Insertion: erupting through the mouth.

Francis. (*Screams*) Paint flung against the canvas. Slashed with the knife. Smeared with a sponge. Ribbed with a rag of corduroy. Wiped off with an old towel. A whole world falling apart in a scream. The history of my time.

He climaxes violently. Abruptly his arms shoot upwards:

immediately **FX:** The Tango.

Frances. (*Cautioning him*) Ah! (*To audience*) It takes two to tango! (*To him*) Don't destroy the yardstick, duckie!

She removes it. Either flings it offstage or sends it upwards to the Gods. He collapses in a heap. Tango ends. She leans forward, looking at the 'painting'.

You know Francis – You'll have to do substantially better than that crud of warmed-over juvenilia!

Francis. Juvenilia? Have you any idea of how I *suffered* to become what I am? *Suddenly his head whiplashes to where the 'painting' was.* It's vanishing! *My* painting is vanishing! Stop it!

She folds her arms.

I order you to stop my painting from disappearing.

A beat.

(*Anxiously*) What about all of my other paintings? Are they going to vanish? Have they vanished? What kind of collectors have you got down here?

Frances. (*Dearie me tone*) Look! It's vanished.

A beat.

There are no collectors down here.

Francis. (*Stamps his foot*) Have it your own way. (*Urgently*) Where are we?

Frances. (*As if to a child*) There is no such thing as the 'here and now'.

Francis. Speak English, dearie.

Frances. You've heard of String Theory?

Francis. No.

Frances. Yes you have. (*To audience*) It posits the existence of up to eleven dimensions, one time dimension, and up to ten spatial dimensions.

Francis. So?

Frances. So your future, and your past, might co-exist. (*To audience*) Maybe your future could exchange with your past!

Francis. So?

Frances. So our senses, and our experiences, don't tell us how the world really works, Francis.

Francis. I see, therefore I am!

Frances. But what are you seeing? Maybe there are spatial dimensions which are so small, or so large, that you simply can't *see* them. (*To audience*) They're invisible, to us, but that doesn't mean that they don't exist.

Francis. So what?

Frances. We see light on our wavelength. But we can't see ultraviolet light, can we – yet it's there. We can't hear beyond our acoustic range, but a dog can.

Francis. Highly instructive no doubt, dearie, but ectoplasm and supernatural phenomena are merely metaphors for psychic disturbance.

Frances. George Dyer.

Francis. (*A long, long beat*) Ah!

Frances. Ah...Can you see it? The red carpet, rolling down the steps of the Palais Royale.

Francis. (*Discovering*) 'By trampling the royal crimson'...

Frances. We all bring about our own destruction, just like Agamemnon...

Francis. (*Amazed that he is 'getting' it*) Unleashing the Furies in the quest for further blood...

Frances. (*Jokingly*) Watching the nobility with which our hero suffers his misfortune...

Francis. In atonement for his tragic guilt...

Frances. Would that be wearing your mother's underclothes? (*To audience*) Or being queer?

Francis. It's a disease. I was born with it.

Frances. You enjoyed it. (*To audience*) Even more when it was illegal!! (*To him*) Now what about this suffering? Ah! Of course. (*To audience*) It purges the spectator's mind through terror and pity, leading to catharsis!

A beat.

Not much chance of that with you here!

Francis. Offence, counter-offence – resolution.

Frances. (*Claps her hands delightedly.*) Now you're getting it!

Francis. Sin provokes sin until justice asserts itself.

Frances. Gosh! At this rate we'll convert you to Catholicism!

Francis. (*Ironically*) You forgot murder and revenge!

Frances. I did? (*To audience*) No problem. (*To him*) Murder. Well, you may as well have murdered George Dyer, and as for revenge, take your extravagantly large choice! (*To audience*) Revenge on your father for not having sex with you? (*To him*) Only joking! (*To audience*) Revenge on your mother for having no interest in you? (*To him*) Closer? (*To audience*) Revenge on your lovers for not measuring up to expectations?

Francis. (*Sourly*) You need a deus ex machina.

Frances. Everything cometh to he who waits!

Francis. (*Unexpectedly*) Are we in God's Zoo?

No response.

Is God the vivisector, the man with the flaying knife? *(Urgently to audience)* We're still in my studio, but we've just gone down to the garage underneath – the Underworld!

No response.

Frances. (*Gently*) You should prepare yourself.

Francis sits down, takes a small hand mirror out of his pocket, and looks at her enquiringly.

Frances. (*Handing him*) Peach Foundation.

(He applies) Lipstick.

(He applies) Scouring powder.

He cleans his teeth with the powder on his fingers.

Light and dark tan bootpolish.

She opens, he mixes on his wrist.

She hands him a brush: he brushes it into his hair

He admires himself.

I think I'd like a good tying up now, please!

Some...sailor's knots!!

Frances. Whom do you see in the mirror?

Francis. (*A beat*) Deakin.

Frances. Maybe you're in Hell?

Francis. Hell doesn't exist. Hell is the here and now. (*To audience*) If I were in Hell, I'd know that I always had the chance of escape!

Frances. How would you like to die?

Francis. (*As a reflex. To audience*) Fast!

A beat.

I thought I *was* dead...

Frances. (*Almost singing. To audience*) You should be so lucky! What does it feel like to be alone in a room, waiting for the hunter?

Francis. (*Looking around*) Time doesn't exist?

Frances shakes her head.

Unconscious scanning? (*Pointing to audience*) Portals to another dimension?

Frances. (*She grins*) Maybe!

The low, insistent military drumbeat begins to surface again. Then slowly, ever so slowly, in the far, far distance, the thunderous gallop of horses, as if on hard unspringy turf.

Faust.

Francis. What?

Frances. You got it wrong Francis. (*To audience*) There's more than one reference. (*To him*) Why do you think the Christian Church always built on pagan sites? Can you hear them, the furies, your very own, personal Eumenides? (*To audience*) What's sauce for the goose, Francis! (*To him*) Whom do you see?

Francis. Deakin's friend: Graham Mason.

Frances. He was your friend too.

Francis. Acquaintance.

Frances. Have it your own way. What do you see?

She is behind him, cradling him. As they both 'see' Mason.

Francis as Mason. (*He becomes him: horrified at the experience of it*) I'm sitting by the window, looking out over the Thames...imprisoned by emphysema. The cylinder of oxygen by the armchair, a bottle of white wine by my elbow... A face like a rotten choirboy...angry...oh so...Angry.

Frances. Deakin didn't want to die like that. Did he?

Francis. (*Coming out of Mason and shuddering: softly*) No.

A beat.

Neither did I. Do I daydream...or do I sleep...

(*Discovering*) Ahh...

> Let the night come slowly, like a wave of viscous honey
> So slowly that the pale canopy of midnight is suspended
> Like an ethereal glow from the first spark of creation
> So slowly that Christ's blood will clot and cleach but never
> Outreach the dumb and sullen canopy of oblivion

He looks up, stricken, as the galloping of the horses drives all too close by.

My immortal soul?

Frances. (*To audience*) I thought you were an atheist? (*To him*) Sorry. Cheap quip. Does Art give meaning to the brief interlude between life and death?

Francis. (*With a ringing declaration*) Yes!

She stands, and taps the buttons on his coat with her whip. He comprehends immediately, undoes them, and lets the coat fall to the floor, revealing him, once again, in suspender belt and stockings. The lights begin to darken. She picks up his coat and drapes it around her shoulders

Frances. Your immortal soul, Francis...is *me*. You...are about...to cease to exist...

As the galloping reaches a crescendo, the image of Head Two is projected onto the back of the stage.

Francis finds himself impelled to roll under it in a foetal position, head upraised but bent back, mouth opening in a snarl.

A trial run for a discarded human being.

Francis.

A new life for a new human being Francis/Me!!!

He howls into the ether above him.

In one swift movement, she lashes at him with the whip as the lights reach incandescence and we close on an image of her, smiling radiantly, triumphantly.

Blackout.

Notes from Brian McAvera

Francis & Frances, as usual with me, had a rather long gestation period. Although I first came into contact with Bacon's work as early as 1966, it was not until shortly after I finished *Picasso's Women,* in the late nineties, that I began to think of a play about him. Six or seven years later I happened to be at a drama conference in England and got talking to a director who programmed an experimental theatre season at Cambridge. He said it was a shame that writers didn't write about visual artists. I remarked that he obviously didn't know my work whereupon he said 'Have you any ideas?' and I replied that I was thinking about writing a play on the painter Francis Bacon who had been born in Dublin. 'Do the first 20 or 25 minutes of it for the late-night slot' he said. That turned out to be only three months away. I said that I didn't work like that, that it took me many years to write a play, and he said, 'well, there's a slot there if you want it'. Three months later I had produced about twenty-five minutes of text. The word had been 'experimental', and I took that quite literally, both in form and subject-matter.

Come ten o'clock on the performance night there were about twenty to thirty people in the audience who were well over sixty, and then in came a bunch of very young people in their mid to late teens. I pondered leaving at speed. After all, Francis Bacon had a very – to put it politely – unconventional sex life, and the form of the play took very large risks in terms of the manner in which the story was told. The excerpt ended at around ten-thirty that night and the audience had to be ejected at 1.30 a.m the following morning as they were still discussing it. I reckoned that I had hit a nerve. But I knew that I wasn't ready to write the rest of the play so I put it to one side. It was to be another six years before I took up the pen (this was one I wrote in longhand) and started work. Some plays, you know in advance, are going to be a bugger to write; others just flow. You can guess which category this one fitted into...

Enter into my life Mr Joe Devlin, artistic director of Focus Theatre who had recently cajoled me into letting them put on *Picasso's Women* in Dublin. He enquired as to whether I was writing anything at the moment. I mentioned *Francis & Frances*.

He suggested that I do a workshop when I was ready. Now the great thing about Joe is that he doesn't put you under pressure and give you a deadline, so I took my time. But when I was ready, we cast and did a number of workshop sessions. Time passed. Joe suggested another workshop as I was at that time running a Residency Project in Stranmillis College in Belfast, so we did a weekend workshop on the play with other actors. Then we did a third one in Dublin again which we played in front of an audience, first in Dublin and then in Wexford. By now I felt that I knew where I was going with the piece so Joe suggested we do a production.

We did a proper casting session, lasting two days. I was fairly confident that I had it cast until, at the end of the second day, two actors unknown to me walked in. I remember, within seconds, turning to Joe and saying 'That's our cast'. Casting is threequarters of a production. Cast correctly and you are on a winner. Cast incorrectly and you will never get there. *Francis & Frances* is a dense, layered and complex play. It needs actors who can do humour as well as tragedy, who have serious technical skills, who can move well, who are 'sexy' and as Francis is the male version of Francis Bacon and Frances the female version, it obviously needs a chemistry between the two leads. These two were stunning.

There were the usual running entertainments. Francis was much in favour of trying to edit down his (very long) part. Frances was more philosophical in this direction. But I think it fair to say that 'we had a ball' in rehearsal. I know writer-directors who are determined that the finished play will correspond, exactly, to what they had in their heads when they wrote it, but that seems daft to me as theatre is about collaboration and for an actor to inhabit a part – as opposed to pulling it on like a glove – one has to go through a process which will allow an actor to find his own way through the role. In the process, hopefully, one will eliminate inconsistencies, find out things you were not perhaps aware of, and enable the actors to share ownership of the script. The only way to do that is to treat the script as if you had not written it. You kick it around with any line being treated as if it were an elastic band being capable of being stretched in all directions; any sequence being explored from multiple angles. You find out what works for the actors. If you do another production with different actors, you will have to start again from scratch.

I very much enjoyed working on this production. When you have actors as gifted and as fearless as Cathal Quinn and Tara Breathnach, every day becomes a city of possibilities. I like to leave blocking until as late as possible so that exploration of the text is paramount. In this particular play I was aware that because of the extreme emotions that it explores, it could easily slide into a psychodrama – which was not what I wanted – so we experimented constantly with music, often in ironic counterpoint to the action. For me the ideal aspect of a theatre play (unlike a film or television script) is that it is not fixed. The performance codes are inherent in the text, but they can be unlocked and explored in a myriad of ways.

For me, theatre does not exist without a live audience. That is what makes it different from cinema or television. The logic of this – for playwrights like myself – is that the fourth wall does not exist; that the audience becomes a part of the play; that, put crudely, Brecht as I understand him was perfectly correct: an audience is simultaneously capable of emotionally engaging whilst intellectually evaluating. If Hollywood prefers to play to the lowest common denominator, it seems to me that theatre should never underestimate its audience. If they are engaged, emotionally and intellectually, who cares whether they 'get' everything on a first viewing? Do you get everything in a novel on a first reading?

Francis & Frances was first produced at the Focus Theatre, Dublin, 13-25 June, 2011.

Francis: – Cathal Quinn
Frances :– Tara Breathnach
Set and Poster Design: – Sarah Jane O'Neill
Lighting Designer: – Colm Maher
Stage Manager/Sound Design: – Sonya Deegan
Photography: – Karl McCaughy
Programme Design and Printing: – A and M Scott
Producer: – Joe Devlin
Written and Directed by Brian McAvera

Appendix

A Word to the Wise (further reflections by Brian McAvera)

This is not a biographical play. I'm not interested in biography as such, but I am interested in what generates 'art' in any medium, and thus am obviously interested in the relationship between an individual's art and his or her life. That 'life' operates within a social, cultural and political context as does the 'art' that the individual produces.

For a very long time now, I have been looking at the work of Francis Bacon. To be precise I first came across it when I was seventeen or eighteen, circa 1966, when working on a summer job in London. I came across a huge pile of a serial magazine called *The Masters*, stacked close to the front door of a bookshop in Holborn. There were one hundred issues, each featuring an artist, with sixteen very good colour plates on thick quality paper, and each issue had an introduction by a recognized authority. Before the summer was out I had bought most of them, including the one on Bacon which was introduced by Sir John Rothenstein, then Director of the Tate Gallery.

In a sense my education in drama and my education in the visual arts went hand in hand. At university I discovered stage-directing and started to write plays. I also started to collect books on art. I had attempted to paint (copying Van Gogh and Degas) but I rapidly recognized that I would never make myself into a major painter. However the experience of trying was useful as it focused one's attention on looking – what John Berger calls Ways of Seeing – and on the tactile quality and rhythmic consonances of paint applied to a surface.

This was also a period when, exploring the world of English Literature, one was coming upon intriguing ideas, many of which seemed to inter-relate to the other arts, such as Auerbach's concept of Mimesis, Empson's ideas on Ambiguity, and Eliot's exploration of emotional precision. Tristram Shandy (that prototype of Ulysses) generated ideas about narrative that are not unlike notions of Performance Art: the time needed for a Performance or the reading of a novel was that which was necessary for the said artwork. Likewise, the narrative did not have to be linear and straightforward.

This was also a period when Resnais (think of *Hiroshima Mon Amour*), early Godard (*Weekend*), and Bergman (*The Silence*) overlapped with the rather jauntier structures of a Bunuel (*The Milky Way*) or those charming but unsettling explorations of disaffected youth as in Fellini's *La Strada*.

All of this is simply another way of saying that I have never seen any reason to assume that the arts were not *all* interconnected. Listening to Chopin and Bartok for example, writing pop songs (which I did for many years) or listening to folk ballads seemed to me (and still does) very much of a piece with reading a novel, watching television, writing and directing, and living one's life. The notion that the arts are a decoration, a luxury, is a barbarism that, in my case, first emerged when I attempted to earn a living in the arts, in Northern Ireland, before and during the Thatcher years.

Anybody is capable of writing a play, though a limited number of people seem capable of devoting a lifetime to it. It is very easy to simply repeat oneself, to find a formula, and please an audience with the familiarity of a warm overcoat. Having learnt to assert myself at university, I took it for granted that part of one's job was to take the audience on a voyage of discovery, not a voyage up the well-signposted features of, say, the Manchester Ship Canal. A large part of this voyage is an interior one. Playwrights are always being told that either they are too literary (which usually means that they are more literate and intelligent than the literary manager) or too undramatic (code for the literary manager not having a clue how the play will function in performance). In real life, there *are* no simple rules for drama: if something works on stage, then it is dramatic.

Language, as the Elizabethan theatre demonstrated, can be very complex and compelling at one and the same time. You can strip it back or you can load it; you can denude it of reference (timelessness) or anchor it in a web of allusion. The problem with a loaded language, as in much of what passes for 'poetic' drama, is that in the wrong hands it has no forward momentum. This is not necessarily a problem in short plays. Much of Yeats is fundamentally undramatic but a good production can disguise the deficiencies as the plays are mercifully short. The nineteenth century poet Robert Browning wrote marvellous short dramatic monologues but once he attempted a longer span the result was stillborn.

What the Elizabethans were really good at was writing a loaded language which had a forward momentum and within which were contained all the codes necessary for performance. Putting it simply they were men of the theatre, and practice taught them what would work, and what wouldn't. As John Arden demonstrated in a marvellous essay on *Henry V* there were what one might call standard directorial codes embedded in the language: how to stage a coronation; how to stage a battle and so forth.

As it happens I don't write in iambic pentameter but I do write highly rhythmic, loaded, stage dialogue. Having directed since my early university days, co-founded theatre companies, and worked in everything from Street Theatre, Youth Drama, and Community Theatre through to professional theatre, I tend to 'see' as I write. Indeed almost all of my plays start in the mind with a visual image or a series of images. The imagery (metaphor and simile being only a small part of stage imagery) emerges from the physicalization of the action. I don't write plays in which well-mannered people stroll around a stage as if in a drawing room. I write plays for a very physical theatre in which the language *itself* is physical.

This is not as strange as it might seem. Medieval monks, so Dom LeClerq tells us, physicalized in a very muscular way the words which they were writing down in their scriptoria. Each word had a muscular response in the throat, even when no sound was being made. The codes in the language – the rhythms, the alliterations, the associations, the images – determine the broad shapes of the staging.

At intervals over the past century or so playwrights have been lectured about the need for visual theatre. Just what, one might ask, is more visual than an Elizabethan or Jacobean play? Just what is more visual than a Roman comedy or a medieval miracle play? As silent cinema demonstrated, via the use of titles, one needs words to anchor thoughts. A great painting can encapsulate a theme or calibrate an emotional response. What it can't do is deliver a compelling, unfurling narrative over one and a half to two hours. The physicality counts: the unfurling, in real time, in front of a live audience; the inter-relationship between actor and audience with no proscenium arch – direct contact, no fourth wall. Just as with reflections in a shop window whereby, under strong sunlight, one cannot be sure what is inside the shop and what is being reflected and so a 'third space' is created, I aim for that 'third space' in drama: an other world (what the Greeks called a heterocosm) in which the Players, and the Played-to communicate directly to each other.

What also interests me, however, and this is where Francis Bacon enters again, is the political. The play charts his Irish childhood in a turbulent and war-torn Ireland, through to his rise to fame through the latter part of the 20th century, and explores how the political landscape of Europe, and his private life, impacted on Francis's imagination to create some of the most disturbing and iconic paintings of the twentieth century. The personal and the political are never divorced, even though individuals like Bacon might want to think otherwise. Bacon has recently been claimed for Irish art (though anything less like an Irish artist or an Irish identity would be difficult to think of) and as his studio has been archeologically excavated and removed to the Municipal Gallery, Dublin (one imagines he would have been vastly amused), it is a good time to consider the question of his identity. When I started out, long ago, on this play, I did not consider him an Irish artist. I still don't in the sense that neither his personality nor his art have any obvious Irish connection but I am now convinced that his childhood imagination was profoundly marked by his experiences in Ireland, and that this childhood imagination is the basis for all of his subsequent work. I am equally convinced that he considered himself British (specifically a Londoner), not Irish.

Set

An empty black box except that the sides and rear of the stage are actually a semicircle, made up of a patchwork of hanging mirrors, most of which are shattered, cracked or damaged. At odd intervals, but in particular dead centre, there are odd normal mirrors.

If possible the mirrors should continue at the left and right of the front end of the stage so that the audience is mirrored, right to the edge, and thus implicated in the action. In effect the audience are mirrored in a shattered, fragmented world, a third space, with the occasional 'straight' mirror acting as a wormhole into a seemingly normal reality.

At the start of the play, ideally projected onto a normal mirror dead centre of stage (but otherwise onto any 'dropped' screen or gauze) is an image of the Francis Bacon painting **Head 2** (actually in the Ulster Museum), or a version of it, which consists of a strange amorphous mass of blubber with, in its centre, predominating as if with the head raised backwards, a set of incisors. There should be just enough light for this image to reflect and refract in the other mirrors. If possible, the floor of the set should be black as well, possibly made out of a reflective substance like aluminium.

The play can be performed, quite minimally, within this space, though the director and designer could take the opportunity for Bacon-like visuals (his trademark distortions). Thus Bacon-like images in the process of deliquescence could continually inhabit this world.

Cast

Francis Bacon: The actor should not attempt to impersonate Bacon, apart from dress and an initial quality of cherubic innocence. He should be old enough to suggest a wide range of experience but young enough to be athletic.

He is 'queer' but not 'gay' (to use his own terminology), enormously attractive, and with an almost magnetic presence. This is a man who can charm any audience. The voice is highly flexible, and to a degree mannered, in that his vowel sounds and inflections are often exaggerated for effect. He can switchblade between an almost Anglo-Irish aristocratically inflected tongue, and a distinctly 'lower-class' ambiance. Occasionally his vulnerabilities shine through.

The persona that he creates is *not* 'camp' – though he quite happily and deliberately uses 'camp' when it suits him but there is always an element of danger. He is, in his own life, a constant actor. He wears a very expensive wristwatch, and carries a small hand mirror in his pocket. For casting purposes, imagine John Hurt; or, at one end of the spectrum, the current Alan Rickman, blended with Eddie Izzard.

Frances Bacon: Think of Frances as the feminine self of Francis. She is dressed as a dominatrix with high heels, stockings, a clinging one piece upper body dressage, legs as long as sin, and a voice which is beguiling, sensual and manipulative. Ideally, she is taller than him, slender rather than buxom, and with a splendidly flowing mane of red curly hair. She is instinct with intelligence and – especially – emotional intelligence.

She too is never far away from the element of danger; and for long stretches she actually is, *literally*, dangerous, but where *Francis* uses language to slide in and out of his different selves (the deliberate elongation of vowel sounds, the schoolboy French phrases, the hauteur of the aristocrat or the louche patois of a sailor) she uses emotional, psychological and sexual manipulation. Initially she is very, very dominant, but there will be a power struggle as to which parts of the composite personality should be ruthlessly suppressed – or emphasized. Despite the dominatrix elements, the quieter and more reflective she is, the better. We become aware that, at times, they blend into each other.

For casting, imagine the early Diana Rigg in *The Avengers* – the notorious Hell Fire Club episode; or a young Helen Mirren.

A brief note on style

There are lots of different ways of staging, and playing, this kind of stuff...

I've written for an ideal staging, but don't feel bound by that. All of my work for the past decade or so has been a) non-naturalistic and b) written with the audience being a part of the play.

In all cases, the actors not only talk to each other but talk directly to the audience, often even throwing a phrase in the middle of a sentence to the audience. The indications as to this style of playing, in the script, are just that: indications.

An actor may comment on another actor, look for support for his stance, joke with the audience, take the piss out of them, play off male against female, or young against old (and vice-versa).

So whether there is a proscenium arch or not, the actors should play as if the proscenium doesn't exist. The closer they get to the audience the better.

I like to involve an audience, which also means taking them on an emotional (and hopefully thought-provoking) roller-coaster, which in turn means that pace – as opposed to pacing – should be swift. No hanging around.

I want the actors, and the director and everyone else, to enjoy themselves; or put another way, this is *play*. Serious play, but indisputably play. This is physical theatre, and the action should be as physical as is possible.

A very brief note on sound

In an ideal world there would be a designed soundscape, as opposed to a (nominal) number of sound effects plus music cues. For preference, a composer should handle the lot, but if this is not feasible, at the very least, both the music cues and the FX cues should be recognizably from the same sound-scape.

The key components, apart from the specifics of musical cues, are the military undertow and the sounds of a roulette ball tumbling along a roulette wheel. For music cues, in the first production, we used a wide range of rock and pop anthems of the fifties and sixties, along with excerpts from film scores and the occasional classical extract. The music was used variously as a) emotional underpinning b) ironic counterpoint c) period context d) as a distancing technique, much in the manner of Kubrick's use of music in *A Clockwork Orange* and e) as a way of using the associations that pop and rock have for an older audience to help them relate to otherwise very dark sexual, psychological and political subject matter.